Financial Exodus

THE FINANCIAL DELIVERANCE OF GOD'S PEOPLE

GUY WALKER

Financial Exodus
The Financial Deliverance of God's People
by Guy Walker

Printed in the United States of America

ISBN 978-1-60647-337-5

www.xulonpress.com

In Appreciation

I want to express my deepest appreciation and love to my wife Carol, who has always believed in me. She has stuck with me *"in sickness and in health and for richer and for poorer"*. I thank God that she is a woman to whom those vows were important, and have caused her to stick with it in some pretty lean times. Someone said there is no substitution for character and she has plenty. I thank God for putting her in my life.

I also want to express my appreciation to Dr. Jim Clark, my spiritual father and mentor. He has also believed in this subject and my ability to speak to it in an articulate manner even when I doubted myself. His command of the Word of God and the English language is formitable, and I hope one day to become like him in these areas of my life. He is a man of forceful insight, and yet great compassion and understanding; much like the Master he serves…our Lord Jesus Christ.

I also want to thank the members of my Church who also believed in the message (and have had to listen to it repeatedly). They are the greatest flock that any shepherd could ever ask for.

And last but not least, I want to thank my Lord Jesus Christ, who has allowed me to endure tribulation in order to perfect the gifts and the callings He has placed in me. Even in the storms of life, or perhaps more correctly, especially in the storms of life, He has always been there. He has loved me when I didn't feel worthy, and He has seen me through every trial and tribulation, all the while teaching me and encouraging me so that I might remember *"who comforts us in all our tribulation, that we may be able to comfort those who are in any trouble, with the comfort with which we ourselves are comforted by God."* (2 Corinthians 1:4, NKJV)

Forward

I count it a privilege to be asked to make remarks concerning this clear mandate to our culture in America today. Guy Walker not only makes his point clear that many believers as well as most non-believers of the Christian faith; that financial stewardship and primarily the huge debt most people have incurred is a pivotal issue their personal survival as well as our national safe keeping is a primary concern if this culture as we know it is to survive. Guy has the means of solution to this vast problem through the principles he shares in this timely work.

Having come through the Great Depression with fifty-five years of ministry experience, having taught and been taught the essentials of stewardship I marvel at the clarity and simplicity of Guy's approach and insight to the problem and solution to the financial quagmire most people are facing as a result of poor financial judgment based upon little to no teaching in their lives.

Guy is uniquely qualified for this ministry of financial ministry and integrity, in that he has had a very strong career in the financial world with both momentous success and critical failures; which served to wake him up to the need of Jesus Christ being LORD in his life and subsequently receiving his "Call" into the ministry. All this has served to release his passion for stewardship which is serving to be a major facet in the lives of everyone he touches and particularly in the lives of believers.

Serving the ministry at the great Barn Church located in the Texas Panhandle at Hereford, Guy and Carol Walker pastor "cowboys" with a passion and commitment to see them grow in Christ through their stewardship in every arena of life. Now these principles of how to properly use your money is available in this volume through clearly defined Biblical principles and precious "cowboy" common sense.

These easy to read and easy to learn lessons make this volume a real tool for proper "money handling" for the individual and for group study. As you proceed through these anointed pages; Guy's experience and practical "cowboy" wisdom will open up a whole new world to you in the area of your personal financial freedom and responsibility

Jim Clark, D.D.
President and Founder of Ministers Training Institute
Baker, LA 70714

Introduction

In the opening verses of the Book of Job, the *"Sons of God"* (angels) come to present themselves to God. Satan decides to mix in with the crowd and see what happens. God, of course notices him, and asked him, *"From where do you come?"* (Job 1:7, NKJV). Satan replies, *"From going to and fro on the earth, and from walking back and forth on it."* Then the Lord asked him, *"Have you considered my servant Job, that there is none like him on the earth, a blameless and upright man, one who fears God and shuns evil?"* (vs.-1:8) The Lord knows that he is familiar with Job before He asked the question. After all, everyone on earth knew Job. He was the richest man in the East, according to the Word of God. How could Satan not know of him? How could he not detest him for the blessings that were exemplified in his life?

Then Satan makes a cynical observation concerning the character of this man. He says, *"Does Job fear God for nothing? Have You not made a hedge around him, around, his household, and around all that he has on every side? You have blessed the work of his hands, and his possessions have increased in the land. But now, stretch out your hand and touch all that he has, and he will surely curse you to your face!"* (Job1:9-11) The Lord response is quick and to the point, *"Behold, all that he has is in your power; only do not lay a hand on his person."* (vs.12). Then Satan went out from the presence of the Lord. The "cosmic wager" had been struck, and Satan under the authority of God Himself, begins to systematically destroy Job's life. He destroys his family, his wealth, his status in the community, and his health; all in an attempt to get him to renounce his faith and curse God, and thereby win the wager.

If you've read the Book, then you already know the outcome. Even though Satan destroys all that Job has and he lays naked with boils on his body from head to toe, and even though his wife urges him to *"curse God and die"*, he refused to compromise his faith. Later Job proclaims, *"Though he slay me yet will I trust Him."*(Job 13:15). The story of Job is *not* one of suffering, or patience…it's one of faith. Job was patient and he was heroic in his resistance towards evil, but the source of his strength lies in his faith. A faith that was extraordinary.

I think God had a very specific purpose in licensing the cursing of Job. It was not that He took pleasure in seeing Job's suffering, in fact, it must have been quite difficult to watch as His servant suffered. I think that the purpose in Job's suffering was twofold. First was to show Satan that he may have great insight as to man's weaknesses, but concerning his strengths he was ignorant. That men of faith have a strength of character and devotion to their Lord that defies explanation. That men of this type seem to have a *"peace that surpasses all understanding"* (Philippians 4:7).

Secondly, He wanted the trials of Job to be recorded for posterity, so that future generations of Believer's might examine their faith, and check its motives. Men have through the ages, followed great leaders, not because they made life comfortable and lavish for their subjects; no in most cases it was exactly the opposite. Following the great leaders of history usually came at great personal cost, often life itself. These Generals, Presidents, and Prime Ministers of history attracted committed followers because people believed in their purposes and vision. They believed that their cause would make the world a better place…maybe not for their own generation, but for the generations to come. In short, their service was based on serving, not receiving. It was the cause that they believed in. This was the motivation behind their faith.

And this was where my personal journey began. After September 11,2001 I was thrust into a crisis of faith. As I watched the television screen from my office, I stared at the image that seemed surreal as I saw the second plane crash into the World Trade Center. I vividly remember the horror of the next several hours as the buildings collapsed...not realizing it at the time that my financial position would collapse just like those buildings. I had invested all that I had in a business that I had started, and had wagered heavily on the future of this business. The main concern of the business was producing a commodity (beef) that would lose 30% of its value in the fourteen trading days subsequent to 9/11. The result...I lost most on my net worth in the next three weeks, and it took me a couple of more months to realize it.

What happened? I was, after all, a giver and a participant in the Covenant of Abraham, grafted in by the Blood of My Lord and Savior. The only thing that could happen to me was wealth and prosperity. All the sudden it wasn't *"pressed down and running over... (into) my bosom"*(Luke 6:38). It was, in fact, running the other way... *into* the other guys *"bosom"*. To say that I was stunned does not do it justice. I became a zombie, both physically and spiritually. My faith was shaken to the core. I had completely lost my balance; this actually occurred years before, when I began to prescribe to an out of balance doctrine commonly called the "Prosperity Message", but I had just been awakened to this fact, like a bucket of cold water in the face, by the events of 9/11.

And so I found myself in the middle of a Spiritual cyclone. Much like Job, caught up in a contest between the forces of heaven and the forces of evil. More than a contest...an all out war, of which my business had just become a casualty. How could God let this happen! Where was He? Did I do something that facilitated this? Was I being punished for some unconfessed sin? For two years the questions continued. And much like an engineer that tests a foundation of a building, and discovers a crack, I found that my faith was defective. It was built on some false premises. When measured against Job's, it was totally inferior. My motives were not entirely pure. There was too much of me in my walk with Christ and not enough Him. Like it or not I had entered into the refiner's flame and the impurities (dross) of my spiritual life was being siphoned off the top.

But every great breakthrough with God comes on the heels of a "faith crisis". The sons and daughters of Israel, could not enter into the inheritance of Canaan, without first facing the faith crisis of the Jordan River. And so it is today. It is trial that brings about the perfecting of faith, and crisis that instigates an Exodus…a forced journey. A journey that will often take us deep into the heart of God, where we find out much about Him, but just as importantly, we find out the truth about ourselves and our motives for following Him. This book is about just such a journey. And I have been compelled by the Spirit to share what I've learned with the Body of Christ, for the path that God has placed me on since 9/11, has enlightened me as to the condition of the Church. I find that my story is not the exception, but the rule. Most of the Church is not in bondage to alcohol, or drugs, or pornography…their in bondage to debt. The effects are the same…they are not free.

God has done miraculous things to set His people free in the past, and He is more than willing to do miraculous things to set His people free now, but first they have to acknowledge that they are enslaved. His people were enslaved in Egypt long before they came to the realization of the fact. They only began to cry out after the demands of their masters became oppressive. I submit that the demands of the financial masters of the average Believer will soon become just as oppressive. The church has to wake up the way that I did, and realize that in every area of their life they may be the image of Christ, but in the area of their personal finances, they are no different from the rest of the world. The Word says, "… *do not be conformed to this world, but be transformed by the renewing of your mind, that you may prove what is that good and acceptable and perfect will of God.*" (Romans 12:2). A good reason to be not *"conformed to the world"* in the area of finances is because the world is broke!

They are deceived and they are in bondage. We, on the other hand, are called to be free (John 8:36). The goal of this book is to become a guide to help Believers come out of the stupor that I was in for so many years, and realize that they are in bondage. My calling in Ministry is to show God's people the way to Financial Deliverance. Don't be mistaken, God wants to bless His children just like you want to bless your own children, but if (heaven forbid) you have a child that is in bondage to alcohol or drugs, the wise parent understands that money given to this child will end up in the hands of those who are supplying the drug. It is no different with God. If you are in bondage to someone who is charging you 28% interest on your credit cards, He knows who will get the money if He gives it to you. Those who are supplying the drug...*credit.*

I was conformed to the world in the area of my finances at one time in my life, and prescribed to an interpretation of God's Word that was out of balance. God has set me on the path of freedom, and forever changed me in the process. Although my suffering has been minimal, it was a painful thing to face the truth about myself, but know this... it's the truth that will set you free.

So what do you really think about Job? A loser...or a hero. In God's heart, he was a hero for the ages. A man that loved his God, not for what He could do for him, but merely because of who He was. The blessings in Job's life were the bi-product of his faith and devotion. Not the cause.

So I say to you, the reader, if you elect to take this journey to freedom you will be forced to answer "the question" from deep in your heart. Be prepared... you may not like the answer. What question you ask? The question is simple...Why do I follow Him? What's my motivation? Is my motivation worthy of the price He paid, so that we could be reunited? When I place the motives of my heart up against the Cross...am I embarrassed? I know I was. My faith was carnal and shallow. My devotion was based on the potential for plunder, not the pursuit of the righteous cause of justice, mercy, love, and freedom.

The impurity of my motives had brought me into bondage to debt and the things of the world. But in the wilderness of my Exodus, I've learned much about myself, my enemy, and my Lord. I've learned how to live free. And I'll only go back to Egypt for one purpose, and that is to lead God's people out. So, here we are...standing on the Banks of the Red Sea. The financial wilderness looks forbidding, but on the other side of the wilderness is the *"Promised Land"*. A place that flows with *"milk and honey"*. A place where God wants to bless you. Do you have the courage to make the journey? Believe me...it's worth it.

G.W.

Contents

Part One: "The Revelation"

Why Would God Want To Prosper His People? –

The Covenant—"I will bless you…and in you all the families of the earth shall be blessed." Genesis 12:2-3

One of the most misunderstood and unbalanced doctrines taught in the American Church today, is the doctrine of God's Prosperity. There have been more books written and tapes made on God's financial blessings than on the doctrine of salvation. It seems to be a subject that attracts much interest. This interest is in a word— "natural". It is a natural thing for a person to desire to succeed in career or business. And God wants His people to be successful so that they might be an influence in a dying world. The issue is motive. God wants to *"give good gifts to His children"* (Matthew 7:11), but God also knows that for every ten men who can withstand adversity, there is only one in that same group that can withstand prosperity.

In the 8th Chapter of Deuteronomy Moses pleads with the children of Israel, not to forget their God who is about to bring them into the Promised Land, and consequently great blessing. When you read this chapter its almost as if Moses has seen a prophecy of the future of the nation of Israel. He reminds them that, *"the Lord your God led you all the way these forty years in the wilderness to test you, to know what was in your heart, whether you would keep His commandments or not."* (Deuteronomy 8:2). And that this testing was to demonstrate that man can't live by *"bread alone, but man lives by*

19

every word that proceeds from the mouth of the Lord." (Deuteronomy 8:3). In verses 13,14, & 17 of that same chapter he said, *"and when your herds and your flocks multiply, and your silver and gold are multiplied, and all that you have is multiplied, when your heart is lifted up and you forget the Lord your God who brought you out of Egypt from the house of bondage…then you shall say in your heart, 'My power and the might of my hand have gained me this wealth.'"* You notice He didn't say, "**if** your hearts become lifted up"; he said *"**when** your heart is lifted up."* Moses seemed to understand intuitively, that the character that had been built-up in his people by the adversity of the wilderness, would be destroyed by the lavishness of unlimited prosperity and wealth.

History, of course, proved his intuition correct. After taking over the Promised Land of their fathers, and enjoying its richness and blessing, Israel became a backslidden-shadow of its former self. Wealth in and of itself, apart from God, has the damaging impact to its holder of exalting "self". And "self" has always been the enemy of God and His Kingdom.

The truth is that we are made in God's image. God is "triune" in nature, or "three-in-one". We, His children, are "three-in-one". The New Testament uses three different words to describe "life". Each one refers to one of the three aspects of our existence that makes us "triune" in nature. When Jesus was teaching the Parable of the Sower in the 8th Chapter of Luke, He referred to the life that chokes out the seed (or natural life) as *"bios"* life. He said, *"Now the ones (seeds) that fell among thorns are those who, when they have heard, go out and are choked with cares, riches, and pleasures of life (bios), and bring no fruit to maturity."* (Luke 8:14, NKJV). He clearly was referring to the natural life in this passage, or the "biological" life. The "pleasures of the biological life" would indicate anything from sexual indulgence to over-eating. Anything that brings our bodies pleasure, however short lived it may be, is something that we don't desire to give-up. When the choices are indulgence, or living by the Word of God, most of us will choose indulgence.

The second reference to man's triune existence was in John 12:25 when He said, *"He who loves his life (psuche) will lose it, and he who hates his life (psuche) in this world will keep it for eternal life."* (John 12:25, NKJV). The Greek word here for life—psuche *(psoo-khay')* is often interchanged in translation with the English word "soul". It refers to the "soulish-nature" of man, or his mind, will, and emotions. It is the root for the English word *psyche*. The psyche of a man is that very complex system of his will, mind, and emotions that make him so unique and so unpredictable. These two facets of man's nature form an alliance that the Bible calls *"the flesh"*. A simpler way to think of the *"flesh"* is to think of the "self-nature". Man's flesh or his "self-nature" is what stands between him and his creator.

The third and most important level of our existence is the spirit. The Greek word used in the New Testament for the spiritual life is *"zoe"*. Jesus said, *"...I am the way, the truth, and the life (zoe). No one comes to the Father except through Me."* (John 14:6, NKJV). "Zoe" is the spiritual nature that has to be regenerated by the "born-again" experience. In the third Chapter of John, the Pharisee Nicodemus was incredulous at the response of Jesus when he had come to Him by the cover of darkness, so as to minimize the impact of his reputation, and confessed that he knew that Jesus was a teacher from God. He said, *"no one can do these signs that you do unless God is with him."* (John 3:2) Jesus, seeing right to the heart of the matter as He always did, responded, *"Most assuredly I say to you, unless one is born again, he cannot see the Kingdom of God."* (John 3:3). That wasn't the response Nicodemus was expecting. He was expecting some explanation from Jesus as to how He had come by His authority which was obviously from God. Nicodemus was stunned by what Jesus had said to him. He himself was no neophyte to the things of God. After all, he was a Pharisee. They were required to know the first five Books of the Bible by memory. They were meticulous tithers, and lived a life consecrated unto God. Nicodemus had even confessed that He believed in Jesus. And yet the Lord's response too him was "you're not saved". That he had to be "born again" to make heaven. Nicodemus protested by asking, *..."How can a man be born-again when he is old? Can he enter a second time into his mother's womb and be born?""* (John 3:4) Then Jesus answered, *"Most assuredly, I say to you, unless one is born of water and the Spirit, he cannot enter the Kingdom of Heaven. That which is born*

21

of flesh is flesh, and that which is born of spirit is spirit." (John 3:5-6)

What Jesus was alluding to was the regenerative experience of having one's spirit brought back to life. God said through His prophet Ezekiel, *"I will put My Spirit in you, and you shall live, and I will place you in your own land. Then you shall know that I, the Lord, have spoken it and performed it," says the Lord."* (Ezekiel 37:14, NKJV). God is clearly saying that there is a process by which His Spirit comes into us. Jesus called this process, being *"born again".*

It was man's spiritual nature that was the casualty in the Garden of Eden when Adam and Eve failed to keep the commandment of the Lord to stay away from the tree of knowledge. God understood that the mind of man would always war with his spiritual nature, and that it would be detrimental for Adam to partake of the fruit of the tree of knowledge before he was ready. Before his spiritual nature had become his dominant nature. It is not that God wanted Adam to be some kind of ignorant robot that followed Him around like a Labrador retriever. It's just that God fully understood that once man's insatiable appetite for understanding was activated, that he would have a tendency to reject the things that his mind could not understand, and that the mysteries of God and who He is are never going to be intellectually palpable to a reasoning mind. That while Adam's nature would insist on understanding, his finite mind would always be woefully inadequate to understand an infinite God. Man has always been required to accept God by faith, not by reasoning.

And after a person has established a faith based relationship with his/or her creator, then God will teach through the communion of man's spirit and His Spirit…the Holy Spirit. The word communion means –"the intimate exchange of thoughts and ideas." God's communication link is "spirit-to-spirit". Not mind to mind. The mind was intended to serve the spirit…not the other way around. So the tragedy of Adam's sin was that man's spiritual nature was assassinated, in effect, by his carnal nature or *"flesh-nature".*

The role of the Son, Jesus Christ, was to provide a mechanism whereby man's spiritual nature could be "reborn" or regenerated. He also demonstrated the power and life of the Spiritual nature that is available to all those who are willing to pursue it. *"For Christ also suffered once for sins, the just for the unjust, that He might bring us to God, being put to death in the flesh but made alive by the Spirit,"* (1 Peter 3:18, NKJV). He demonstrated a pathway that would *"bring us to God"*. The process that He modeled was to kill the "flesh" so to speak, and allow the Spirit to live. Fortunately for us, we do not have to literally "kill the flesh". By deliberately over-coming reasoning, and accepting Him and His sacrifice by faith, the sacrifice itself is spiritually imputed to us. We have to accept the Cross even though it is foolishness to our natural mind and its reasoning ability. *"For the message of the cross is foolishness to those who are perishing, but to us who are being saved it is the power of God."* (1 Corinthians 1:18, NKJV).

When we demonstrate to God that we are willing to believe and not necessarily understand. That we are willing to take authority over our "soulish-nature", and *"walk according to the spirit"* (Romans 8:1), then He touches our spirit and brings it back to life and then He does something even more wonderful. He puts His spirit in us, and our spirits commune together (share intimate thoughts and ideas). God in essence, restores what Adam lost in the garden, and we become intimate with Him again. We have been *"born again"* and many of us mature in the spirit and become "spiritual" in nature. Or put another way, our spiritual or *"Zoe"* nature becomes dominate and our flesh remains under subjection to it. We *"walk according to the spirit and not the flesh"*.

For far too many Christians, this process of transformation stops at their Calvary experience and they never become spiritual. They remain carnal...driven by the impulses of their flesh-nature. The Word of God is clear on one issue—your flesh nature and God are an enmity to one another. It says, *"For the flesh lusts against the Spirit, and the Spirit against the flesh; and these are contrary to one another, so that you do not do the things that you wish."* (Galatians 5:17, NKJV). It also says, *"So then, those who are in the flesh cannot please God."* (Romans 8:8, NKJV). The "flesh-nature", which we've identified as the "self-nature," is simply man's "natural state". Man in his natural state—is an enemy of God, because he is led by his "flesh". So when we seek to "prosper", the question is: are our motives natural, or spiritual? In other words do we seek personal gratification or do we seek to make a difference for God?

■ Reasons God Wants to Prosper His Children Financially

1. To Be An Influence

So this begs the question, "If the evidence is overwhelming that when God's people prosper financially, they turn from Him and begin to live in their flesh, why would God desire to prosper any of His children." The answer is influence. A history professor (who shall remain nameless) once said that it was unfortunate that fate had placed Israel in between Egypt and Babylonia. His reasoning was that since these were the two Super-Powers of antiquity, it was inevitable that Israel would be crushed as these two civilizations contended for world dominance. They were trapped with nowhere to go, the Mediterranean Sea to the west and desert to the east. These two great powers, one to the north and one to the south, left the children of Israel in a sort of geographical vice. He went on to say that if they had been located in some other area, say Europe, etc., they could have continued to develop unimpeded for thousands of years with no formidable enemies. But since they were located on the main trade routes between these two powers it was just a matter of time before they were conquered by one of them. Seems logical doesn't it?

The problem with this logic is that it is logical only from the viewpoint of a secular historian, with no or little understanding of God's plan and purposes on Earth. The reason that Israel was located between the banks of the Jordan and the shores of the Mediterranean Sea was precisely so they would be located between two Super-Powers. It was not a misfortune of fate. It was their destiny. God placed His people on the main trade routes of the historic period, so that they might be an influence. If you are going to be an influence on the world of the lost, you have two ways that this may be accomplished. One is through military strength, and the other is through commerce. God chose commerce. I believe that as history progressed

He ordained the birthing of America. A nation that would exert influence in both areas, commercial and military strength. Israel, however, would always receive its strength and protection from the Supernatural power of the God of Abraham, Isaac, and Jacob. He was their inheritance (Jeremiah 10:16). So long as the Children of Israel followed hard after their God and "turned not to the left or the right from His commandments" (Deuteronomy 28:14), He protected them supernaturally.

He reveals His plan to the prophet Jeremiah:

Jeremiah 33:9 (NKJV)

[9] Then it shall be to Me a name of joy, a praise, and an honor before all nations of the earth, who shall hear all the good that I do to them (Israel); <u>they shall fear and tremble for all the goodness and all the prosperity that I provide for it(the nation of Israel).</u>'

[1]

Just think about that for a minute. His plan was to prosper His own covenant people (Israel) through trade, to such a degree that it would scare Israel's natural enemies. It was only after Israel committed spiritual adultery with the gods of the indigenous peoples of Canaan, that their protection from superior military powers was withdrawn. But secular history demonstrates that even though they had been carried away into captivity in Babylon by the ancient Babylonian King Nebuchadnezzar, they prospered in that great city no longer as farmers and shepherds, but as shop-keepers and administrators of the King. The prophet Daniel, for example was described as having "an excellent spirit" and prospering in the courts of the Kings of Babylonia as an advisor and administrator. So much so that He became the most successful of the "satraps" or governmental ministers of the King (Daniel 6:3). The blessings of prosperity continued to flow to His covenant people, even when their idol worship had caused them to be removed from the lands of their inheritance. In fact, when the Persian Kings began to allow the repatriation of Judah by the Jews, starting with King Cyrus in 559 B.C. and ending with Darius II in 404 B.C., only 42,000 of the esti-

---

[1] *The New King James Version*. 1996, c1982. Thomas Nelson: Nashville

mated 1,000,000 Jewish exiles elected to return to their homeland. The reason – in spite of captivity, they had prospered in Babylon, and were reluctant to leave their prosperous farms and businesses.

2. He Promised He Would –

If we understand anything at all about God, it has to be that He is a covenant maker and a covenant keeper. God's covenant people will always prosper, no matter where they reside, or under what circumstances. This was His promise to the descendants of Abraham; that they would be blessed and that through them all the families of the earth would be blessed (Genesis 12:2-3). And furthermore, according to Galatians 3:29, *"... if you are Christ's, then you are Abraham's seed, and heirs according to the promise."* Those who are "in Christ", are covered by the Abrahamic Covenant. This is one of the six Biblical covenants that are eternal in nature. Abraham himself, as we know from Genesis 13:2, was "very rich". He was prominent among the local Kings of Canaan largely due to his vast wealth. Abraham's fortune was made in the livestock business. His and his nephew Lot's herds became so vast, that there was contention between their respective herdsman as to available water and grass in Genesis 13. Abraham chose peace over conflict when he asked Lot to pick the territory that he wanted and to "separate" from him. He says to Lot in Genesis 18:8-10, *"Please let there be no strife between you and me, and between my herdsmen and your herdsmen; for we are brethren. ⁹ Is not the whole land before you? Please separate from me. If you take the left, then I will go to the right; or, if you go to the right, then I will go to the left."* He knew full well that Lot would choose the "well watered" country to the east. He knew that he would be left with the desert. He chose financial hardship over "strife" with his "brethren". In this decision Abraham proved once more to God that he was made of the right stuff. He set an example for Believers in business as to the attitude that must be maintained to walk in God's blessing and abundance. This event in Genesis testifies to the heart of Abraham. Wealth was not as important to him as family. He understood that his wealth had come from God and not by his own efforts. Therefore it was up to

God to sustain it, not him. He understood that relationships were precious...not gold.

After Abraham demonstrated his character by making a hard choice for peace in his household, God rewarded him in Genesis 13:14-15 when He tells Abraham, *"Lift your eyes now and look from the place where you are—northward, southward, eastward, and westward; for all the land which you see I give to you and your descendants."* This is the Biblical claim that the nation of Israel stands on today concerning what has come to be known as the Holy Lands of Zion. Just think of it. Because one faithful man chose to pursue family instead of finances. Because one faithful man had his priorities right before an all mighty God. Because one faithful man was willing to trust in God and not in wealth, an entire peoples were blessed. Not only did God give Abraham everything that he could see, but he gave it for an eternity to his descendants. A blessing that Satan has been trying to steal ever since. A Land so sacred, that many have died defending it. Defending this covenant that was made between God and Abraham; a man justified not by his righteousness, but by his faith in God (Genesis 15:6).

Down deep in this Biblical account is the secret to abundance. Examine Abraham closely, and you will find God's requirements for increase. Abraham had just completed a 1500-mile journey by faith. Faith that God would give him a "promised land". A place where God would establish him and in the Lord's own words, "make him a great nation." It was when Abraham first entered Canaan at Shechem, that God appeared to him and told him that He would give him this land (Genesis 12:7). Then Abraham traveled south all the way to Egypt before returning to the mountain just east of Bethel, where he had constructed an altar to God immediately after receiving the vision from the Lord concerning his inheritance. This was a sacred place to Abraham; a place where he "called on the name of the Lord". A Holy place that reminded him of God's original promises concerning the Land he was to inherit. It was here, at this altar...this sacred place...that years later, Lot would stir up contention concerning their feuding herdsman. How dare he be so irreverent. In fact, close examination of the scriptures reveals that Lot clearly did not understand the source of his blessing. He was blessed because of his relationship with Abraham. He did not seem to have an intimate relationship with God. He looked at the natural realm as the source of his blessing. Good grass and good water. He clearly did not possess the understanding of divine provision that his uncle had. Of course, God did not appear to Lot. He appeared to Abraham. But instead of seeking a relationship with God like Abraham's, he sought better land and water.

3. Expression of Our Creative Gifts Will Always Cause Us To Prosper

I wonder what was going through Abraham's mind as he asked Lot to choose his preferred pastures and separate from him. This was *his* inheritance that he had traveled over great distances and suffered great travails to possess. In an instant, he gave it away. I wonder if he gave a thought to how God would have reacted to this foolish act. You see, I think that Abraham was a great herdsman and had a great trading instinct. But I don't really think money meant all that much to him. You see people who place a high value on money, will always fight for the choicest property. They cannot help it. It is the way that they are made.

But if you examine many of the "self-made" millionaires of modern times, you find one similarity. That is that they didn't do it for the money. Wealth, in and of its self, is a pretty poor motivator. Most great fortunes are amassed by people that have extraordinary creative gifts, and simply desire to express that creativity. Bill Gates for example has always been driven by his fascination with excellent software, much of which he created or helped create. He has recently changed his title at the computer software giant Microsoft, Inc., from CEO to Chief Software Architect. Why? Because when you become the richest man in the world, you can do whatever you want to. And when you get to the place where you can do whatever you want to, your true motivation becomes apparent. Bill Gate's true motivation is to create. Create software. This is what makes him tick. Not money…in and of itself. How do I know that, you ask? Because he has given $24 billion of it away: around half of his total wealth. What a man does with his money speaks volumes about what is in his heart.

4. He Will Test What Is In Our Hearts Through Prosperity—

The character of Abraham is contrasted with that of Lot in this passage. Abraham, who was probably the richest man to ever live, was willing to give it away in the name of peace. He told Lot, *"let there be no strife between us, for we are brethren."* You see it was not that Abraham was afraid of a fight, he just didn't want to fight with his own family. There were many times in the Genesis accounts when Abraham was forced to take up arms to protect what was his. But he was not going to war with his nephew over grazing rights. He would take his chances in the wilderness.

So he gives away the best parts of what God had given him. How could God continue to bless someone who was so foolish with what He had given them to steward? How foolish this must have seemed to the nephew Lot in his carnal mind. He might have prided himself on "out-trading" his uncle. But God had the last word in the matter. Abraham's heart had to be heavy. His nephew must have been a disappointment to him. He was quick to seize the opportunity and take advantage of his uncle. Then God appears to Abraham and says look around. I'm giving you everything that you see (Genesis 13:15).

All through Abraham's experiences in Canaan, God was testing his heart. When Abraham proved to God that his relationships were more important than money. When he demonstrated genuine love and compassion for Sarah, Lot, or even Ishmael, God promoted and increased him. Of course the final and toughest test occurred on Mount Moriah, were God ask Abraham to sacrifice his only remaining son, Isaac; the seed of the promise.

By now, Abraham has had to send Ishmael and his mother out of the camp. His heart was broken, for he truly loved the boy, and tried to get God to accept him as the "seed" of the covenant. God refused however, and told him that Sarah would become pregnant with Isaac and he would be the "seed of the promise". Ishmael, who was born out of the will of the flesh, would never be the seed of God's covenant. Sarah and Abraham had conjured up a scheme to "help God" along with His promise that Abraham would be the father of many nations.

Sarah had allowed the enemy to plant strongholds in her mind that would cause her to make a grave mistake. *"So Sarai said to Abram, "See now, the Lord has restrained me from bearing children. Please, go in to my maid; perhaps I shall obtain children by her." And Abram heeded the voice of Sarai."* (Genesis 16:2, NKJV) Sarah was convinced that she was the stumbling block to the fulfillment of the promise. The mistake that Sarah made was not realizing that its not who **we** are that matters in the miracle…but **whose** we are. Its not about us…its about Him. Most believers who struggle in receiving from God, struggle not because they don't believe in God or His miracles; they see themselves as unworthy to receive such favor. They fail to understand that when God looks at them, all He sees is the blood of Jesus on them. That they are not justified by the way they have lived or the choices they have made.

They are justified in the eyes of God by what they have believed. *"But as many as received Him, to them He gave the right to become children of God, to those who believe in His name: who were born, not of blood, nor of the will of the flesh, nor of the will of man, but of God."* (John 1:12-13). What makes them "heirs to the Promise", is their faith in Jesus Christ. If you have been "born again", you have become eligible to receive. Its not what you did that matters… its about what He did. The New Covenant that we are party to is established by His Blood, not by our works. Our lives in and of themselves, don't warrant these kind of blessings, but we walk in *"unmerited favor"*. Grace is by definition, *"the unmerited favor of God."*

Sarah just couldn't see that it wasn't about her…it was about Him and what He wanted to establish on Earth. So she began to ask herself, "What are we going to do? I'm not getting any younger and neither is Abraham." The result was Ishmael; a son born not by the commission of the Spirit, but out of the will of the flesh. God could not and would not use him as His seed. If Sarah had focused on God's word, and not on her own inadequacies, she would have saved herself and the rest of the world a lot of grief. You see Ishmael is the progenitor of the Arab races, and they have warred with the "Seed of Isaac" for thousands of years.

So God's promise of prosperity tests us in two ways. Can we wait patiently for its fulfillment in our lives, or do we decide to "do something" and thus give birth to some Ishmaels. How long are you willing to wait for God to fulfill His promise in your life? It seems to me that we spend an inordinate amount of time waiting on God. In fact ninety percent of our time in the Kingdom we spend waiting. It only takes God a minute to manifest the miracle in the natural, but we may have been waiting on the promise of that miracle for many years. So He tests us to see if we will wait or take matters into our own hands.

The real test occurs after the promise has manifest. God said in Matthew 6:24, *"No one can serve two masters; for either he will hate the one and love the other, or else he will be loyal to the one and despise the other. You cannot serve God and mammon."* Mammon is the Biblical term for wealth. God will release some prosperity in our lives to see who is going to serve whom. Can we remember that money is not our master. Are we strong enough to be master over the money or will we become slave to it? And in so doing, become separated from God, since He will not compete for glory with anything or anyone. Notice that the word didn't say that we couldn't steward wealth, and serve God. It said that we couldn't serve wealth, and serve God. It's all an issue of perspective.

The truth is that the Greek word for prosperity—*euodoo (yoo-od-o),* is used very rarely in the New Testament. The most prominent passage where it is used would be 3 John 2, *"Beloved, I pray that you may prosper in all things and be in health, just as your soul prospers."* John is saying that he is praying for our prosperity, but only in accordance with the prosperity of our soul. In other words, he is praying for balance in our lives. The more prominent term used is increase—*auxano* (owx·**an**·o). As we will learn in later chapters, God is waiting to increase whatever you will give to Him. Then He waits to see what you do with the increase. Do you serve it, or do you sow it. Are you after more seed, or are you after things. He wants you to have the things, but He doesn't want them to have you.

Clearly, this business of prospering His people is tricky, to say the least. I have isolated seven tests in the Word of God that we must pass, so as to release the ***increase*** in our lives. Make no mistake, God wants you to pass the test and become blessed; " *"And you shall remember the Lord your God, for it is He who gives you power to get wealth, that He may establish His covenant which He swore to your fathers, as it is this day."* (Deuteronomy 8:18, NKJV). Never forget…He is a covenant-maker and a covenant-keeper!

Welcome to Babylon

"And Babylon, the glory of kingdoms, The beauty of the Chaldeans' pride, Will be as when God overthrew Sodom and Gomorrah." **(Isaiah 13:19)**

"And I heard another voice from heaven saying, "Come out of (Babylon), my people, lest you share in her sins, and lest you receive of her plagues." **(Revelation 18:4)**

In 1 Chronicles chapters 11-17, David is finally recognized as the King of Israel after the death of King Saul and his sons. One by one, the tribes of Israel make their way to Hebron, where David and his army are encamped. It was at this time that their numbers where accounted for and a pledge of loyalty was offered to their new King. As each tribe is enumerated in the Biblical account of chapter 12, there was an interesting footnote added concerning the house of Issachar. It says, *"of the sons of Issachar who had understanding of the times, to know what Israel ought to do, their chiefs were two hundred; and all their brethren were at their command;"* (1 Chronicles 12:32). The *"sons of Issachar"*, seemed to recognize what was happening and the prophetic significance of it. As Ministers of the Word of God, I wonder if we understand the times in which we live. And if we do not, clearly, our congregations cannot.

The evidence is overwhelming that we are in the last days, and although it is not within the scope of this book to expound on the prophecies concerning these times, it is its purpose to bring clearer understanding concerning their impact on today's financial climate. The Bible tells of a coming political, religious, and financial system which it refers to as *"Mystery Babylon"* (Rev. 17:5). If we are going to address the current financial condition of the average Believer, then it is imperative that we understand the times, and to understand these times you must look towards the Prophets. Prophecy, after all, is nothing more than the foretelling of history, and although I believe the Lord when He says, *"...I also will keep you from the hour of trial which shall come upon the whole earth..."* (Rev 3:10), I also understand that events of the magnitude of the Tribulation-period, do not happen over night. Hitler and the Third Reich, for example, did not appear on the world scene in a wisp of smoke and a snap of the fingers. It took years of political unrest and specific conditions had to develop, for a noble nation like Germany to become deceived enough to empower a mad man as its leader. Historical events build on one another and transpire slowly. Just like the "supertankers" of the world of ocean going ships, the "ships of state" must be turned ever so slowly.

So therefore, the follower of Jesus Christ would do well to heed the Lord's words when He said that *"no man knows the day and the hour"* of His coming, but we should, *"learn this parable from the fig tree: When it's branch has already become tender and puts forth leaves, you know the summer is near. So you also, when you see all these things, know that it (the second coming) is near—at the doors!"* (Matthew 24:32). We might not know exactly when these prophecies concerning His *"glorious appearing"* will take place, but we should be able to read the signs and know that He is near, since historical events do not transpire over night, but instead cast a long shadow in time. Anyone who wanted to be honest with themselves should have seen the Third Reich rising in Europe long before Hitler became Fuehrer. In this same fashion, any beginning student of Biblical prophecy understands that the greatest historical event in the story of man is about to take place. We are standing in the shadows of His coming.

And we know by the word of the Lord spoken through His Prophets, that just prior to His return and victory, this Babylonian system will be established on the earth. He will, of course, crush it upon His return, along with the counterfeit trio trying to pass themselves off as the Holy Trinity...Satan, the Anti-Christ, and the False Prophet. But for a seven year season called the Time of Jacob's Trouble (Tribulation), Babylon will become dominate on the earth again.

This Babylonian system will be a tribute to man's intellect and ingenuity; a monument to the deception that man can do things his own way. Adam chose, in the Garden, to eat of the Tree of Knowledge and in so doing was cursed to live by his own moral judgment and intellectual capacity instead of by God's leadership by the Spirit. He was warned that He would die if he ate of the fruit of the Tree of Knowledge, and His "spiritual-nature" did die immediately upon his transgression. He was doomed to try and live out the rest of his days in the strength of his flesh. The heart of Satan's mission is to deceive men/and women into believing that they can make it without God; that the knowledge of the "natural-mind" is sufficient, and in fact, should be the source of their glory instead of their service to God. The "natural-man" thinks he has no need of God. This is the essence of the Babylonian system, the pride of man's technological achievement. A machine for wealth creation. A universal system that encompasses the whole world. A monument to man's intellect.

God's preemptive strike against the Babylonian System —

God has dealt with the rise of this "one-world" system in the past; another monument to man's ingenuity and determination to possess the attributes of God without entering into a relationship with Him. In Genesis chapter 11, the descendants of Noah gathered on *"a plain in the land of Shinar, and they dwelt there."* They said, *"Come let us build ourselves a city, and a tower whose tip is in the heavens; let us make a name for ourselves, lest we be scattered abroad over the face of the earth"* (Genesis 11:4) The Lord came down and examined their work, and was impressed with their ability and ingenuity. *"And the Lord said, "Indeed the people are one and they all have one language, and this is what they begin to do; now nothing that they propose to do will be withheld from them."* (Genesis 11:6). God could see that man was going to continue to sin willfully; living by his "soulish-nature" (mind, will, and emotions), in spite of the judgment of the Flood. He was compelled to take a preemptive measure and *"... go down and there confuse their language, that they may not understand one another's speech."* (Genesis 11:7). Prophetically speaking, it was not time for a "one-world" system. It was much too early in history for man to rule himself through one government, led by one man, from one Capitol City. This event had to be reserved for the pages and the times of Revelation. Only then had it been ordained for a universal political, religious, and financial system to manifest itself on the earth. So He struck their language and they no longer had the ability to communicate corporately. Confusion ensued, and the place became known by the name "Babel", which means confusion. Overtime the name of the city evolved into "Babylon"; Land of confusion. Just as Jerusalem is the blessed city of God, so Babylon was and is cursed by Him, and its ruins are located just a few miles south of the modern city of Baghdad in the country of Iraq.

Saddam Hussein went from the Palace to a prison cell, because he too tried to rebuild this cursed city before it's time. History has shown that to get in the way of God's prophetic design is not a good career move. Just ask the first Babylonians who ended up leaving the *"plain of Shinar"* for points unknown in a state of confusion. One minute they were building a Tower, and the next they couldn't even understand each other. Hussein also harbored lofty intentions for the evil city of Babylon. His heart's desire was to rebuild it to its former glory. He had bricks made that had his name on one side and the ancient Babylonian King Nebuchadnezzar's on the other. These bricks were used to reconstruct some of the City's walls. In fact, he thought he was the reincarnation of this Babylonian ruler who conquered Jerusalem in 586 B.C.

What he failed to recognize was that Babylon would be rebuilt one day, and then supernaturally destroyed by the wrath of God, similar to the way He destroyed Sodom and Gomorrah (Isaiah 13:19), but that day would be intricate to the timing of God's prophetic plan. First it was destined to become the headquarters for the most sophisticated financial system ever devised by man. This system will be, in fact, much more than just a financial system. It will be truly universal. When John, the Apostle of Jesus Christ and the writer of the Book of Revelation refers to *"Mystery Babylon"* in the seventeenth chapter, he is referring to a political, religious, and commercial system to which the world has bowed down. This system, just like the prophetic fig tree, is starting to put on some leaves, and we must understand it better so as to recognize it in its infancy.

No more politics as usual—

The political aspects of the Babylonian system are relatively simple; the world willingly accepts a leader who they think can "deliver the goods", as they say. He will be charismatic and will come disguised as a peacemaker in the beginning of his political career. The prophecies in Daniel indicate that he will gain access to, and political control over the oil fields of the Middle East *"peaceably"* (Daniel 11:24). He will divide the *"plunder"* (profits) from this undertaking to his politically cronies. There will be, according to scripture, ten of these kings who follow him and are the Lieutenants of his power machine. They will gain control of the world's primary energy supply, and within the geographic boundaries of the original Roman Empire, they will form an unholy alliance of nations that will, in effect, control the world. This political system will, **not** be democratic…it will be demonic. This leader, who the Bible refers to as the *"little horn"* (I'll bet he *loves* that), and who John refers to as simply the "Anti-Christ", will hold power because the world wants him to. They believe in him. They think he is Christ. It is the ultimate deception. Half-way through his tenure as the ruler of the world, his true colors will come out. He will turn on God's people (the Jews) and persecute them with great malice and vengeance. Fortunately, if you're a Believer, the Lord has made you a promise: *"…I also will keep you from the hour of trial which shall come upon the whole world, to test those who dwell on the earth."* (Revelation 3:10) I don't know about you, but I hate that I'm going to miss it. Sounds like fun but I've got a dinner date…with the Lord. He calls it His marriage supper, and all things considered, I'd rather be there with Him in heaven than down here watching the world fall into a powerful deception. Again, we're not particularly interested in what happens after the Church is raptured and *"caught up in the air to be with Him"*, but we are interested in the shadows of His coming and what they mean to us. Already we see the political winds blowing in the direction of a revised Roman Empire of prophecy. Five Arab countries form an alliance with five European countries to form the last gentile power to ever exist on the earth. If the war in Iraq has done nothing else, it has exposed the deep ties that Iraq, Iran and other Muslim states have developed with Western European countries. It's not nearly as difficult, in light of these revelations, to envision a political climate that fosters the creation of such an alliance and the fulfillment of Daniel's prophecy (Daniel 2:41-45). The Prophets clearly tell us the politics of the world are about to make some abrupt changes, and you cannot make such drastic political changes without capturing the hearts and minds of the people.

A "One-world" Ecumenical Religious System —

Enter stage left…the false prophet. Revelation 13 tells of the coming of a "false prophet" who will finish off the deception of "those not written in the Lamb's book of life". Again, those who are Believers before the Lord calls His Church to be gathered to Him (we'll be on a seven-year vacation), will not witness the official ordination of this person as the leader of the world's religious system, but once again we're looking for shadows; evidence that these events are at hand. Ecumenical means, of course, "worldwide or universal". Translation—watered down enough to suit everybody. The 21st century Christian Church has, generally speaking, begun this process of neutering the Gospel so as to keep from offending anybody. Even though Christ prayed for unity among His followers; to the rest of the world, He brought division between them and Believers, of which, He seemed unconcerned. In fact, He said Himself, *"For I have come to 'set a man against his father, a daughter against her mother, and a daughter-in-law against her mother-in-law';"* (Matthew 10:35). His clear intent was to sort those who believed, from the rest of the world, no matter who it tore them from. If He gave little thought to offending the mother of a daughter who was a Believer, I doubt He would worry about violating the religious sensitivities of Buddhists, for example. Christ has always brought division. To attempt to water down the Gospel enough to please everybody, robs it of its truth and power.

Yet this is the precise purpose of the Babylonian religious system. To draw everyone who remains in the world into a universal religion, and thereby give the people of the world a false sense of security and peace, while the Anti-Christ and his cohorts, loot and pillage the governments of the world— all in the name of world unity. This false prophet will also do great signs during the Tribulation, even causing, *"fire to come down from heaven on the earth in the sight of men,"* (Revelation 13:13). He will cause a great statue of the Anti-Christ that is erected in his honor, to come to life and speak. This ought to convince any remaining skeptics as to the Anti-Christ's self-proclaimed deity. Of course, another effective deterrent to unbelief will be the fact that the false prophet will have anyone who refuses to bow down and worship the statue killed. These guys really know how to build a church of committed members, and fast!

Then there is the sticky issue of explaining to the rest of the world what happened to roughly a third of its population at the rapture. You've got to have some talking statues and a little hell-fire and brimstone to sway them after that, I'll bet. Revelation 13:6 says about the Anti-Christ, *"... he opened his mouth in blasphemy against God, to blaspheme His name, His tabernacle, and those who dwell in heaven."* The word *"blasphemy"* is not an everyday word for most of us, so if you're like me, maybe you need to check out its definition to get the drift of what John is saying. According to the American Heritage Dictionary, *"blasphemy"*, is any contemptuous or profane act, utterance, or writing concerning God, and I would like to add—or His people. He and his false prophet will be *"talkin' trash"* about God, His name (or power), His tabernacle (which they promptly defile), and *"those who dwell in heaven"*. Who might that be I wonder? I doubt it's the angels...its just not good P.R. to trash angels. I suspect it's those of us who have been raptured. They're probably going to tell the world that we were sent to hell for preaching to everybody all the time. I'm not sure *what* they will be saying, but I know it will be *"blasphemous"*, and its intent will be to discredit the fulfillment of the Prophetic event called the "rapture of the Church".

Who said, "Religion and business don't mix"? —

Then there's the final "church-building" strategy that the Babylonian religious system will employ, and it may be its most effect. It's referred to by John as simply *"the mark"*. According to Revelation 13:16-18, after the false prophet breathes life into the statue of his boss, the Anti-Christ, he then requires everyone to express their devotion by receiving *"a mark on their right hand or on their forehead."* Without this mark, which is probably actually a RF transmitter of some type, no one may *"buy or sell"*. This technology is available today, and is being used, in fact, in places like Mexico, where all their top government officials have been "implanted" with one of these devices so that in the event of their abduction or kidnapping, they could be located by authorities no matter where they might be taken. All that is required is for the police to take a receiver (set to the frequency of the respective transmitter); place it in a helicopter, and the target can be located in a matter of minutes. These devices are also being touted by the financial community as the perfect remedy for credit card fraud. Simply place a scanner at every cash register, and every time a credit card is used, require the customer to pass his or her hand through the scanner so as to verify the identity of the cardholder. Better yet, eliminate the card altogether and just have the customers scan activate the electronic transaction of crediting and debiting to the proper accounts. After all, the computer systems could care less about the card you're carrying—they just want the ID information off of the magnetic strip on the back. This exact same information could be easily accessed through a RF transmitter implanted in the hand of every consumer, with markedly reduced incidents of fraud, no doubt. It's very difficult to steal someone's identity, when you've got to steal one of their appendages to get it. It will all seem very practical and reasonable I'm sure.

But what's interesting is __who__ institutes this ID system. It's not the computer geek from the data processing department who has the pocket protector full of various colored pens which have some obscure purpose that only an MIT graduate can discern. Nor is it the tough guy who seems angry most of the time and has that curious scare on his face, and heads up international security. No...it's the false prophet; the leader of the counterfeit religious system. Why is he concerned with streamlined data-transfer? Why is he concerned with increases in the efficiency of the world's financial systems? Is he after enhanced targeting capability similar to that used by *"The Terminator"*, so as to track down those who refuse to bow down to the image of the Anti-Christ and worship him? Perhaps. But if we're not careful, we'll miss a deep Spiritual truth about two things; our concept of God and our concept of money. The goal of the enemy has always been to link these two concepts in our mind; righteousness and wealth. The Jews of Jesus' day were overtly religious as demonstrated by their attempt to live strictly by God's law. Jesus said. *""Woe to you, scribes and Pharisees, hypocrites! For you pay tithe of mint and anise and cummin, and have neglected the weightier matters of the law: justice and mercy and faith. These you ought to have done, without leaving the others undone"* (Matthew 23:23). They carefully weighed out the tithe received in trades that involved spices, and yet treated the poor mercilessly. They showed no compassion or mercy on them, but instead saw their poverty as the result of their unrighteousness and sin. There is no doubt that sin produces poverty and sickness, but their measure of righteousness became exclusively in accordance with a man's wealth. If you had it...you were righteous. If you didn't...you were "unclean".

The Babylonian religious system says, "You worship me, you get wealth. Otherwise you starve." And the leader of this universal religious system is the one who decides who gets access to markets and who doesn't. He determines who's *"blessed"* and who's not. They willingly worship a god who they think will make them wealthy. Jesus warned of a powerful spirit that would deceive men and draw them away from God. He said, *"No one can serve two masters; for either he will hate the one and love the other, or else he will be loyal to the one and despise the other. You cannot serve God and mammon"* (Matthew 6:24). The Aramaic word translated as "mammon" literally means riches. The issue is not having riches,

it's worshiping them. We will cover this important spiritual principle in subsequent chapters, but for now we need to understand
that the spirit of mammon will compete for our allegiance, and will
attempt to draw us away from the true source of all wealth—the
God of Abraham, Isaac, and Jacob. As we stated in the introduc-
tion, it's vital that we examine our motives for following Christ. Its
certainly true that He wants to bless us and prosper us, but if that is
our sole reason for pursuing a relationship with Him…we've given
our hearts to the demonic spirit called "mammon".

The power of this demon is strong, and reigns on the earth right
up to the *Day of the Lord*. Jesus warned that the condition of the
Church would deteriorate just prior to His coming, largely due
to the effects of this spirit on Believers. The last-days Laodicean
Church of Revelation 3:14-22, is rich in material things, and yet
they are dead spiritually. Their anemic spiritual condition is largely
due to the fact that they have become self-sufficient; they've got
money and therefore have need of nothing else. Mammon satisfies
the "soulish" appetites of "self-gratification", but can never feed the
spirit. A Church that is content with having "things", can never have
Him.

So it is little wonder that the Babylonian system of religion is
strongly tied to wealth and its hold on the human soul. The spirit of
mammon has always endeavored to capture man, and imprison him.
The *"mark of the beast"* is not about financial freedom…it's about
financial bondage, and the stage has been set. No one has to use
much imagination to envision a centrally controlled world financial
system that knows everything there is to know about everybody,
and rewards those it favors, and persecutes those it does not with a
terrible vengeance. The technology exists, and is in fact already in
place, to allow for the manifestation of the Babylonian system at any
time. Christians are going to have to decide whom they're going to
serve. It's either Him, or mammon. There are no other alternatives.

The book of Revelation is difficult to interpret, because it is not
written in a chronological order. It jumps around from the time of
the Apostles, to the birth of Jesus, to the time of the Tribulation, etc.
We do know, however, that this Babylonian system will be built
during the Tribulation and destroyed upon the Return of Christ at the

end of the Tribulation time period. And most of us strongly believe that the Church will be raptured in the beginning days of this period. In the 18th chapter of Revelation, the Bible gives the account of this destruction of Babylon as the angel proclaims, *"Babylon the great is fallen, is fallen..."*, and the rest of the chapter is devoted to a narrative describing her destruction. So the words of the *"voice from heaven"* seem a trifle strange which occur in verse 4 and say, *"Come out of her, my people, lest you share in her sins, and lest you receive of her plagues."* These instructions for the people of God could, of course, refer to the people who are left behind but get saved during the Tribulation, yet it's fairly clear that they are not **in** the Babylonian system since no one who takes the mark can be saved according to Revelation 14:9-10. I believe that in the light of the book of Revelation's irreverence for chronological order, these words are directed to those who live before the Tribulation period starts. They are a warning to Believers to be in the world, but not of the world. The world's financial systems are already, I believe, entrapping and oppressing God's people since they have chosen to conform to them. The Babylonian system is not here, but her shadow has been cast and can be seen now. At all cost, Believers must renounce the world's financial systems and refuse to become ensnared in its allure. We must, at all cost, get free.

The danger is that we confuse prosperity with righteousness, and being wealthy with being *"in Christ"*. Like the sons of Issachar, we must reckon ourselves to the prophetic clock of scripture, and understand that the world's financial system is designed to entangle and bring bondage on the Covenant people of God. The secret to avoiding the trap, is to recognize it. The angel of the Lord is crying out, *"Come out of her my people lest you share in her sins, and lest you receive of her plagues"*

Is Money Evil?

It is said that for money you can have everything, but you cannot. You can buy food, but not appetite; medicine, but not health; knowledge but not wisdom; glitter, but not beauty; fun, but not joy; acquaintances, but not friends; servants, but not faithfulness; leisure, but not peace. You can have the husk of everything for money, but not the kernel.
-Arne Garborg

Jesus' admonition for the lukewarm Church at Laodicea— *"Because you say, 'I am rich, have become wealthy, and have need of nothing'—and do not know that you are wretched, miserable, poor, blind, and naked— I counsel you to buy from Me gold refined in the fire, that you may be rich; and white garments, that you may be clothed, that the shame of your nakedness may not be revealed; and anoint your eyes with eye salve, that you may see."* (Revelation 3:17-18)

"Money talks...but all mine ever says is good-bye."
-Anon.

Many well meaning people misquote the famous passage from 1 Timothy 6:10 which says, *"For the love of money is a root of all kinds of evil...*" They incorrectly state that "money" is the root of all evil, instead of the "love" of money. Money is not a person, it is a thing; therefore it can be neither "good" nor "evil". Similarly, a brick is an object and not a person, so therefore it also is morally neutral. It can be used to build a hospital or church, or it can be thrown through a window in a riot. The constructive or destructive use of the brick has nothing to do with the brick itself, but everything to do with the hand which holds it. In this same fashion, money can be constructive, and it can be destructive. It can bring life or it can bring death. It can serve, or it can be served. The difference is determined by the hand that is holding it.

The scripture is very clear on one point...it's the Lord's desire that we have money. Proverbs 22:4 says, *"By humility and the fear of the Lord Are riches and honor and life"*. Another Proverb says, *"...I may cause those who love me to inherit wealth, That I may fill their treasuries"* (Proverbs 8:21). And finally Psalms 35:27 says, *"... And let them say continually, "Let the Lord be magnified, Who has pleasure in the prosperity of His servant."* He wants His children to have riches and honor and life, and the said riches are not just some metaphor for spiritual fulfillment. No sir, He's talking about a "full treasury". He wants those who love Him to inherit and have money, and He finds pleasure in them having it. Poverty does not make us more spiritual, it just makes us poor.

So the Word of God states that God recognizes our need to have money; He wants to give it to us (be our source for it), and yet He recognizes there are real spiritual dangers inherent in our having it. The risk is that if He gives it to us, it we will take our eyes off of Him and put them on it. Financial prosperity has always caused problems for God and His relationship with His children. The danger is that we become infatuated with the "booty and plunder" as the Word puts it. Again the issue is motive. What's your motive for following God? Are you seeking His face or just His hand? He will test men's hearts until He knows the answer to the question.

In fact, the first test for the generation of Israelites led by Joshua into the "Promised Land", was whether they could keep their hands off the plunder in Jericho. When the Lord instructed Joshua concerning the attack on Jericho, the first city to fall at the hands of the Israelites in the Canaan campaign, He told him that the gold and silver of the city was His. He said, *"But all the silver and gold, and vessels of bronze and iron, are consecrated to the Lord; they shall come into the treasury of the Lord"* (Joshua 6:19). They were not to be touched or to become the possession of anyone else.

Of course, you know the rest of the story. How a man named Achan took some of the gold for himself and brought the armies of Israel into a curse. After conquering this great and highly fortified city with relative ease, they were subsequently routed by a few farmers with pitchforks in a little village called Ai. The cause of the curse was investigated and discovered and dealt with. Achan was exposed, stoned to death, and burned for good measure. Joshua was serious about keeping the children of Israel and their relationship with money in order. He needed God's blessing much more than he needed a greedy soldier. I wonder how different our lives would be if we looked at things the way Joshua did?

The Four Purposes of Financial Blessing—

So God wants us to have riches and life and honor; but not at the expense of our relationship with Him. There are four purposes that God has for blessing His children with financial wealth. If we will examine these purposes, we can get a better understanding of the role money is to play in a Believer's life.

1. We are blessed to be a blessing—

We're blessed to bless others, not to hoard stuff. How does God get financial blessing to His people? Give up? Through other people. If you receive a financial blessing in your life, God's signature will not be on the check. It will be someone who God has instructed to give you the money. It will usually be another Believer, but occasionally it will be a non-believer. God has used non-believers all through history to bless His people. In fact, in Genesis chapter 12 He told Abraham, *"I will bless those who bless you, and I will curse those who curse you."* He put no stipulation on the givers spiritual conviction, and history has born out the validity of His promise.

This covenant was like all the other covenants in the Bible, it is forever; extending to all the generations of Abraham's descendants. All the nations and people who have blessed and defended the Jews (Abraham's descendants) have been blessed. And all those who have cursed them, have been cursed. With the exception of the Arab countries (which are necessary for the fulfillment of prophetic events yet to come), every nation that has persecuted the Jews has perished from the earth. The Jews are still here, but their adversaries have all vanished.

Furthermore, all the nations that have stood with Israel and blessed her, have been blessed; the greatest example being the United States of America. Since America stood with the United Kingdom for the establishment of Israel as a nation in 1948, after the atrocities that they withstood during World War II, both nations have been blessed and continue to lead in the world. Secular historians might make the argument that these two nations prospered because they won World War II. The problem with that argument is the USSR. The Soviet Union, was their ally during the war, but chose to persecute the Jews. They have perished from the earth. The USSR refused to recognize the God of Abraham, Isaac, and Jacob, or the covenants that He had made with His people, and it cost them their very existence on the earth. Am I saying that if they had blessed the Jews they would still be a Superpower? Would there still be a cold war and an East verses West arms race. Not necessarily, because if they had a heart for God's covenant people, they would have had a different heart towards their own people and the rest of the world. The blessings of the Lord would have had the effect of drawing them closer to the love of God and thereby softening the hardness of Communism. Their downfall was not that they chose to make an enemy of America and the west, but that they chose to be an enemy of God and His covenant people. The rest is history.

When God made this covenant with Abraham, He told Him, "… *in you all the families of the earth shall be blessed*" (Genesis 12:3). The theological implication is that the "seed" of Abraham would be the conduit through which the rest of the world would be blessed. Either through helpful acts of kindness done to them (I will bless those who bless you), or by becoming a member of the family. When you do a good deed for the family of Abraham, you reap a nice reward, albeit a one time thing. Become a member of the family, however, and you're in line for the inheritance. Those of us who are Believers in Jesus Christ belong to Him. *"And if you are Christ's, then you are Abraham's seed, and heirs according to the promise'* (Galatians 3:29). So if we're grafted in, as it were, and have become the *"seed"* of Abraham through our faith in Christ, then the Abrahamic covenant becomes a spiritual reality in our lives; and the words that He spoke to Abraham are very relevant for us. He said, essentially, you are blessed to be a blessing.

There is purpose in the financial blessing that God pours out on the world through the seed of Abraham, and the main one is to be God's agent of blessing on the earth. The purpose is not—"having", it is "being". Not having stuff, but being a blessing to the ones to whom God directs us.

Money is the only natural thing that can be converted into spiritual blessing by handling it properly. Jesus said, *"Do not lay up for yourselves treasures on earth, where moth and rust destroy and where thieves break in and steal; but lay up for yourselves treasures in heaven, where neither moth nor rust destroys and where thieves do not break in and steal"* (Matthew 6:19-20). The implication here is that when we sow the money that God gives us into Kingdom works, it is thereby converted into *"treasures in heaven"*. And He goes on to say, *"For where your treasure is, there your heart will be also"* (Matthew 6:21). God can tell a whole lot about where our heart is by what we do with our money. Are we focused on having blessing…or being a blessing. Therein lies the truth of where our treasure is. It is either on earth, or is it in heaven? It's actual location can be determined by our actions.

What would it be like to write a check to Reinhard Bonke for a million dollars and then watch as he puts on a crusade in Nigeria and wins a million souls for Christ in one night. Where in the natural realm can you find a return like that? A dollar a soul. What kind of treasure would that equate to in the Kingdom of Heaven. Most people say, "If I had a million dollars, I'd give it to him in a minute." But the truth of the matter is, if we won't give a thousand dollars, we certainly wouldn't give a million dollars. And if we won't give a thousand dollars, there's a good chance we wouldn't give a hundred dollars. And if we won't give a hundred dollars, would we give ten dollars…if it were the last ten dollars that we had? Search deep in your soul for the answer to these questions and you will probably find out why you don't have a million dollars. I have a close friend who says, "God will give you whatever you can steward." I believe that. The Word says, *"It is required of a steward that he be found faithful."* (1 Corinthians 4:2). If I can't give Him everything that's in my hand when He asks me to, even if it's just ten dollars, I'll never hold a million dollars in it. The issue is…where's our heart? How bad do you want to be a blessing? Or are you only interested in being blessed?

2. We're blessed to be a witness —

God wants His people to walk in blessing so that the non-believing world will marvel. *"You prepare a table before me in the presence of my enemies; You anoint my head with oil; My cup runs over."* (Psalm 23:5). David is saying that God intentionally blessed him so that His enemies could see it. It was His plan for the blessing to be obvious. Just think of it. God's desire was for the abundant table to standout, to be obvious, not so much to other Believers, but to the world. He wanted them to be drawn to the supernatural nature of David's provision as a clear indication of God's blessing and anointing on His man. Now when can an "abundant table" be more obvious than in difficult economic times? David was living in the *"strongholds of the wilderness"* at the time. Not a likely place to find abundance. So if God's strategy is to bless His servants in a time of financial distress, so as to witness as to His love and protection, then doesn't it follow that He would more than likely bless His children the most in times of economic contraction and even depression?

He even told the prophet Jeremiah, *"Then it shall be to Me a name of joy, a praise, and an honor before all nations of the earth, who shall hear all the good that I do to them (His people); they shall fear and tremble for all the goodness and all the prosperity that I provide for it (the Nation of Israel).'"* (Jeremiah 33:9). This prophecy was given to Jeremiah during the worst times in Israel's history; at least since their occupation of Canaan. It was at the time of Nebuchadnezzar's occupation of Jerusalem. Their lands were occupied and their property had been confiscated by the Babylonian king, and it looked bleak. But God makes a proclamation that He had not forgotten His covenant even though Israel had forsaken their part in it. And He would bless them in distressing times to the point that it would strike fear into the hearts of their enemies. That's what I call a witness. In the worst of economic times, God's people have always prospered, and they always will, because it brings glory to their Father, the God of Abraham, Isaac, and Jacob.

We must always remember that it is God's will *"that none should perish"*. It's always about the lost. Everything that He does is about evangelism and witnessing to the non-believers. God can bless His children during good economic times...when every one is prospering, but He can be glorified when He prospers them in horrendous economic times. It's about His glory, not ours. My prayer is that His people will be encouraged, because in later chapters we will make our argument, convincingly I hope, that the end to naturally prosperous times is just ahead. However, that is when the "supernatural" prosperous times will begin for *"those who love Him and are called to His purposes"*.

"For the eyes of the Lord run to and fro throughout the whole earth, to show Himself strong on behalf of those whose heart is loyal to Him..." (2 Chronicles 16:9). He's looking for someone to *"show Himself strong"* through. If you're strong in the natural, in other words if you've got it made financially, I'm glad for you, but God has a hard time "showing Himself" through you. He's looking for someone whose financial mistakes are obvious to the whole world. He's looking for someone with a few financial enemies out there. He's looking for someone He can set a table for, and the whole world's going to know that it was "supernatural provision." What's required is someone who is in covenant with Him (believes in Jesus Christ as Lord and Savior), and whose finances are in a mess. This person must also be willing to pull up stakes and leave Egypt (the world) financially. Their hearts must be willing to embark on a "Financial Exodus"—to forsake the world's systems and ways of

doing business, and follow the *"pillar of cloud by day"* and the *"pillar of fire by night"* (Exodus 13:22). It's the journey to freedom and prosperity.

But those who make the journey will walk in prosperity like you've never known before. All that is required is that we allow Him to lead us across the Wilderness of transition, where our thinking is transformed, to the place of blessing called the "Promised Land". In the wilderness phase of our financial journey, He will provide for our needs. We will be fed manna from heaven and be given water out of a rock, but we will not prosper there. When our thinking has been transformed and we have been delivered from a "slave mentality", we will be ready to enter into the land of His promise. This is not a physical place, but a spiritual place where we no longer think like the world, *"but have been transformed by the renewing of our mind."* (Romans 12:2). It is here in this place with Him that He will begin to *"strike fear in the hearts of our enemies"* through His radical prospering of His people. We're blessed to be a blessing, and to be a witness. We've got to pack out financial bags and leave the Sea of Red behind.

3. We're blessed to finance the Gospel around the world—

"And God is able to make all grace abound toward you, that you, always having all sufficiency in all things, may have an abundance for every good work." (2 Corinthians 9:8) We're blessed so that we might *"have an abundance for every good work"*. God wants the Gospel preached to the world. *"How then shall they call on Him in whom they have not believed? And how shall they believe in Him of whom they have not heard? And how shall they hear without a preacher? And how shall they preach unless they are sent..."* (Romans 10:14-15). God has provided us with the means to finance His work around the world. It takes money to buy access to tele-communications technology. It takes money to send a missionary to another continent. Money is not a problem for God since it is all His anyway. The issue is finding a willing vessel through which He can funnel His provision to His cause. He has to test the "conductivity" as it were, of every Believer.

Again, it's an issue of the heart. Are we more interested in a new bass boat, or the souls of hungry Africans? Is it important that we live in a more fashionable house and neighborhood, or are we willing to do without, in order to sow into God's work in China? What will have the greatest impact for the Kingdom of God? Our social standing in the community, or sending $500.00 per month to feed hungry people and preach the Gospel to them. The answers to these questions indicate our "conductivity".

Grace and electricity have much in common. Electrons flow from one atom to the next in a current that we know as electricity. The size and quality of the wire that conducts the electricity determines the amount of electricity that can flow through. The electrical current is produced by huge generators in the power plant, and it passes through various wires to get to the household or factory where it energizes a motor or computer or other electrical device to produce something. Grace originates in God and is passed through a conductor called faith. Faith resides in the hearts of God's people. Its size and quality will dictate how much grace can pass through to the need.

When it reaches the need it is energized and produces something in the natural that is very real and tangible. It might produce a coat for a child in the winter time that is on the verge of freezing to death. It might produce a meal in Africa for a family that is starving to death. It might produce a crusade in South America where, in the words of the Lord, the *"Gospel is preached to the poor."* The point is it's never a question of the amount of grace. He gave His only begotten son so that none should perish. The magnitude of God's grace is almost incomprehensible in light of the Cross. What limits God's grace in a specific situation is not the willingness of God to provide; it's the wire through which the provision flows.

In the example of electricity, the conductivity is determined by how easily the atoms of a specific metal will "give-up" their electrons so that they are passed from one atom to another by the induction of electrical current. Copper is a very conductive material, where as rubber or plastic will not conduct electrical current at all. The difference is in their respective molecular composition. One readily gives up its electrons, while the other stubbornly holds on to his. The condition of a Believer's faith determines their "conductivity". Those who willingly "give-up" their money as directed by the induced current of God's grace and instruction, are good conductors. Those who "give-up" their money begrudgingly, are not. One will have the opportunity to be used profoundly by God to help many people in their life time. The other will always scrape to get by and wonder why they never seen to have enough provision.

God has obligated Himself to always provide seed to a sower. *"Now may He who supplies seed to the sower, and bread for food, supply and multiply the seed you have sown and increase the fruits of your righteousness,"* (2 Corinthians 9:10). The sower's potential is defined by his or her "conductivity". The more conductive they are the more seed that will be provided. The issue is how much of the seed are we taking for ourselves. There is no question that He wants us to have *"all sufficiency in all things"*, but the *"abundance"* is for *"every good work."* Satan's number one strategy is to steal and devour your seed. We will discuss this strategy in later chapters, but for now we must recognize that we are blessed to be a blessing, to be a witness, and to finance His work on the earth.

4. We're blessed to be an influence in the world—

I had a history Professor in college that made a statement in a lecture one semester that caused me to contemplate the role of God's people in the world. He said, "It's unfortunate that the people of Israel chose to settle along the Mediterranean Sea, in between two of the greatest powers of antiquity; Assyria to the north and Egypt to the south. Unfortunately, geography would bring about their inevitable downfall as these two superpowers vied for supremacy, causing the territory between them to become the first logical target for conquest." The location of the nation of Israel was, in his words, "unfortunate".

The conquering of the lands of Canaan by the Israelites was not some random act of fate…it was God's plan. He told them that He had given these lands to Abraham and his seed through his son Isaac. Isaac's son Jacob (later changed to Israel by God) was the chosen heir, and therefore the descendants of Israel had covenant rights to this land. It was chosen for them by God. It was their manifest destiny to possess it and pass it on to their heirs for an eternity. Zion, in fact, was chosen by God as His eventual dwelling place (Zechariah 8:3). The term Zion originally was used to describe the City of David, but over time has been used to describe the sum total of the inheritance of Israel. This land is important to God, and Israel's covenant rights to it are important to Him. Anyone who has tried to take it from them throughout history has been cursed. Joel chapter 3, proclaims harsh judgment on those who *"divide up My land"*. The covenant nature of the lands of Israel must never be taken lightly, no matter the political expedience. Dividing up God's land is never going to be successful.

So what was God thinking exactly when He chose this land for His dwelling place and the heritage of His people? Did He not know about the Assyrians and the Egyptians? Did He not know that the kingdom of Babylon would also rise up and use the trade routes through Israel to trade with the Egyptians? Did He not recognize this political and geographic peril that my history Professor so quickly diagnosed? The answer is—of course He did. But as long as Israel was following Him, they were protected supernaturally. The Assyrians, under the leadership of their king Sennacherib, tried to conquer Jerusalem, but because king Hezekiah (the king of Judah), was in good standing with God, the Assyrians lost 185,000 soldiers in one night. Mysteriously! Judah's army never had to fire an arrow. Sennacherib and his army packed their bags and got out of town, then he was subsequently killed by one of his sons at the altar of one of his gods. It didn't pay to try and take covenant lands as long as the Israelites were in right standing with God. *"Blessed is the nation whose God is the Lord, The people He has chosen as His own inheritance."* (Psalm 33:12).

God purposely placed His people between these superpowers because the trade routes between them would have to run right through the nation of Israel. Israel would prosper by this trade, but even more importantly, they would become an influence on these nations. God has always understood that commerce is a means of influence. Jesus said in the parable of the minas in Luke 19:13, *"So he called ten of his servants, delivered to them ten minas, and said to them, 'Do business till I come.'"* This parable is about the work that His disciples are charged with in His absence (in body only). They are told to take what He has given them and engage in commercial activity until He returns. Moreover, He goes on to say that we will be judged by what we've done with the provision when He comes back.

Did we engage in business activity that created jobs and influenced people, or did we have to give it to Mastercard to cover the 31% interest charges on our purchases of "stuff"? We are not blessed to facilitate the expansion of our credit limit, we're blessed so that we can engage in business and have influence. There is nothing wrong with having "stuff", but if "stuff" is what's on your heart, then you're not a very good conductor of God's grace. We cannot be an influence when we're broke, but we can be a great influence when we're employing people and influencing the moral compass of an industry through our good standing in that industry.

God's intention has always been for His people to be involved in commerce and thereby be in a position to witness to non-believers. It was no accident that Israel was located on the main commercial routes between two superpowers...it was the plan. God blesses us to be a blessing, to be a witness, to finance the Gospel, and to be an influence in the world.

An often quoted scripture concerning financial blessing is Deuteronomy 8:18. The passage says, *"And you shall remember the Lord your God, for it is He who gives you power to get wealth, that He may establish His covenant which He swore to your fathers, as it is this day." (Deuteronomy 8:18, NKJV).* The Hebrew word interpreted as *"wealth"* in this passage is *"chayil"*. It appears in the Old Testament 243 times. It is translated as "army" 56 times, "man of valour" 37 times, "host" 29 times, "forces" 14 times, "valiant" 13 times, "strength" 12 times, "riches" 11 times, "wealth" 10 times, "power" nine times, "substance" eight times, "might" six times, "strong" five times, and translated miscellaneously 33 times. You see the simple translation of "wealth" is somewhat of an over simplification. If we had to try and summarize all these translations we might say that *"chayil"* is a, *"powerful creative force of influence which produces wealth."*

So we could say in a paraphrase translation of the passage, *"Remember the Lord your God, for He causes you to walk in a powerful creative force of influence which produces wealth so that His covenant shall be fulfilled with you as it has always been with His people; the covenant which says that you shall be blessed and through you all the families of the earth shall be blessed."* It's clear by this scripture that God's intent is for His people to be a force of influence that exerts itself inside as well as outside the Church. We're to use our wealth to influence a lost and dying world…not to facilitate insatiable materialism. The Disciple of Christ walks in frugality coupled with diligence which produces wealth which in turn facilitates influence in the world. This is God's plan.

The Spirit of Mammon —

Jesus was concerned, primarily, with two groups of people during His ministry; the poor and the wealthy. He wanted the poor to have hope and be treated well by those that were wealthy, and He wanted the wealthy to be aware of a powerful spirit that He called *"mammon"*. He said, *"No one can serve two masters; for either he will hate the one and love the other, or else he will be loyal to the one and despise the other. You cannot serve God and mammon."* (Matthew 6:24). Mammon is the English translation of the Aramaic word *"mammonas"*, which means wealth *"personified"*. Wealth personified means that the person takes on the personality of opulent wealth. They become arrogant and judgmental.

The Spirit of mammon is a lying spirit that convinces its host, that the highest and best use of their life is the pursuit of it (wealth). People afflicted with this spirit have literally fallen in love with money. They are more than willing to abandon their families to pursue it. Like all demonic spirits, it is very deceptive. Those who are afflicted with it are convinced that they are not affected by anything evil. They are the "producers" of this world. What would the world do if they weren't working 16 hours a day? How would the cause of commerce ever be advanced if they weren't in the harness pulling it along? This is their mindset. They cannot see that their pursuit of mammon is destroying all of their relationships.

They literally lust for the *"personification of wealth"*. It's not the money they want, they will tell you. No it's what the money buys. They want social status and power. People afflicted with this spirit see money as power, and power is what they lust for. They're not about to give it away, because to give money away is, in their minds, to weaken their power base. They are more than willing to give it away if there is some political advantage that can be gained from it. Maybe public recognition that will enhance their need to be a social leader.

It's ten times easier to raise money for political campaigns than it is for the work of the Church, because people who hoard money are commonly afflicted with this spirit. When they give to a political candidate, they are buying power and influence. Since they thirst for power, giving to a politician is an investment that allows then to leverage their money and increase their power. Giving to political campaigns is actually satisfying to a spirit of mammon.

As with all demonic afflictions, the spirit becomes their identity. Just as an addict becomes a *"junkie"* or a *"drunk"*, so someone oppressed by a spirit of mammon becomes a power monger. And just as it's nearly impossible to convince the alcoholic that they are afflicted with the spirit of addiction, those walking in mammon also are deceived. They are "doing good" for the community as far as they are concerned. They are not doing it for recognition and power... they're just advancing the cause of "freedom" and commerce. Therein lies the power of the deception. They become active politically in the name of protecting freedom, when they themselves are in bondage and they can't see it.

Look at the relationships in this person's life and you can detect a spirit of mammon very quickly. There is usually a pattern of divorce. They have poor relationships with their own children. They have basically sacrificed everything on the altar of their god—mammon. They have "close friends" who are only close because of the wealth that they represent. The friends usually are afflicted with the same spirit, and are drawn to them because "they understand them". That doesn't mean that they love them. Let the person lose his wealth and you will be able to count the friends that stand by him on one hand. While he represented opportunity and access to more wealth generating power, he had hundreds of friends. If he goes broke, he'll be fortunate to have one.

All in all, the spirit of mammon is no different than any of the other demonic spirits that you will encounter. It has come to, *steal, kill and destroy"* (John 10:10). At the end of this person's life, he will have amassed great amounts of wealth, and have no one to leave it to. At some point in his or her journey, he will realize that he has spent a life time climbing to the top, only to find that the ladder was leaning against the wrong wall. At this point he will usually turn to drugs or alcohol to numb the pain. The only relationships that he has are all predicated on his money, and by now he has figured this out. Therefore he trusts no one, and his spiritual condition becomes extremely dark indeed.

He has become a casualty of the spirit of mammon. Jesus said we can't serve Him and mammon. And more specifically He said we will *"love one and hate the other"*. Again, mammon is not money. It is a spirit that attaches itself to money. It is arrogant, deceptive, and full of pride. It lusts for power and influence. It loves money because it sees money as the objective of life. Believers need to recognize it and hate it; for if you hate mammon, you will love God. If you hate mammon, you will refuse to serve it, and you will serve God. If you hate mammon you will not love money…you will use it. You will use it to bless people, to be a witness for Christ, to finance His Gospel, and to be a positive influence in the world.

Money can't buy happiness, but giving it away can—

"It is said that for money you can have everything, but you cannot. You can buy food, but not appetite; medicine, but not health; knowledge but not wisdom; glitter, but not beauty; fun, but not joy; acquaintances, but not friends; servants, but not faithfulness; leisure, but not peace. You can have the husk of everything for money, but not the kernel."-Arne Garborg. Money is not evil—it's our love of money that is the root of all evil. It can buy the husk, but it can never buy the kernel. It cannot make us happy unless we're willing to give it away, but it can ruin our lives if we fall in love with it and begin to hoard it. There is purpose for the money that He entrusts us with.

We need to be mindful of what that purpose is. We need to look at money as "seed" and not riches. *"He who trusts in his riches will fall, But the righteous will flourish like foliage."* (Proverbs 11:28). They flourish because they are continually sowing.

Is Debt a Sin?

"The rich rules over the poor, And the borrower is servant to the lender." (**Proverbs 22:7**)

"You must pay at last your own debt. If you are wise, you will dread a prosperity which only loads you with more." — Ralph Waldo Emerson (1803–1882)

"Debt is the prolific mother of folly and of crime." — Benjamin, Earl of Beaconsfield Disraeli (1804–1881)

According to the teachings of our grandparent's church, you would have difficulty discerning the fact that debt was not a sin. They preached like it was, and for good reason. In the Church of that period, they never confused debt and prosperity. In fact, debt was a symptom of poverty. Those who were truly wealthy, in those days, were not borrowers…they were lenders. Want to hear a startling fact! The same is true today. Men and women, who have accumulated great wealth in the twenty-first century, were never in the habit of borrowing…at least for personal consumption. They may have borrowed to finance business inventories, but they never borrowed to consume. They paid cash for items such as furniture, meals, clothing, and many of them would only drive a car that they could pay cash for. It seems that no matter the period of history, the wealthy have had a general disdain for debt.

The Church has a responsibility to teach the wisdom of God to its flock, and the early Church was doing just that. They were teaching what God has to say about debt, namely that it is unwise and dangerous. Debt is not a sin... it's just dangerous. Wealthy people knew it then, and they know it now. It's the rest of us who think it is our civic duty to spend money that we don't have, and in many cases, will never have.

In fact, debt has become such a way of life that the Church today doesn't even speak on the subject. It's just not spiritual enough for them. If they did, their congregants would simply respond with a "mind your own business" attitude. So the Church adopts the attitude of, let's just stay away from the controversial stuff. After all, we've got payments to make ourselves because we're not living the word of God in the area of finances either. We can't offend anybody, because we've got to keep our numbers up. The consequence being, no one tells the truth from the pulpit concerning what God's word teaches about having debt in your life. Everyone has their head in the sand thinking, *"Maybe if we can't see the enemy, he won't see us."*

I've got news for you, he's already seen us and he has already gotten many of us in the trap. We've got to let God lead us out, but first we have to admit that nothing oppresses us spiritually like adverse financial conditions. You can have the most dedicated Choir member in the world, faithful and full of the spirit...until she gets her electricity shut off. All the sudden the spiritual goes right out the window, and the natural comes in like a flood. She's not coming to choir practice. She's not reading her Bible anymore. She won't pray out loud and over people anymore. Why? She's worried and nothing steals our spirituality like worry. Financial oppression is one of Satan's most effective strategies to drive us into our selves, and away from God. When we're financially oppressed, we close our spirits, and nobody can speak into them, including God. Just what the enemy is looking for.

Spiritually it's a dangerous thing, this business strategy called debt, and we need to have a closer look at it.

God's word calls for a credit system—

God's initial intent was that those of His children, who had been blessed, would lend to their spiritual brothers and sisters who had need. He said, *"If there is among you a poor man of your brethren, within any of the gates in your land which the Lord your God is giving you, you shall not harden your heart nor shut your hand from your poor brother, but you shall open your hand wide to him and willingly lend him sufficient for his need, whatever he needs."* (Deuteronomy 15:7-8). He clearly intends for His people to have access to credit. The goal here would be that those of the brethren (fellow believers) who have endured hardship would borrow from their brothers and be able to start again. God emphasizes that those to whom He has given land (provision and blessing), have a responsibility to lend to those within their gates (sphere of everyday life, and of the faith), in order to help them with their needs. All good bankers get real satisfaction from watching an account develop into a thriving and successful business enterprise.

This type of lending creates economic opportunity and produces a proliferation of wealth. There is no question that business lending produces commerce and commercial enterprise is a Biblical concept. Abraham and Isaac, and Jacob (the Patriarchs of the faith) were extremely successful businessmen. Although I can find no Biblical documentation of their having borrowed from anyone, there can be no question that the blessings of God that manifest in their lives came in the form of material prosperity. God understands the value of commerce, and He intends that His people participate in that process. The issue here is not business borrowing…we're talking about the dangers of borrowing to consume.

There is danger in all types of borrowing, but consumer borrowing is the most deadly. God's instructions are that he who has been blessed should not close his hand to the "needs" of his brother. Not his wants. Our generation has been borrowing to satisfy a voracious appetite of wants. I don't need a $450.00 Orvis Trident fly rod, but to hear me talk, you'd think I couldn't live another day without it. I've just about convinced myself that it has become an absolute necessity. I remarked to my wife Carol, *"After all, my friends all have one. I'm only thinking about my witness in the circles of serious anglers. You know I've been called to minister there. That's right. It's my ministry. How can I possibly win any of those brothers to the Lord by using "run-of-the-mill" fly fishing equipment? I need that new fly rod for my ministry. Just think of how many souls this might turn into for the Kingdom."* Her response was the same as your's. I've just successfully converted a want into a need...at least in my own mind. She didn't buy it either. Borrowing to meet life's needs during a season of adversity is Biblical. Borrowing to satisfy the desires of our flesh is not, and it is this category of debt that is destroying us.

All in all, I'd rather be a lender than a borrower. What about you? The only caveat here is that lenders in the Kingdom of God do not behave like lenders in the world. God said, *"You shall not charge interest to your brother—interest on money or food or anything that is lent out at interest. To a foreigner you may charge interest, but to your brother you shall not charge interest, that the Lord your God may bless you in all to which you set your hand in the land which you are entering to possess."* (Deuteronomy 23:19-20). That's right! Your motive has to be purely philanthropic, if you're going to be a lender in God's Kingdom; lending in the Kingdom of God is motivated by a spirit of charity, not profit taking. He said you may charge a foreigner (someone who's not saved) interest, but not the brethren. For the loan to a brother, however, He says that He will take care of the interest. The interest will come to you in the form of blessings that will surpass mere dollars.

A Kingdom lender walks in blessings that are too numerous to list. Just suffice it to say that they range from financial, to social, to spiritual. I'm convinced that Kingdom lenders are the only members of the body that walk in the fullness of God's provision. What makes a Kingdom lender? It's someone who lends to help and strengthen someone who has no ability to do anything for them. They do not lend for the interest that the loan might accrue (obviously). They lend because they love and believe in the brother or sister to whom they are extending the credit. I knew a man who paid for a young girl's college tuition to nursing school. He knew she couldn't afford it, and he believed in her ability and diligence. After the young woman graduated and landed a job in the nursing field, she came to the man to make arrangements to repay the loan. Over her objections he insisted that the terms of repayment were that she do the same thing for another young person when she achieved the financial means.

Many years later, at the man's funeral, the young woman wept as she shared the story of her providential encounter with this "Kingdom Lender". She shared how this man's generosity had changed the course of her life and that of the generations who would follow her. She had been bound in a generational curse of poverty, but the obedience of this man had facilitated the breaking of that curse. Now she was in a position to pay for the college education of her own children, and the child of another family bound by the same generational curse. Now that's "return-on-investment". God's credit system is meant to bring life...not bondage.

The Kingdom lender of our story understood that the real interest comes from the Lord Himself, and that the goal is to help a brother, not bring him into bondage. In the Kingdom system of lending, it is required that the debtor be released from the debt obligation every seven years (Deuteronomy 15:1-2). This is known as *"the Lord's release"*. God's position is that His people shall be free, not oppressed. This is a central theme through out His word and is very important to Him. Just ask Pharaoh. The prize he received through the oppression of God's people was some great looking pyramids. The cost of it was the life of his first-born son. I'm quite sure that if we could interview the Egyptian King of Exodus, he would confirm our suspicions that the price he paid exceeded the value of the prize, and if he had to do it over again, he would gladly let His people go. *"Now the Lord is the Spirit; and where the Spirit of the Lord is, there is liberty."* (2 Corinthians 3:17). The Lord is about freedom, and so is His lending system.

To those who observe the *"Lord's release"*, God makes certain promises. In Deuteronomy 15:6 He says, *"For the Lord your God will bless you just as He promised you; you shall lend to many nations, but you shall not borrow; you shall reign over many nations, but they shall not reign over you."* To those who believe and observe the tenants of His system, He promises that they will become financial leaders, and that they *"shall lend to the nations"*. Furthermore, they never have to worry about becoming a debtor. Their financial strength will increase, not decrease. This is His will for His people… financial freedom and strength. Not bondage and weakness.

The First Step to Bondage: Adopting a Debtor's Mentality

According to Proverbs 22:7, nations that borrow from other nations will serve the nations they're indebted to. Modern economist, nix this notion as "old-fashioned". God's word says that the borrower is slave to the lender, and I'm betting on the word. Not modern economic theory. We have become, in fact, a nation with a debtors-mentality. We've become callused to the dangers of debt, and it is reflected in our own government. When the national deficit is increasing at the rate of $2.43 billion dollars per day, and is at a current level of $27,968.36 for every man woman and child, who call themselves U.S. citizens, and it is not the number one political issue in the public forum, you have fallen into a debtor's mentality. If our government is running a few trillion in the red, why should one of its citizens be concerned with personal credit card debts of twenty or thirty-thousand dollars?

The movie *Remember the Titians*, is about a football team in the south that had just integrated under court mandate during the racially charged '60's. The immediate challenge of the coaching staff was to get these black and white players to accept each other and direct their aggression towards the opposing team instead of their own teammates. During "two-a-days" (training camp), some of the white offensive linemen seemed to block with much less intensity when the play called for their black half-back to be the ball carrier. This fact did not escape the attention of the black players on the defense; who responded by tempering their zeal for tackling of the same individual. The net result was sloppy football, which irked the coaching staff. Their response was to extend the length of practices in the stifling Virginia heat, until the quality of the play improved. Finally, Gerry, the best player and unspoken leader of the team (who is white), confronts Julius, the other captain (who is black) in a nose-to-nose heated exchange, about the poor tackling of his kindred. Gerry, the white captain is about to blow a gasket, as he heatedly complains about the slacker attitude of the black players on the defense (he seems impervious to the fact that the "all-white" offensive line's blocking is inexplicably poor) and he questions Julius's leadership. Julius's sweat-soaked response is classic, as he screams back through the sweltering heat, *"Attitude reflect leadership—cap'um!"*, and then he spits.

Some times I just want to spit, when I think about the attitude of the leadership in this country. After Bill Clinton was caught in a compromising position with the young intern, Monica Lewensky, youth Pastors across American, who are really in touch with what is going on in our young people, reported a huge increase in oral sexually activity in teenage kids. Both inside and outside the Church, I'm sorry to say. It seems they had learned something from the nation's top leadership, and that something was that oral sex was not real sex. Therefore, if it wasn't real sex…it couldn't be real sin. *"Attitude reflect leadership…cap'um!"* Oh, deep down these kids knew better, especially those who had teaching in Church, but we're all looking to justify sinful behavior. And while we began this chapter by declaring that debt is not sin, **$8,363,536,754,922** of it might be. That's the amount of the national debt as of this writing. Of course, everyone knows this figure will increase by tomorrow, so by the time you read this, the number we print here will be irrelevant. That ought to scare somebody. We've mortgaged the future of our children with prodigal living. We've followed the leadership of our nation into a "debtor's mentality". We don't seem to be able to grasp reality. The reality is that we've become a debtor nation and according to the Word of God, we cannot remain strong because we've become enslaved by our own insatiable appetite for "stuff". Fiscal discipline has become blasé!

A "Debtor's-Mentality"—Defined

A "debtor's-mentality" is essentially a "slave-mentality". Or to put it another way, it is a stronghold in a person's thinking pattern that corrupts truth and causes them to get in agreement with a lie. As we stated in Chapter One, it took an amazingly long period of time for the Hebrews of Exodus to admit that they were in bondage. The reason that it took them so long was that they could not perceive truth. No one goes into slavery willingly. The enemy uses subtle deception to build strongholds in the thinking of the intended victim, and they will enter into bondage on their own. After all, who perceives themselves as a slave while driving around in their new Escalade? If the Escalade were paid for, then the perception of prosperity might be accurate, even though it's hard to rationalize prosperity in the owning of an automobile that will lose $17,000 in value the first year he owns it. But if the driver borrowed the money to buy it, or worse yet, signed up for the "Smart-lease" (this is a pseudonym…it should be called a "Dumb-lease" since in reality it works like 15% car loan), then simple math would lead us to the conclusion that owning an asset that will depreciate (lose market value) faster than the loan balance decreases does not yield wealth. In fact it diminishes wealth. It doesn't matter how good it makes you feel to be seen in it, feelings don't pay off bank loans. Dollars do and this financial arrangement is costing him money.

In a similar fashion, the drug addict needs the drug to feel good and thereby numb the pain of life. No one forces her to take it. She does it willingly. The more she does it, the worse she feels about herself, so the more drug she needs. Oh, she has tried to stop, but she fails…and when she fails she feels worse about herself, so now she needs more of the drug to numb the pain. She eventually gets to the place where she no longer believes that she can ever live without the drug. She has become slave to the drug, and the enemy has successfully set-up a stronghold from which he will systematically destroy her and everyone around her in time.

The woman in our example has developed a full-blown "slave-mentality" by now. She justifies her behavior generally through a powerful mental deception called "denial".

"Well if I really wanted to, I could stop using meth. But you know it makes me more productive at work (she seems oblivious to the fact that she is unemployed and hasn't been able to hold a job down for two years). But I could stop anytime", she makes excuses. "You know it's not really my fault. My mother was mean to me and my husband was a scoundrel (he's long since left), and a girl's got to do what a girls got to do", she struggles to cope with the things she has done to maintain this illusion she calls life. But the one thing she cannot bring herself to do, is to admit that she's an addict. Just as our Escalade driver in the previous example cannot seem to grasp the fact that in his attempts to "medicate" his self-image with an artificial sense of prosperity he is actually destroying himself; so the drug addict maintains the illusion of "well being" through a chemical that is actually destroying her. Both do irrational things to try and promote a false sense of "well being". Both have developed a "slave-mentality". Both need deliverance, and both need to know the truth to be free.

The "debtor's mentality" and the "addict's mentality" develop exactly the same way. From a search for fulfillment, and the consequences of trying to extract it from things that have no to capacity to provide it. The result is frustration and bondage. Just as the "meth" gives her a high for a few hours, so does driving the Escalade off the dealer's lot for him, but in the end the high always gives way to reality. And reality will be dealt with in one of two ways. Either they will own the truth, and accept responsibility for the choices they have made, or they will medicate themselves with another "hit". If they face the truth about themselves and their situation, they will have taken the first step to freedom.

If they deny the truth, their bondage will only become deeper and harder to shed later. In the decade of the 1990's household debt grew annually at the rate of 2% faster then did personal income. Two percent doesn't sound like much, but when the trend stays in tack over a ten year period, the result is devastating to American families. A 2% trend over a decade will make an economist hyperventilate. So you can understand why the people who study such statistical data are stricken with terror when they see that the outstanding credit balances in the U.S. have increased from 1996 to 2000 at the rate of 9% per year to $633 billion dollars. From 1992-2000 disposable income rose 47%...personal spending rose 61%. When you spend more than you make, guess where you make up the difference. That's right...you borrow it.

A good portion of the economic boom that we have experienced in America the last few years has come from rising home values that have allowed consumers to refinance their home equities. They have taken proceeds from these home equity loans and paid off stifling credit card debt. The problem is they have not changed their behavior.

This conclusion is supported by the fact that they have not cut up their credit cards. In 70% of households that have refinanced home equities to payoff credit card debt, they have run their credit card balances back up to previous levels or more. Now they have mortgaged their home equity, and there is nothing left to refinance. Heaven forbid that home values should ever decrease as they did in the decade of the eighty's. The resulting negative impact on the financial worth of Americans would be devastating since most of their net worth is in their home.

We've been afflicted with a "debtor's-mentality". A debtor's mindset, frankly, does not believe that it can live in this world without debt. He or she equates the absence of debt with an absence of a nice car to drive or a nice house to live in. There is no question that most of us could not buy a house without a mortgage, but if we learn to think with a lender's (or investor's) mindset, we will shortly be able to pay cash for a car. Remember the word of God said we're to be lenders and not borrowers (Deuteronomy 28:12). I have found that most people are one or the other. The classification of the person as a lender or a debtor has less to do with what they owe and more to do with how they see themselves. How they think.

The word says, *"For as (a man) thinks in his heart, so is he..."* (Proverbs 23:7). Our lives are propelled in the direction of our most dominate thoughts. The thoughts that are most dominate in our mind will spring from what we believe in our hearts (or spirit). Paul said, *"...and be renewed in the spirit of your mind,"* (Ephesians 4:23). The word of God is designed to transform our mind through a renewal process that causes our thought patterns to be changed and no longer conform to the world's thinking patterns (Romans 12:2). By faith in the word, our deepest beliefs about who we are and who He is are dealt with. Believers are charged by the word of God to think of themselves as lender's (investors) and not borrowers (debtors).

According to Proverbs 23:7, we will not think it in our mind until we believe it in our hearts. Pretty hard to think of yourself as a lender when American Express is calling every hour on the hour wanting more money, isn't it? In fact, the most dominant thoughts that occur to those of us who've experienced financial crisis, don't line up with God's word at all. Thoughts like, *"I'm just a loser"*, *"I've always been a poor steward"*, or, *"God's word on prosperity is for someone else...He obviously doesn't love me or I wouldn't be going through this,"*. We've got to take such thoughts captive (2 Corinthians 10:5), and make them obedient to Jesus Christ. Christ's thoughts are that we've been grafted into the vine and the blessings of Abraham (Galatians 3:14); that we're a blessed and a called people (1 Peter 2:9); joint heirs with Him to the Kingdom of God (Romans 8:17); that we're worth dying for, because that's exactly WHAT He did (Mark 10:45). If we succumb to the negative thought patterns of the world, instead of the powerful truth of the word of God, we'll fall into a debtor's mentality (among other things), and we'll never be able to see ourselves as lenders or investors.

Debtors are willing to put up with a severe task master, rather than risk the unknown and dare to try and be free. Lenders are courageous, and not afraid to be different. Debtors want instant gratification; lenders are patient and committed for the long haul. Debtors don't want to endure any pain, even though pain is inevitable for someone living in an illusion of well being and will only get worse the longer the illusion is propagated. Lenders have an ability to face and deal with the truth about themselves and their situation and are willing to endure some pain to make progress. Debtors always blame others for their situation; lenders "own" their problems and never fool themselves into believing that it's someone else's fault. The worst effect of shifting blame to others is that you rob yourself of the empowerment you need to change the situation. When you accept the responsibility for the problem, you have equipped yourself to make the changes necessary to overcome the problem. You stop the cycle of denial and start the process of learning and correction. Debtors have confused wealth with having "stuff"; lenders see wealth as being financially free (and they get the "stuff" eventually anyway).

Debt is Satan's Strategy to Steal Our "Seed" —

Perhaps the most lethal aspect of debt is that it provides the enemy an opportunity to steal our "seed". The Kingdom of God operates on the "Seed Principle". Jesus said, "*...the kingdom of heaven is like a mustard seed, which a man took and sowed in his field, which indeed is the least of all the seeds; but when it is grown it is greater than the herbs and becomes a tree, so that the birds of the air come and nest in its branches.*" (Matthew 13:31-32). Jesus was saying that the things of the Kingdom seem insignificant in the natural realm; the mustard seed being the smallest of all the seeds in the garden. But when the things of the Kingdom are sown in the fertile ground of faith, they produce something that becomes more extraordinary than anything else in life. The mustard seed starts out as the smallest (most insignificant) seed, and ends up the largest plant in the garden.

The "Seed Principle" is about the unseen potential of the thing that is sown. I heard a minister say once that, *"God is a God of seed. If you need a tree, He will send you an acorn. In that acorn is the tree that you need, but also in that acorn is a forest if you have faith enough to see it in the Spirit. What you make of the seed that He gives you is up to your ability to believe and see with the eyes of the heart. With faith and diligent hands, the seed can reach a potential that will stagger the natural mind."* God is a God of potential. The seed that He supplies us has the potential to bring us a harvest of *"some hundred-fold, some sixty, and some thirty."* (Matthew 13:23). Whether it's a hundred-fold or a thirty is entirely up to us. How big is your faith and how resolute is your will. Have you hardened your will in agreement with His, or are you still *"wavering between two opinions"* concerning this seed that you've been given? When you look at the acorn, do you see a tree or do you see a forest? Or do you still just see a seed? The answer to these questions will determine the size of your harvest.

Another aspect of the "Seed Principle" is that seed will produce after its kind. In other words, if I plant wheat, I'm not going to get corn. In the Kingdom of God everything operates on this principle. If I need mercy, then I need to sow the seed of mercy. If I want love, then I need to sow the seed of love. If I need forgiveness, then it is essential that I sow forgiveness. In fact, if I have not forgiven those who have trespassed against me, then I shouldn't expect that God would give me anything. He'll not even hear my prayers. Of all the lethal spirits that can get hold of a Believer, the spirit of unforgiveness is the most deadly. It cuts us off completely from God. (Matthew 18:21-35) and (Mark 11:25-26). So if you feel that God's not meeting your financial needs, check for any unforgiveness. Ask the Holy Spirit to help you and allow Him to search your spirit. If it's there, He'll show you. When you find it deal with it immediately, so that you can receive from God again. Your seed may be dormant because you have fallen into unforgiveness. Sow forgiveness...harvest forgiveness.

Sow money...harvest money. God is obligated by His word to provide seed for the sower. *"Now may He who supplies seed to the sower, and bread for food, supply and multiply the seed you have sown and increase the fruits of your righteousness,"* (2 Corinthians 9:10). He is bound by His word as well to, *"...to make all grace abound toward you, that you, always having all sufficiency in all things, may have an abundance for every good work."* (2 Corinthians 9:8). Satan knows that if the seed gets in the hands of the sower, it will be sown into "good works". His plan for stopping this process is to steal the seed before it gets there.

How does he hijack the thing that God provides that is filled with potential? The seed that is sown into "good works" will change the world. The seed that has the potential to bring forth a hundredfold increase to the sower. His strategy can be summed up in one word. Interest. The penalty extracted for living above our means. The price that the world's system requires in exchange for satisfying the appetite of the flesh. Our flesh sees it, and has to have it. We're not inclined to wait...the flesh won't wait on its own accord. It has to be ruled by the spirit, else it will consume us into oblivion. The world is more than willing to alleviate that urge of the flesh to consume (after all it created the urge in the first place). All it will cost is 20%. That's no step for a stepper.

The only problem is that God is trying to transfer the wealth of the "unjust" to the "just" according to Proverbs 13:22. And when you're in bondage to credit cards that are charging you 30% interest…you're in bondage to the "unjust". Anyone that will charge you usurious interest rates is not just. Therefore, God knows that the seed that He would like to provide for you, will end up in the hands of the very people He's trying to extract it from, namely the "unjust". Satan has, in effect, cut you off from your provision. Hope that new Armani suit that you put on your credit card lasts a while, because until you begin to understand that you've become slave to the Master (Card), and have allowed yourself to be chained to the "unjust", you're not likely to see much more seed.

Satan has neutralized the financial execution of God's plan through you. You've been transformed from a sower of seed into an eater of seed. Giving you money would be the equivalent of giving a drug addict money. It will all end up in the hands of the unjust and will never make it to the "good works" for which it is intended. You have developed a full-blown debtor's mentality, and God dare not trust you with the precious provision for the Kingdom. After all there is a missionary somewhere in Africa who is living on pinto beans and saving soles like crazy, and God needs your seed to be planted in his ministry. If you're in bondage to Capital One then there is a good chance that Capitol One will end up with any seed He sends your way instead of the missionary. Therefore you no longer become a viable conduit for supplying "good works". Satan has stolen your seed.

If you've just realized that I'm talking about you here, the good news is that all you have to do to be delivered from bondage is repent, and become "renewed in the spirit of your mind". Recognize the truth of your financial situation, and ask God to deliver you. The question that we asked earlier was, "Why did it take God 430 years to respond to the bondage that His people were suffering in Egypt?" The answer; "It took 430 years for them to face the truth about themselves and their situation. It took that long for them to admit that things were not going to get better next year or with a new Pharaoh, and that they needed super-natural intervention to be set free."

Freedom begins with what we believe and what we consequently think. Wealth is not about what you drive or where you live; it's about knowing who you are, and understanding you're not

Pharaoh's slave. According to Galatians 4:7, because of the work of the Cross, those who believe are no longer slaves, but have been made sons of God. *"...born, not of blood, nor of the will of the flesh, nor of the will of man, but of God"* (John 1:13). It's time for God's people to break free of the bondage of the world's financial systems. It's time for us to start thinking like sons and daughters rather than slaves. The world's systems are judged according to the word of God (1 John 2:17), and are consequently passing away. They are going to take those who have become entrapped in them down as well (Revelation 18:4). Personal finance guru Dave Ramsey says, *"Do what the world's doin', and you'll get what the world's getting'... and they're broke."* The truth of this statement is beyond question. 1.49 million bankruptcies filed in 2001 (a record) is a barometer of things to come.

It's time God's people were no longer conformed to this world, but where transformed by the renewing of their minds (Romans 12:2). Some how...some way, we've got to learn how to think like free men and women again, thereby breaking the bonds that Pharaoh and his system have placed on us. It's time to begin the journey to freedom, and freedom has never come without revolution. Jesus Christ was the most profound revolutionary to ever live. He attacked the traditions of men and caused us to question the wisdom of conventional wisdom". He taught radical principles like, to keep it you've got to give it away, to receive you've got to give, and those who lose their lives for His sake and the Gospels will actually find them. He shook their beliefs and caused them to reevaluate their perception of the truth. He launched twelve men on a radical new path that eventually caused the great Roman Empire to fall in on itself, like a house of cards.

He said, *"You shall know the truth and the truth shall set you free."* (John 8:32). The truth is that God's people are in bondage financially to a judged system that will perish along with everything else that man has tried to create in his own image. Now that we've accepted the truth about where we are, we can begin the journey to the land of His Promise. A journey deep into our own hearts that wakes us from the fog that we've been living in. A journey that brings us from slavery back to the rightful place of an heir. Let the journey begin.

Which Way To The Red Sea?

*"And Moses said to the people, "Do not be afraid. Stand
still, and see the salvation of the Lord, which He will
accomplish for you today. For the Egyptians whom
you see today, you shall see again no more forever. The
Lord will fight for you, and you shall hold your peace.""*
(Exodus 14:13-14)

**"There is nothing wrong with America that the faith,
love of freedom, intelligence and energy
of her citizens cannot cure."**
-Dwight D Eisenhower,

**"The last of the human freedoms
is to choose one's attitudes."**
-Victor Frankl

**"One who restrains his appetites avoids debt."—
Chinese proverb**

"**O**k, already! I get the message." "I'm in financial bondage."
"So…which way to the Red Sea?"

The answer is simple; "Follow Him." This is the secret to deliverance. Follow the Lord and He will lead you out of bondage and into freedom. Your path will take you through the wilderness and into the Land of your inheritance; The Promised Land. The place where you will prosper in Him.

"Then the Lord spoke to Moses and Aaron, and gave them a command for the children of Israel and for Pharaoh king of Egypt, to bring the children of Israel out of the land of Egypt." (Exodus 6:13). God gave two commands. One was for the children of Israel, the other one was for Pharaoh their oppressor. He promptly placed both parties in a position where they had little alternative except to obey. If there are some of you reading this who have reached the end of your rope, I have good news. As Moses said to the people, *"Stand still and see the salvation of the Lord..."* I want to warn you, it's a frightening thing to be standing on the banks of the Red Sea as your enemies are closing ranks on you and about to mount an all out attack. And I want to make clear that what we advocate in this book is not inaction, but the exact opposite. We're going to call those of you who have recognized their bondage to powerful, purposeful, positive, action.

However, in this passage from Exodus, Moses is instructing his people to "standstill". To not run. To witness the destruction of their enemies and to understand that the Lord will fight for them. To take their eyes off the natural and place their hope in the super-natural. If the task at hand is not bigger than you, then you don't need God. He will purposely lead you to a place where there are no alternatives. What were the Israelites going to do...swim? He will vanquish your enemy right before your eyes. They trusted the Lord and He lead them right to a place of no options. Are you there yet?

In this passage He gave a commandment to Pharaoh to turn His people loose. What's interesting about this is that He knew Pharaoh would not recognize His authority when He issued the decree. But after the Tenth Plague, He also figured that Pharaoh would gladly cough-up the people He had oppressed, and that He would be glorified among the non-believing gentiles in the process. If you're in a desperate situation financially, *"standstill and see the salvation of the Lord"*, and watch as He works on your behalf. He will command Pharaoh to turn you loose, and Pharaoh will; whether He wants to or not. Sooner or later, Pharaoh (the world's system) will give up, but God will not. *"He is not a man that He should relent"* (1 Samuel 15:29).

God will take care of Pharaoh. What you as a Believer have to do is follow Him. *"And the Lord went before them by day in a pillar of cloud to lead the way, and by night in a pillar of fire to give them light, so as to go by day and night. He did not take away the pillar of cloud by day or the pillar of fire by night from before the people."* (Exodus 13:21-22). It's the Lord who will lead you through the tough terrain of the wilderness. He will take the form of a cloud of shade and protection in the heat of the day, and the warmth of a fire in the chill of the desert night. But even still, it will not be an easy journey. There are four things that you will have to pack in order to make it through this life changing passage to freedom.

■ Four Essentials For Financial Freedom —

1. Faith

The first requirement is faith. Faith is the only thing that God responds to. *"And without faith it is impossible to please God, because anyone who comes to Him must believe that He exists and that He rewards those who earnestly seek Him."* (Hebrews 11:6, NIV). The essence of faith is the abandonment of our trust and confidence in our own resources, and conversely, our total confidence in His love and His resources. You must seek Him diligently; then you must believe that He's a *"rewarder"* of those who do so. *"Now the Lord is the Spirit; and where the Spirit of the Lord is, there is liberty."* (2 Corinthians 3:17). His intention is to reward His people with freedom. Financial freedom is an important issue to God. He doesn't want you to stay in bondage.

If He knows you intimately enough to know the number of hairs on you head (the ones that came out in the comb **and** the ones that are still left in your scalp), according to Matthew 10:30, then He knows about your financial situation as well. And more importantly, He knows the way out. Always remember, however, that without faith you cannot make it. He will lead you to a place that looks like the end of the road, but if you'll do what Moses said, *"stand still"*, you'll see the salvation of the Lord. You see the one attribute that Moses had developed in his years in the wilderness, is that he had gotten good at tuning the noise of the world out, and hearing God clearly.

We will talk later on this subject in more detail, but for now suffice it to say that if you're saved you have His spirit, and if His spirit is in you then you hear His voice. Most of us hear God, but what we lack is faith in our spiritual ears. We talk ourselves out of what He's asking us to do, based on the premises that we've "missed" Him.

The events of 9/11/2001 brought the overnight demise of my financial condition (I lost most of my net worth in the subsequent 10 trading days of the Chicago Mercantile Exchange). Along with all my money, I lost my faith. Faith in just about everything. Well almost everything…I knew God was real and all-powerful. But I lost my confidence in my relationship with Him. What had I done to bring this on my self? Job's friends all asked the same question, "What was your sin that brought the judgment of God upon you Job?" My friends never openly asked me this question, but I promise they thought it. A few of them decided that they would just fill in the blanks themselves. They did a little analysis, and rendered their own verdict as to the cause of my financial demise. The rumors and gossip that ensued could trace most of its origin back to my "friends". Herein lies the danger of the prosperity Gospel. If you're broke, you're a sinner. This is the only conclusion that you can come to if your relationship with God is based on dollars and cents. If He blesses those He loves (materially), and He curses those He doesn't, and you're broke, then you must fit in the latter category. This is exactly the way the Pharisees thought in Jesus' day.

Their attitude was, "The poor are getting what they deserve, because if they were righteous, they wouldn't be poor. So why should we help them. They need to deal with their "sin issues" first. Then we'll see if we can help them financially."

This attitude drove Jesus crazy; in fact, when He announced the beginning of His ministry in Luke 4:18, He read from a scroll in the Temple out of the prophecies of Isaiah concerning the Messiah. He opened the scroll and proclaimed, *"The Spirit of the Lord is upon*

Me, Because He has anointed Me To preach the gospel to the poor; He has sent Me to heal the brokenhearted, To proclaim liberty to the captives And recovery of sight to the blind, To set at liberty those who are oppressed; ". Then He goes on to say, "*...Today this Scripture is fulfilled in your hearing.*" (Luke 4:21). The Good News or gospel was about to be preached. Prophecy was about to be fulfilled, but the Pharisees weren't celebrating. Maybe you noticed the gospel is to be preached to *"the poor"*. The oppressed were to be set free. The religious system of the Pharisees that viewed the wealthy as righteous and the poor as sinners, was about to be shaken to its very core.

"What was the 'Good News' for the poor?", you asked. It was that their condition is not who they are. Just because the circumstances of life and the consequences of discrimination by the wealthy class, had helped to afflict them doesn't mean that God doesn't love them. And that financial disadvantage in this life, would lead to advantage in the next one (James 2:5). Jesus was saying, "The religious aristocracy may look down on you, but I don't!" Once the bonds of class discrimination are loosed, many of them will prosper. Generational curses of poverty will be broken off them by His own Blood.

According to the statistical evidence, over 35% of us will experience a significant financial disruption to our lives in the next 5 years. A firestorm just like the one that I passed through, caused by circumstances totally outside of my control. It was in the fierceness of the storm, that I lost by bearings because the compass I was using was faulty. My confidence in my relationship with Christ was based solely on His provision...not His love. It was based *"on the things that are seen"*, not on the *"the things not seen"* which are eternal in value (2 Corinthians 4:18). The invisible qualities of justice and mercy and love are what my faith should have been built on. Instead I was basing the proof of His love for me on houses and boats and airplanes. My faith was defective and it was weak and in the storm...it was failing. Looking back on this season of trial, I know that He was speaking to me and trying to lead me out. I just didn't have enough confidence in my ability to hear His voice. I eventually made it to safety, but the trip was a lot harder than it had to be. Moses had developed an ear for God that never failed him. Whether the seas of life were tranquil or rough, he could always discern His voice. And the root of this ability to hear is unshakeable faith.

If you're a Believer in Jesus Christ, know this; He loves you and you're important to Him. And He's more than willing to let you go through some financial adversity to cause you to reexamine your relationship with Him. The question we have to answer is, "Is my relationship with Him built on the Rock, or is it built on 'having stuff'?" Is your walk with Him spiritual, or is it carnal?

When the storm comes (and there will be one), what your faith is built on will determine whether you make it to shore. You need to believe and not doubt, as God begins to lead you to freedom. The circumstance that you're in, may be the very thing you need to confront your own spiritual issues. Trust in His voice and follow the cloud by day and the fire by night. Believe in His goodness. Believe in His mercy. Believe in Him!

2. Agreement

The second thing you will need for the journey, is agreement. If you and your spouse are going to make it to Canaan, you have to get in agreement over where you are now and where you're going. *"Can two walk together, unless they are agreed?"* (Amos 3:3). Recognize that there is power in agreement. *"Again I say to you that if two of you agree on earth concerning anything that they ask, it will be done for them by My Father in heaven."* (Matthew 18:19). When you and your spouse get in agreement concerning your financial deliverance, it is going to come to pass. As long as you have faith, come together on His word, and listen to Him concerning your finances, your deliverance will "draw nigh".

Blaming each other is a useless and futile exercise. You need to share the responsibility and both participate in the solution. Both of you have to repent, and both of you are going to have to have faith. I recommend that you forget the things that are behind and reach forward to those things which are ahead, pressing in toward the prize which is the upward calling in Christ Jesus (Philippians 3:13-14). Dwelling on the past will only drive the two of you apart. What's important is planning your future. Get in agreement concerning your financial goals. You need to make mutual sacrifices. Blaming all your financial problems on your partner and requiring them to make all the sacrifices to "right the ship", will not work. This is an opportunity to sow some mercy. After all, there's a strong possibility that you will need some mercy some day. Remember, love does not keep an account of offenses. (1 Corinthians 13:7, NIV).

If you're the partner in the relationship that made the decisions that brought economic hardship on the family, I've got three words for you...shake it off!!. The viper bit Paul and attached itself to his hand after the ship wreck on the island of Malta, and the scripture merely says, "… *he shook off the creature into the fire and suffered no harm.*" (Acts 28:5). If you will "shake it off" just like Paul, the serpent (the devil) will do you no harm, but if you allow it to linger, a spirit of guilt and condemnation will establish a stronghold in your heart. Until you are delivered of this spirit, you will not have the confidence you need to press on. According to Romans 8:1, there is no condemnation in Christ. There is only learning and repenting and moving forward in Him. Remember, success is merely the intelligent application of failure. Failure is necessary. Failure can be constructive. Learn from your mistakes, and move on. It's the devil who wants us to dwell on our losses. Not God.

Remember men, most women have a big security need. There may be times when you just need to hold her and reassure her that it's going to be alright. Show her that you love her and that you're committed to this relationship no matter how the finances look. It doesn't cost a lot of money to be romantic. Buy her a single rose and take it to her work. Set it on her desk and kiss her on the cheek and walk out. See what her reaction is when you get home. She doesn't need diamonds...she needs you. Speak to her romantic nature. Convince her that you are her white knight and you've come to rescue her. Invest in her. Not by spending money you don't have on her, but by spending your time on her. She'll soon forget about bill collectors; especially when you take steps to insulate her from them. You handle those calls.

And remember women, this is a serious dilemma for most men. They feel like failures and men abhor failure. Many men start entertaining suicidal thoughts while in financial stress. You need to stroke their ego a little. Honor him. Let me say that again…Honor him!!! I don't care if his "get rich" schemes have brought you to the verge of bankruptcy. You can talk candidly about the family's financial decision making, but never and I mean never dishonor him. Men live for honor. What in the world could possibly cause a man to take a sword and a shield and charge down a hill into a mass of other men bearing the same types of weapons, knowing that there is a high probability that he will not survive to see the sunrise again? The answer is…Honor!! You can crush him, or you can make him into a valiant knight and protector. Make your financial problems into a courageous fight for the castle, and convince him that he's your Sir Galahad and he will defend it, and you, heroically. Crush him with guilt and condemnation, and you'll lose him. Oh, your financial crisis will pass. They always do. But the man you married will be gone. He may be present in the physical, but the spirit of the warrior will not likely return. His heart is in your hands. Be extremely careful with it.

In fact, you both need to watch over your thoughts and your words. The power of life and death is in the tongue (Proverbs 18:21). When in crisis, speak words of life. Stop hurting each other with them. Forget the past. Look to the future. You and your spouse need to go somewhere and get alone with God. Seek a vision for your life as a couple. Get in agreement about your future. Then embark on the path to healing and victory. You will find that whatever it is that you want to do together will require money. And most of the time your vision will require you to be financially free (out of debt). Your future begins in the area of your finances. Fight for the castle.

At some point, agreement has to become more than lip service. The evidence of financial agreement is a budget plan. When you have established your financial goals, you need to get in agreement over every dollar that comes into your possession each month. Develop a "cash flow plan" that satisfies your financial goals as a couple. Settle the argument over how the money is going to be spent in advance, when you develop your cash flow plan. Stop fighting over bank over-draft charges and start preventing them. There are many excellent computer programs that are very helpful in the area of personal finance, such as MS Money, and Quicken. But the bottom line is, until you sit down and get real about your cash flow vs. expenses, you will never meet any financial targets. (See sample in the Appendix)

After you have come together in agreement, be accountable to one another. Remember, it's about mutual sacrifice. It's about sharing the pain to achieve the gain. Don't spend money for new golf clubs if it's not in the cash flow plan, unless you talk to her about it. Never violate the plan, without consent from your partner. After all, you're doing this together. This will stop the painful and destructive money fights that all couples have. These arguments are damaging and if they go on unabated, they will bring death to a relationship. Agree on a plan; then execute the plan. This will alleviate that out-of-control anxious feeling that is lodged in the pit of your stomach. You will gain a sense of purpose, victory, and control over your finances. There is power in agreement! The Sherriff of Nottingham is no match for a couple with a vision of their future and a determination to follow God's leading to get there.

3. A New Attitude

The third thing you will need is a changed attitude. Victor Frankl said, *"The last of the human freedoms, is to choose one's attitude."* To make the journey will require you to develop new habits, and habits are the product of attitude. This new attitude has to be built around the revelation of spiritual truth.. *"Then Jesus said to those Jews who believed Him, "If you abide in My word, you are My disciples indeed. And you shall know the truth, and the truth shall make you free.""* (John 8:31-32). Notice that these Jews were believers. But it was not enough that they merely believed in Him; they had to abide in the Word of God in order to know the truth. And the truth that they would come to" know", would "set them free."

Jesus even referred to the Holy Spirit as *"the Spirit of Truth"*. In the fifteenth Chapter of John, the Lord explains that the primary benefit of His death, Resurrection, and ascension (next to making atonement for our sins), was that the *"Spirit of Truth"* would then come. He further explains that there are other things that He needs to teach us, but we *"cannot bear them now..."* *"However, when He, the Spirit of truth, has come, He will guide you into all truth..."* (John 16:13). The Holy Spirit's main function is to lead us into *"all truth"*. Not just the truth about Christ and who He was, but the truth about ourselves as well. We know according to 2 Timothy 3:16, that the Word of God was authored by the Holy Spirit. So in essence, Jesus was saying that if we read the Book and develop an intimate relationship with its author, we will know the truth and this knowledge will liberate us from the bondages of the enemy.

You see, Spiritual power cannot manifest in my life, until I have a revelation of Spiritual truth. For example, Christ died for me and my sins over 2000 years ago, but it did not become a reality in my life until, at the age of 39, I received a revelation of the Cross. All of the sudden, out of the blue, like a bolt of lightening, I understood that I was a sinner and that I needed a savior and that He was it. I was in a Church when this miracle happened, but the preacher was not even speaking on the subject of salvation. In fact, I couldn't tell you what he was speaking about. All I know was that I had an encounter with *"the Spirit of Truth"*, and revelation about Christ was imparted to me on a spiritual level. I suddenly knew and believed and confessed and was thereby saved, according to Romans 10:9. And I haven't got a clue as to how this process was accomplished. I just know that it was…and that I was forever changed by it. By a miracle, I stepped from death into eternal life, and what triggered this process was a spiritual revelation about Christ and about myself. I was a sinner, and He was my Savior.

Fundamentally speaking, it is the truth about ourselves that will set us free. Jesus said that when we *"abide in His word"*, we shall experience this phenomenon called revelation. Abide means to remain or live in. It represents serious commitment, not a passing infatuation. We do not see the world as it is. We see it as we are. We have a lens that we view everything around us through. The composition of this lens is determined by our spiritual condition. Most of us have a crack or a smudge on our spiritual lens caused by the traumas of life and the resulting deceptions of the enemy. He is after all, the *"father of all lies"*. Deception is his trademark, and unless our lens has been cleansed by the Blood and the Spirit of Christ, we're in essence, deceived.

Our attitude is the direct result of what we perceive as the truth. When we get in agreement with lies, we develop an attitude that produces deceived thinking. And the way this manifest in our financial lives is that we think we're OK, when in truth, we're in real danger. We think we're prosperous because we've been "blessed" with a large credit line at the bank; the very thing that the devil would use to destroy us if given the chance. We no longer understand the term ownership for example. We think because our name appears on the title or deed that we own it. We don't own it...the lender owns it. If you don't believe me, just get three payments behind and see what happens. You'll find out pretty quickly that you've been deceived by your perception of ownership. The truth is you're not an owner; you're an "interest payer". Or better yet, think of yourself as an "interest slave". Try using this term instead of owner, and see if it doesn't change your perception of that new Navigator that you just financed for seven years with no money down because you've got "good credit".

"Man...I really like that new Navigator I saw sitting in your drive way. Do you own it?", your neighbor asks.

"No...not really. I'm the 'interest slave' that has been assigned to it", you respond.

Your neighbor thought you were a little weird. Now he knows it for sure. But which answer is closer to truth. It is the truth that will set you free. Remember, *"The rich rules over the poor, And the borrower is servant to the lender"* (Proverbs 22:7). The fact is, with a 10% interest rate over seven years, you will pay nearly $81,000 for an automobile whose original cost was $58,000. You paid almost 1/3 of the original purchase price in interest. It sounds like you're an interest slave to me.

But if you've adopted an investor's mindset instead of a debtor's mindset, you would understand that an automobile is not an investment. It's an expense. The reason it's not an investment is because the car mentioned above will lose $26,000 of its value the first two years that you own it. Your payments are $962.87 per month, and you've paid a total of $23,108 out-of-pocket at the end of two-years. You still owe $45,317 on the loan. Add this to what you've spent in payments so far and you'll see that you've got $68,425 in an automobile that is now worth $32,000. This deal has cost you $36,425 dollars in the first two years and you're not out of it yet. This is why an automobile is not an investment…it's an expense and in this case a very costly one. The truth is, you just cannot afford to pay interest on luxury automobiles. Those with an investor mindset pay cash.

You think there's no way to pay cash for a Lincoln Navigator. Well I beg to differ. The first thing you have to do is overcome your showroom fever and resolve that you will let someone else take that "hit" to value that occurs as soon as you drive a new automobile off the lot. What if we shop for one that is low mileage and around two years old. Remember, a car is not an investment unless you're a vintage car collector, and then it is a dubious one. The goal is to try and figure out a way to drive a nice car with minimum cash outlay. The investor sets a financial objective; then she works toward that goal. She doesn't insist on instant gratification. She's patient. She develops a plan. She wants to buy a good clean used Navigator and she knows that one two years old will cost about $32,000. She doesn't have the money now, so this is where her thinking is dramatically different from the "Debtor". The debtor has to have it now, so he jumps out and borrows the money at 10%, and makes payments of $962 per month and is "upside down" (negative equity), after the first year. The Investor calculates an annual inflation rate of 4.5% per year, and thereby reckons that the used Navigator she wants will cost her about $36,500 in three years.

She then opens up a mutual fund account and pays $810 per month into it for three years. She gets a 12% return on her money (this is the average for the better funds over the last several years). She has accumulated the $36,500 dollars she needs to buy a clean used Navigator and she has only contributed $29,136 dollars "out-of-pocket". The interest she has earned on her fund accounts for the rest of the money she needs. She has purchased a luxury automobile of her dreams for $29,136 "out-of –pocket" cash, and the car is worth $36,500 the day she buys it. Meanwhile, our Prince of Impulse from the previous example ends up paying $80,800 "out-of-pocket" for his car and it is never worth what he owes against it until the 6th year of ownership. She has an "Investor's" attitude, and so therefore she thinks like an investor. He just doesn't think; he responds to his emotions. It's not a miracle. It's math.

I want to emphasize there is nothing inherently wrong with owning a Navigator; just pay cash for it. Or at the very least, finance as little of the purchase cost as possible. Our investor in the previous example, now has a free and clear automobile that she can drive for a year or two and trade up for a newer model. She continues to contribute $810 per month to her "sinking fund" (that's a fancy word for a savings account), and after two years she trades her now four year-old car in on another Navigator that is two years old. By now the cost to buy a two-year old Navigator has risen to $38,200 (remember the 4.5% inflation). The value of her car has depreciated to around $21,500 (based on current depreciation rates for this make and model of car). She buys the newer car for a trade difference of $16,700. By now there is $21,200 dollars in her sinking fund. She buys the newer car, and has around $6,000 left in her fund. If she continues to do this repeatedly for 10 years; trading up every two years while continually making the payments to the fund she will have her sinking fund fully funded and it will now produce enough income to purchase her a newer automobile every two years without any further contributions. In other words, she has paid $97,200 "out-of-pocket" over ten years ($810 per month for 10 years), and has basically provided herself a Lincoln Navigator to drive that is never more than 4 years old for a period of 22 years before she depletes her fund. That's what I call getting the most bang for the buck.

Remember our "debtor" in the first example. He financed the whole purchase for seven years, and paid out $80,800 out-of-pocket and all he had to show for his trouble was a worn out old Navigator that nobody wanted. Our "investor" spends $16,400 more over three more years and drives in style for 22 years of her adult life and never has a car that she can't depend on. She shall *"lend to many nations and not borrow..."* (Deuteronomy 15:6). And it all begins with a new attitude that facilitates a new way of thinking. Thinking like a "lender/investor" and not a "debtor".

The key element of your new attitude has to be that you basically renounce credit. Buying things when you don't have the money to pay for them is the root of our financial problems. Yes I know they're running that big-screen TV on a special, and offering it for "90 days same as cash". That means they let you take it home and you don't have to pay for it for 90 days and they won't even charge you any interest. That's a good deal you say. Read the fine print on the purchase agreement. If you don't pay the purchase cost in full within the 90 day time period, interest starts from the date of purchase (usually 22% or better), and you're "buying on time" again.

You say, "Well I have the money to pay for it."

Then do it when you purchase it.

Or you say, "Well I have most of the money to pay for it. When my tax refund gets here I can pay it off." That's fine, but you're still spending money that you don't have. Wait until you've got the cash, then go in and buy a demo that has a little scratch on the bottom that is hardly noticeable. Offer them ½ of the retail price and wave those "Ben Franklins" in front of them and see what happens. They'll sell it, I promise. And you'll have a big-screen TV that is paid for, which has a scratch that nobody can find, with money left over.

Quit paying for groceries with credit cards. I don't care if you pay the balances off every month and you get all those "frequent-flyer" miles for using it. You'll spend a third more on impulsive purchases when you pay with plastic. When you count out cash money to pay for things, there is an emotional connection. This is your money. You had to work twenty hours of over-time this week to get this money. You'll put that "coffee-latte" stuff that cost $6.00 per bottle back on the shelf, and reach for that old Folger's can that cost $5.00 and makes enough for ten gallons of coffee. Plastic separates us emotionally from the sweat of paying for the purchase. Therefore, our impulses run rampant. You'll save enough on groceries over a life time to buy your own airplane. Then you can fly as frequently as you want to.

"And do not be conformed to this world, but be transformed by the renewing of your mind, that you may prove what is that good and acceptable and perfect will of God" (Romans 12:2). The world is living on the impulses of their flesh, and they're broke and don't know it. We're called to **not** be conformed to their way of thinking. They embrace debt as a solution. We see debt as a dangerous trap.

They think "buy now and pay later" is wisdom. We know that it is an invitation from the enemy to come into bondage. They think we're crazy. We understand that they're deceived. Paul makes an important observation about those who are filled with the Spirit of God (or Truth), and those of the world who are lost. He said, *"But he who is spiritual judges all things, yet he himself is rightly judged by no one."* (1 Corinthians 2:15). They have an excuse. They're without the Spirit of Truth. Believers, on the other hand, should be able to discern the truth.

Believers need to reject debt as a solution and see it for what it is. It is the problem. Believers need to renounce all consumer debt (cars, TV's, furniture, etc.) and look at mortgage debt on real estate with a wary eye. Buying "real" assets on time and paying interest on something that is going to increase in value is not unsound. The issue is, do you have the intention of paying it off, or are you content with making payments for the rest of your natural life? The answer will reflect the attitude. The world accepts mortgage payments as a necessary part of life. They will finance a house for 60 years if it will keep their payments lower. They are "interest-slaves", and they don't care. They do not have the ability to *"judge rightly"*, for they are without the discernment of the Spirit of Truth. Believers enter into such arrangements carefully and with the intention of paying the debt off in 15 years. Not sixty. They are sensitive to the dangers of debt.

"One who restrains his appetites avoids debt." The Babylonian system is designed to ensnare. *"...Come out of her, my people, lest you share in her sins, and lest you receive of her plagues."* (Revelation 18:4). God's people need to *"come out"* of the credit system. It starts with a new attitude.

4. A Hardened Will—

As I sat in the banker's waiting area, the whole situation felt surreal. I had come to try and explain how I was going to repay a loan for which the collateral had just vanished into thin air. It was two years after my reversal of fortune brought on by September 11, and I had been unable turn my financial situation around. You see, that was the problem. I was trying to do it. My faith in my relation-ship with God had suffered badly, and I was no longer trying to hear him. My emotional state was such that I couldn't discern His voice any longer. I felt that I had committed sin in my stewardship, and had therefore been disqualified from His mercy and grace. In addition, people who I owed money to were making wild accusa-tions concerning my integrity. Even though I knew that the devil is the accuser of the brethren, I started to get in agreement with him. I was in a weakened emotional condition, and I just didn't have the strength to fight. My health had taken a turn for the worse. I had suffered a mild heart attack brought on by the stress of trying to cope with things over which I had no control. I had even started to get in agreement with the enemy when he offered me thoughts of suicide. I had a million dollar life insurance policy, and I thought (albeit briefly) that it would take care of everything. The bank would be paid, and my wife would have something to start over on.

I had entered into the dangerous ground of a passive will. I had always been what the Bible calls a *"pleaser of men"* by nature. Looking back, I see that God was in the process of changing this part of my character. Paul said, *"… For if I still pleased men, I would not be a bondservant of Christ."* (Galatians 1:10). I was allowing my will to be pushed in the direction of everybody else's will. Not my own. I was trying to do what the bank wanted, what my partners wanted, what my friends wanted. God was no where on the list. I had allowed my mind to get in agreement with the devil, and not the word of God which says that because of the Blood of Christ I am the very *"righteousness of God"* and that the *"righteous have never been forsaken"* (Psalm 37:25). I let the devil tell me that I had messed up and therefore had been forsaken by God, and I was agreeing with him.

As I sat in that bank lobby that day, it felt like I was trapped between two realms; the Spiritual and the natural. My peripheral vision became fuzzy. At first I thought I was having another heart attack, but it was something else. I was having an encounter with the Spirit of God. Something was being touched deep inside of me. I felt strengthened. I felt something rising up inside of me. I had come to the end of myself…He was waiting for me there.

I came to when I heard the banker's secretary tell me he was ready to see me. When I first arrived, I had no clue what I was going to say to him. As we shook hands and exchanged greetings, I suddenly heard myself declare, "This is the plan I would like to talk to you about this morning." Where was that coming from! I didn't have a plan! But I heard myself laying one out. Who was this guy who was using my voice? I realized it was me, or more accurately, the Spirit in me.. The shame and embarrassment were gone and my voice took on a tone of authority. Something had happened and it had been super-natural. I was through being the victim. I was through letting other people control and dictate my financial future. As Joyce Meyers says, *"I was in a mess, but I was not going to stay in a mess. God was bringing me out."*

I had left the paralysis of condemnation and shame to which my passive will had led me, and was stepping onto the solid ground of the spiritual authority which I had inherited from Him. I was a *"joint heir with Christ"* (Romans 8:17). I had let the devil nearly steal more than my money. I almost let him steal my relationship with Christ. I don't care if you've made some bad decisions that have brought you into financial hardship, He will not forsake you. *"For a righteous man may fall seven times And rise again, But the wicked shall fall by calamity* ", (Proverbs 24:16). The righteous are in one of two positions. Either up or getting up. Not staying down. Notice the scripture doesn't say, "the righteous never fall down." Failure is a money back guarantee in life. How we react to it is the essential thing. John Maxwell says, *"Life is 10% what happens to you, and 90% how you react to it."*

When we enter into financial failure, we have to remember that failure is the breeding ground of success. And there is *"no condemnation in Christ"*…only learning, repenting, and moving forward. It doesn't matter what people think. We clearly cannot make people around us happy, and serve Jesus Christ. If you are like I was, and you've always gotten your self-worth from your ability to make the people around you happy, I have one word for you. Stop. You can't serve Christ with an approval addiction. *"The fear of man brings a snare, But whoever trusts in the Lord shall be safe"*, (Proverbs 29:25). If you're going to fear someone, fear Him. *"And do not fear those who kill the body but cannot kill the soul. But rather fear Him who is able to destroy both soul and body in hell,"* (Matthew 10:28). The beginning of wisdom is a healthy fear of the Lord (Proverbs 1:7). And conversely, a sign of wisdom is when we're not moved by the opinions of man. Only God's opinions matter. You're not who they say you are. You're who He says you are, and He says you're an heir to a vast Kingdom.

I received another spiritual revelation that day in the bank lobby. Christ died to bring me victory over my circumstances. Not to prevent me from having them. It's in the trial that my faith is perfected (James 1:2-4). I realized that God was *"chastening"* me to draw out some imperfections in my character. *"For whom the Lord loves He chastens..."* (Hebrews 12:6). Chasten means to "subject someone to discipline." It suddenly dawned on me, God only chastens a son. He judges a sinner. I had not blown it. It was still His will that *"I be the head and not the tail"* (Deuteronomy 28:13). And what had brought me to near self-destruction, was a passive-will; a will that accepted everything that had happened to me as mere fate. God had made me certain promises, and when the opposite began to manifest in my life, I bought the devil's argument that I had brought this on myself because I had sinned in my stewardship. "I had taken foolish chances. I had been arrogant in my confidence in my own ability to read market trends", I thought.

I came to a startling realization. It's not about me!! It's about Him!! These promises that I had been standing on didn't have anything to do with what I had done or not done. It was about what He had done. All I had to do was to remain in Him (John 15:7). It was on Calvary that my financial freedom was won. I was in a war; a war that began eons ago in a whole different age when Lucifer rebelled in heaven and was cast to the earth. In the Garden the devil had tried to destroy God's greatest creation. Man. When the devil tempted Adam and Eve and they fell into sin, God proclaimed a curse on the devil. He told him, *"... I will put enmity Between you and the woman, And between your seed and her Seed; He shall (crush) your head, And you shall bruise His heel."* (Genesis 3:15). Jesus Christ had no natural father. Mary became pregnant by the Spirit; making Christ truly the *"Seed of the woman"*. I was a Spiritual descendant of Christ, and there was *"enmity" (hatred)*, between me and the seed of the devil. God had declared it, not me. Therefore, the devil doesn't like me.

Why was I so surprised that he was trying to steal my inheritance? And why was I letting him? He had me convinced I was being punished. But I was not forsaken, I was in training. God was teaching me how to fight the enemy when he attacks the area of financial provision. I was in bondage, and God was delivering me in order to show me how to lead others to freedom. The thing that the devil had meant for my harm, God had meant for my good. The devil was trying to destroy me. God was trying to refine me. I had snapped out of the trance the enemy had me under.

I was beginning to take authority over my situation and to harden my will and get it in agreement with God's word. A passive will is a dangerous thing in the middle of a storm. In a prophecy about the coming Messiah in the Book of Isaiah, the Lord said, *"For the Lord God will help Me; Therefore I will not be disgraced; Therefore I have set My face like a flint, And I know that I will not be ashamed."* (Isaiah 50:7). Christ declared that no matter how things looked, His Father was helping Him. And that in the end, He would not be ashamed or disgraced, but what He had to do was to *"set (His) face like flint."* He had to harden His will in agreement with God's will and never look back. He couldn't afford to be double-minded. If He had of been, the devil would have talked Him out of the Cross. How disastrous would that have been for us? We would be in a hopeless condition right now, if Christ had become "double-minded".

This is precisely what we've got to do if were going to be delivered from our financial affliction. We have to renounce the world's credit system and "purpose in our hearts" that were going to follow God. To those of us who have the courage to *"set our face like flint"*, God makes us a promise. He says, *"...Do not be afraid. Stand still, and see the salvation of the Lord, which He will accomplish for you today. For the Egyptians whom you see today, you shall see again no more forever. The Lord will fight for you, and you shall hold your peace."* (Exodus 14:13-14). One afternoon, in the lobby of a Bank, I saw the water starting to fall in on my spiritual enemies. I got a revelation about God's love and His mercy. It's without end. He was going to fight for me.

When I walked into the bank that afternoon, I thought my life was over. Little did I know, it was just starting. I resolved that I would no longer live like the world, but would live for God. I was going to follow Him to freedom, and the first thing I had to do was renounce credit. A fitting thing to do while sitting in the lobby of a bank, don't you think? But from that moment, I began to get free. And I began to learn how God's financial system really works. I began to learn about the true nature of His heart and His provision. I was about to learn the meaning of stewardship.

Part Two: "The Journey"

Seven Steps to Freedom and Excellent Stewardship

Step One: Face The Truth
And Take Authority

"Adversity is the first path to truth." -*George Gordon Byron*

"You cannot change what you will not confront"
—*John Hagee*

"There is desirable treasure, And oil in the dwelling of the wise, But a foolish man squanders it." (Proverbs 21:20)

"For as the body without the spirit is dead, so faith without works (action) is dead also." (James 2:26)

The first ingredient to financial revelation is a desktop calculator. Financial issues stir deep emotions in most of us; therefore we spend much of our lives in financial ignorance. We don't really want to know why we can't seem to get all the bills paid each month. We delude ourselves into believing that it will work out some way. "God will provide", we proclaim. God will provide, but He provides to those who are not in denial concerning their financial problems and are trying to deal with them. Too many times we use the "faith" argument to escape personal responsibility.

"The Lord said all I need to do is believe. He didn't say I had to learn how to balance my checkbook"

Do we really expect a God, who has never squandered anything, to bless us when we've not balanced our checkbook in two years, and are consequently paying $250.00 per month in over-draft charges? God is waiting for us to get real about our situation and face the truth. All freedom begins with the truth, and the quicker we face it, the quicker He begins to act on our behalf.

So the first step to our deliverance is simple math. We must sit down and add up our expenses and compare them with our income. Jesus asked a simple question. *"For which of you, intending to build a tower, does not sit down first and count the cost, whether he has enough to finish it—"* (Luke 14:28). The answer is—a lot of people. The truth is there are very few people who really know and understand where they are financially. Most of us live our lives from paycheck to paycheck, and have few if any long-term financial goals. Even fewer of us have a written plan for the expenditures that we incur on a monthly basis. This is commonly called a budget.

I like to refer to it as a Freedom Plan (see appendix). You see after you have taken the time to add up your monthly expenses and compare them to your monthly income, the expenses always out number the income. How do I know that, you asked? Because your credit card balances are out of control. What credit cards do is allow us to go through a succession of months in a negative cash-flow position (we're spending more than we're making), and not have to deal with the financial truth that we're living above our means. We merely put the deficit on the credit card. So the impact of the truth of our situation is somewhat delayed, yet it is inevitable. The bill always comes due. Only now the bill has increased because we're trying to finance our deficit at 21% interest.

What the Freedom Plan does, is it pierces our self-imposed igno-rance with reality, so as to put an end to the delusion that every-thing's OK. "Adversity is the first path to truth." When we confront it...we can change it; but not until then. What prevents us from facing the reality of our financial situation is our emotions. It's just too painful to come to grips with the ocean of red ink that our life-style is creating. Emotion is always the enemy of the Spiritual. Paul said, *"For if you live according to the flesh you will die; but if by the Spirit you put to death the deeds of the body, you will live."* (Romans

8:13). Emotions are of the realm of the "soulish" or carnal nature. Whatever the Spirit commands us to do will be opposed by the flesh or carnal nature, because they are constantly at war with one another (Galatians 5:17). The path to freedom is not going to "feel good" in the beginning, but it will be <u>well</u> worth the discomfort when we get to the end. We have to take authority over our emotions and commit to dealing with the truth.

In fact, living by our emotions is what got us here in the first place. We bought that expensive exercise machine that we saw that beautiful young woman demonstrate on television, because we want to "feel" better about ourselves. If you're a woman, you want to look like her, and if you're a man you want to be attractive to women who look like her. You want to know how she got that wonderful figure? By getting up a 5:00 AM and running two miles every morning. What's required is a sweat suit and a pair of tennis shoes. Not a $1500 machine, that we put on a credit card and that's going to end up costing us $3000 by the time we finally get it paid for. What we need is not equipment, we need discipline. If we haven't learned how to discipline our "flesh-nature", we're going to end up using our exercise machine to hang clothes on anyway. Man! That is an expensive valet isn't it.

The Freedom Plan is the first step to financial discipline. It will give us a sense of control and purpose. There is comfort in having a plan. A plan identifies where we are, and where we're going. It becomes our roadmap to our future. The emotional pain of the present is converted into the mission of the future. *"For I know the plans I have for you," says the Lord. "They are plans for good and not for disaster, to give you a future and a hope."* (Jeremiah 29:11, NLT). Remember, God is in charge of your future, and He has a great future planned for you. This brings us to an important crossroad.

The Balance

I find that most Believer's who have slipped into financial hopelessness, have confused the spiritual concept of "Resting in Him", with allowing the enemy to steal your future through inaction. Let me explain. According to Hebrews 3:16-4:11, the faithful Believer is called to enter into the rest of God. What does that mean exactly? This passage is referring to the incident described in the Book of Numbers chapters 13 & 14, where God's people who had been delivered out of Egypt and the bondages of Pharaoh, were asked to enter in and possess the provision of God's Promised Land. They refused after the report of the scouts who were dispatched into the land on a reconnaissance mission. The scouts admitted that the land was truly plentiful and *"flowed with milk and honey"*, but it was inhabited by people they described as giants, *"and we were like grasshoppers in our own sight, and so we were in their sight."* (Numbers 13:33). Translation: they were afraid and intimidated by the things that they saw as the obstacles to their freedom; namely, the giants.

The writer of Hebrews says, *"So we see that they could not enter in because of unbelief."* (Hebrews 3:19). After witnessing God's supernatural power to deliver them from their enemies at the Red Sea, they did not have enough faith to believe that God could give them victory over the giants who were occupying their inheritance. What was their plan you ask? It was to select a new leader and return to Egypt. They were willing to live in slavery, rather than believe God for freedom and victory, because they were intimidated by the challenges that lay ahead of them. God found this inexcusable, and He condemned this generation to die in the wilderness, rather than enter into His provision for their future.

All except two men who were of the scouting party; Joshua and Caleb. Both of which had advised the Israelites to press in and believe in the power of God to deliver and defend His people. God says, *"But My servant Caleb, because he has a different spirit in him and has followed Me fully, I will bring into the land where he went, and his descendants shall inherit it"* (Numbers 14:24). He recognizes that Caleb and Joshua have a different Spirit. They're not ruled by a Spirit of Fear...but a Spirit of Faith. They believe that God wants them to possess the Promised Land of their inheritance and that He will give them victory over everything that stands in the path of its fulfillment! The others were afraid of failure. They could only see in the natural. They had not learned how to trust in the supernatural power of God, and His purposes for them.

Interestingly enough, although Caleb and Joshua have to spend forty years in the wilderness while this generation of non-believing cowards dies off, they both live to see the Promised inheritance of God's rest come to pass in their lives. Joshua, of course, becomes Moses' successor and leader of the nation of Israel. And as the invasion of Canaan is initiated, Caleb asks Joshua if He can possess Hebron, which is the very stronghold of the "Anak" or giant race of people who struck terror in the hearts of the Israelites. Caleb's argument to his old friend and fellow soldier is, *"And now, behold, the Lord has kept me alive, as He said, these forty-five years... and now, here I am this day, eighty-five years old. As yet I am as strong this day as on the day that Moses sent me; just as my strength was then, so now is my strength for war, both for going out and for coming in"* (Joshua 14:10-11). Joshua gives his consent, and an eighty-five year old warrior, who refuses to doubt the power of God to give him victory over his enemies, throws the giants (who caused so much pain and anguish in the hearts of his people just by appearing insurmountable) off the land and runs them out of town. Caleb proved that he had a *"different spirit in him."* He proved that he had the faith and determination that it took to enter into God's rest and his provision.

"It's a great story, but what has it got to do with me?", you asked. Quite frankly, everything. It has everything to do with you and your journey to freedom. Because the question you have to answer is, "Are you a *'grasshopper'*, or are you a *'giant-killer'*?" If you see yourself as a "grasshopper", someone who is unworthy of God's grace and intervention, then you will never have the strength to face the giants that are going to be in your path to freedom. So what, if the neighbors saw them tow your Jaguar away, as the electric company pulled your meter. This is your journey not theirs. You cannot let people define you, nor can you worry about what they think of you. The word says that you cannot be a pleaser of men and a bondservant of Jesus Christ (Galatians 1:10). It's interesting what the scouts said, *"and we were like grasshoppers in our own sight, and so we were in their sight."* How we see ourselves is how others are going to see us. Do not allow the enemy to put shame and condemnation on you because of the financial mistakes you have made. There is no condemnation in Christ (Romans 8:1). There is only learning from mistakes and repenting.

If you see yourself as a "giant-killer" (one who is on a mission to possess the promises of God and not some counterfeit concept that is merely "materialism" in a spiritual cloak) you will conquer your enemies. A giant-killer is not concerned with the opinions of others, because he or she knows that they have not dealt with the giants in their own lives. Those who judge others (who are in the struggle), are living an illusion of freedom. They have the trappings of success, but look in their mailbox, and you will see the bondages of Egypt (the world's system). They owe Pharaoh, and they're trying hard to conceal the fact that they're falling behind on their brick quota themselves.

A giant-killer has faith in God's plan and purpose for his life, and understands that, "...*that all things work together for good to those who love God, to those who are the called according to His purpose.*" (Romans 8:28). God will use his adversity to strengthen his faith and mold him into a better vessel of His grace. He is not moved by what he sees, but is moved by the truth of the Word of God and what God says about his situation. If the Israelites had been moved by God's Word, and not the emotions that were generated by what things "looked" like, they would have entered into the rest of God instead of the condemnation of the wilderness. The same applies to us in our quest for freedom. We must not be overcome by natural circumstances and we must look for God's hand and His intervention on our behalf.

So what does God mean when He calls us to enter into His "rest". Being a giant-killer doesn't sound very restful to me. Does "resting in Him" mean that we do nothing except fast, pray, and believe? Or to take a self-improvement course and think positive thoughts about our impending bankruptcy?

It is important to remain positive, and you absolutely need to fast and pray. Furthermore, without faith in Him and His word, you're not going to get out of the starting gate. Before you know it, you'll be wanting to elect a new leader and head back to Egypt. So we never make light of the spiritual disciplines that are important in a time of trail. They are essential to your victory. What people seem to be confused about is what results are to be expected from their spiritual life. What your fasting and praying and believing will produce is a clarity of His voice…not the supernatural incineration of American Express by fire and brimstone.

The virtue that Caleb and Joshua had developed which endeared them to their creator and King so much was not a sort of "kamikaze faith"; they were not reckless ideologues living a fanciful existence that had no relationship with reality. No sir, what they had was spiritual discipline. What they had was a spiritual ear that discerned the voice of the Lord no matter how difficult the circumstance. The aspect of their character that God so admired was not a "John Wayne" mentality that caused them to have an overwhelming desire to charge the enemy with a revolver blazing from each hand and the reins of their trusty steed in their teeth. No it was more important than that. It was total obedience. The Lord said, *"But My servant Caleb, because he has a different spirit in him and has followed Me fully…"*

Resting in Him does not mean we sit on the front porch and standby prayerfully as the enemy carries off everything we own (or should I say, "we and the bank own"). Look to the spirit that was in Caleb, and you'll get a revelation of what it is to "rest in God". Caleb had a heart for the fight. He was a giant-killer at the age of eighty-five. He comforted himself at night with thoughts of slaying the sons of Anak. The dream of redeeming his inheritance and destroying those who had stolen it caused him to have a fire in his belly.

Yet Caleb never—and I mean never, took any action without the leading of the spirit of God. He was a man who craved action, and by his own description, had a *"heart for war"*. But he was totally submitted to the Spirit of God, and Joshua, his leader and spiritual authority. Caleb heard God's voice and he *"followed (it) fully"*. In this manner he had entered into God's rest. Not through inaction, but through deliberate action…at the behest of the Commander of the host of heaven. What Caleb rested from was planning his own strategies and battle tactics. Not from the battle itself.

Let me be very clear on this point. You will fight…or you will perish. God has never called His people to inaction. To those who have fallen into *"surety"* (debt), the Word of God says, *"Deliver yourself like a gazelle from the hand of the hunter, And like a bird from the hand of the fowler."* (Proverbs 6:5). This implies intensity of effort. No...the provision of rest He has made for us lifts the worry off our shoulders. Jesus said, *"Come to Me, all you who labor and are heavy laden, and I will give you rest. Take My yoke upon you and learn from Me, for I am gentle and lowly in heart, and you will find rest for your souls. For My yoke is easy and My burden is light.""* (Matthew 11:28-30). Rest of the soul is not just eternal rest, but also relief from emotional stress in the present life. What makes the burden light is not that you'll not be required to do anything. What makes the burden light is that He will accept the responsibility for the success of the actions taken according to His command.

If we will allow Him, He will become our platoon Captain when we've become pinned down by enemy fire. He will take our mess and lead us to safety and victory. All we have to do is do what Caleb did...follow Him fully. We have no chance of making the journey across the Wilderness to the Promised Land of financial freedom without the leading of the Spirit. It's true that we use the desktop calculator to define our current position, but then we must pray, fast, and believe in our ability to hear His voice. He will impart a vision of our future and help us make a map (Freedom Plan) that will take us to where He's called us to go.

Financial freedom requires the perfect balance between the natural and the spiritual. We have to act in the natural with the intensity of the gazelle in the areas of work and diligence, but we must never stray over the line into the realm of the "flesh". To be in the flesh means to have become confident in your ability rather than God's. Everywhere the Bible uses the word "flesh", as in "flesh-nature", just write in the words "self" or "self-nature". The flesh is the alliance made between the soul (mind, will, and emotions), and the body.

We are created in God's image and God is "triune" in His nature. This is to say He is "three-in-one"; Father, Son, and the Holy Spirit. His children also have three aspects to their existence...body, soul, and spirit. *"Now may the God of peace Himself sanctify you completely; and may your whole spirit, soul, and body be preserved blameless at the coming of our Lord Jesus Christ."* (1 Thessalonians

5:23). The destination of your spiritual journey is to become sanctified in all three aspects of your life...body, soul, and spirit. To become sanctified (made Holy or set apart for God) completely, is to become *"transformed into His image"* (2 Corinthians 3:18). This is God's plan for every Believer.

When Adam was formed, he also was formed in three parts. *"And the Lord God formed man (Adam) of the dust of the ground, and breathed into his nostrils the breath of life; and man became a living being."* (Genesis 2:7). Adam's natural body was formed out of the minerals and elements found in the earth, just like mine and yours. Then God breathed the breath of life into his nostrils. He put His spirit in Adam's biological body. The word translated in the NKJ version as *"being"* is the Hebrew word *nephesh*. In most other places in the Old Testament, it is translated "soul", and for our discussion let's use the term "soul" here. What this passage is saying is that God breathed His Spirit into Adams biological body, and by these actions Adam's soul (mind, will, and emotions) were formed and he became a *"living soul"*.

In the garden, God had instructed him that he would surely die if he ate of the Tree of Knowledge. What caused the Fall of mankind in the garden was Adam's disobedience in his eating of the forbidden fruit, the fruit of the Tree of Knowledge. Did he die? Not in his biological nature. This aspect of his nature lived for another 930 years. What died when Adam ate of the Tree of Knowledge was his "spiritual-nature", and since it is "by the Spirit" that we know the mind of God (1 Corinthians 2), Adam lost his ability to commune with God. His "soulish" nature had conspired with his biological nature and they had snuffed out his spirit.

The most damaging thing that happened to Adam was that he was "on his own", from here on out. He had elected to live out of the power of his own intellect and understanding, rather than the infinite mind and power of the intellect of God. He had traded a Cray supercomputer for a slide ruler. Consequently, Adam failed in every area a man can fail in, and he cursed his descendants to do the same.

The mission of the "Son of Man", Jesus Christ, was to reintroduce man's spiritual life. He said, *"...I am the way, the truth, and the life. No one comes to the Father except through Me."* (John 14:6).

The Greek word He used for "life" in this passage was *"zoe"*. This term referred to the spiritual life. He is the way back to the restoration of what Adam had lost in the Garden so long ago. *"For as by one man's disobedience many were made sinners, so also by one Man's obedience many will be made righteous."* (Romans 5:19). His obedience to the Cross caused a "release of the Spirit" that was of epic proportions, in fulfillment of the word of the Lord as spoken by the mouth of the Prophets.

Christ told the Pharisee Nicodemus in John Chapter Three that he was not saved. This shocked this great man of God who by holding the office of Pharisee was required to have the first five Books of the Bible (Pentateuch) memorized. Furthermore. He had confessed to Christ that he believed that He was the Son of God. So he knew and believed the Word, and also believed in and confessed Jesus Christ as the savior and Son of God. But Jesus told him that he had to be "born again" to be saved. It seemed absurd to the old Pharisee who replied, *"How can a man be born when he is old? Can he enter a second time into his mother's womb and be born?"* (John 3:4).

"Jesus answered, "Most assuredly, I say to you, unless one is born of water and the Spirit, he cannot enter the kingdom of God. That which is born of the flesh is flesh, and that which is born of the Spirit is spirit. Do not marvel that I said to you, 'You must be born again.' The wind blows where it wishes, and you hear the sound of it, but cannot tell where it comes from and where it goes. So is everyone who is born of the Spirit."" (John 3:5-8). Man had lost his spiritual nature in the Garden. The Son of Man had come to restore it. Those who have a spiritual encounter with the risen Son, will experience a rebirth of their spiritual nature. Not only will this bring eternal life, but it will also restore their ability to commune with and hear from, a Living God.

If the "born again" Believer will pursue God and His ways, he or she will find that their "spiritual-nature" will become dominant. When we walk in the Word, prayer, and in fasting, our spirit that was restored in our salvation experience, becomes stronger. If we pursue these spiritual disciplines, eventually our spirit will totally dominate our flesh. "Self" will die and Christ will live in us and through us. Paul said, *"I have been crucified with Christ; it is no longer I who*

*live, but Christ lives in me; and the life which I now live in the flesh
I live by faith in the Son of God, who loved me and gave Himself for
me.*" (Galatians 2:20).

The crucifixion of the "flesh" facilitates the "release of the spirit".
"*For Christ also suffered once for sins, the just for the unjust, that
He might bring us to God, being put to death in the flesh but made
alive by the Spirit,*" (1 Peter 3:18). When we put the flesh to death by
denying its Lordship, we bring the spirit to life. It's the flesh nature
that craves food when we fast, and it's the spirit that is strengthened
through the intentional denial of these "lusts". The way the flesh is
crucified is not by the physical act of crucifixion. It is by the act of
the Believer's will that refuses to allow it and its impulses to dominate his life.

Or it comes through an experience of great adversity in our lives
in an area where we usually are very confident of our own abilities.
I was very confident in my own business abilities, and yet this was
the very area where I was afflicted by circumstances over which I
had no control. God used the financial adversity I faced to crucify
my "self" nature. He knew I was over-confident in my own abilities, and consequently far too "self-reliant". He called me to start
this business, and I thought it was my future. Imagine my surprise
when I discovered that it was actually my Cross. The very areas in
which I was most capable and self-sufficient were the areas that had
to be nailed to the Cross if I was going to be used seriously by God.
Could it be that God is trying to kill something in you, namely your
financial self-reliance, so He can resurrect you? As the flesh dies, the
spirit becomes more and more dominate. And we eventually get to
the place where we're "Spirit-led".

The Spirit dictates to the body the truth of its healing by the truth
of the Word of God. The Spirit speaks to the emotions and causes
them to remain calm in the hour of adversity, much like a Coach
calms down his players when they're behind by a touchdown in the
Championship game with two minutes left on the clock. The players
instinctively look to their Coach for guidance and reassurance, and
if he is calm, they become calm. In the same manner, the "Spirit-
led" believer's mind looks to the Spirit and His truth in the heat of
Battle...not to the power of his own reasoning.

This is Caleb's great strength. In his chest beats the heart of a warrior, but his instincts to make war, were always under the command and control of the Spirit of God. He rested in God, and His plan. Caleb understood that the impulses of his flesh were unreliable and dangerous, so he prayed *"continuously in the Spirit"* as he sharpened his sword. To rest in God is to trust in and be confident in His leadership; not to refuse to fight.

Faith Without Action Is Dead—

The real difficulty in our pursuit of Financial Freedom, is maintaining the balance between the natural and the spiritual. In fact, the test in life— is the balance between the spirit and the natural. In Caleb we see a man who is led by the spirit into action. Action that is ordained of God. In the Book of James there resides a controversial passage of scripture that caused Martin Luther, the father of the Protestant Movement, to state that the entire Book of James should be thrown out of the New Testament. This passage has to be interpreted carefully, or it will mess with your theology of salvation by faith as opposed to works. James 2:14-16 says, *"What does it profit, my brethren, if someone says he has faith but does not have works? Can faith save him? If a brother or sister is naked and destitute of daily food, and one of you says to them, "Depart in peace, be warmed and filled," but you do not give them the things which are needed for the body, what does it profit?"* The proper syntax of the Greek language ties the sentence *"Can faith save him?"* to the second sentence *"If a brother or sister is destitute of daily food …"*—not the first sentence, *"What does it profit, my brethren, if someone says he has faith but does not have works?"*.

This is an extremely important distinction, because it changes the meaning of the passage from a theological issue concerning the doctrine of salvation, to a practical issue of how does one save someone who is starving to death by prayer and faith only. James makes the argument that the person of faith should be stirred to feed the hungry person...as well as pray for them. He goes on to say, *"For as the body without the spirit is dead, so faith without works is dead also."* (James 2:26). Faith in God stimulates action...not idleness.

Yes, it's true that many times, the action that God calls us to is "waiting". *"But those who wait on the Lord Shall renew their strength; They shall mount up with wings like eagles, They shall run and not be weary, They shall walk and not faint."* (Isaiah 40:31). Caleb waited for forty-years, and yet he was a warrior… a "man of war". And while he was waiting, God was renewing his strength. This issue of being led by the Spirit is the key to all victory in life. In the area of our finances, it is imperative that we allow the Spirit to lead us through the wilderness.

Knowing the Truth Will Lead to New Priorities

The first step to becoming led by the Spirit of God, is the recognition of His truth. By now, I hope you have been enlightened to the fact that man's financial systems are like him…flawed. They are a snare and we should endeavor to be delivered from them *"as the gazelle delivers himself from the hand of the hunter."* Then we need to renounce the world and its systems. *"Do not love the world or the things in the world. If anyone loves the world, the love of the Father is not in him."* (1 John 2:15). I'm not saying that bankers and the institutions they lead are inherently evil. Many types of business lending are needed to stimulate commerce and various forms of economic activity. It's the world's attitude towards "consumer lending" that the Believer must renounce and become free of. We are consuming more than we can pay for, and it is destroying our future.

Once we have committed to God and His ways over the world's ways, we need to sit down and allow God to help us devise a plan. He will call us to reorganize our financial priorities. This will require you to "take authority" over your financial future. You will determine your financial priorities in accordance with God's Word. Our Freedom Plan is built around this reorganization of priorities. We deal with the primary categories of your monthly expenditures in order of importance: Tithing, contingency fund, housing, utilities, food, transportation, clothing, medical/health, personal, recreation, debts.

Perhaps you notice that debts are the last category. This is consumer debt. The car loan and the mortgage are covered under transportation and housing respectively. It is moved to the bottom and it will remain at the bottom until they are paid-off. You've got to stop going hungry so you can make your Visa payment. When the credit card company calls you and threatens you with a bad credit rating if you don't get your payments caught up by Friday, you need to tell them that you've renounced credit and in fact, it's too much credit that has gotten you here in the first place. What you need is not more credit, it is less debt. Their collection people are trained to make you feel bad about yourself and to stimulate an emotional response that causes you to move them to the top of the priority list and write them a check.

You have to remember that you have reestablished your priorities. You have now taken authority over your finances. You need to pay your creditors, and are called by the Word of God to do just that. *"The wicked borrows and does not repay, But the righteous shows mercy and gives"* (Psalm 37:21). We're not advocating that you refuse to repay what you've borrowed, we're saying that you've got to take authority over the terms of repayment. In the next chapter we'll deal with the methods of renegotiation, but for now it's important that you feed your family and keep a roof over their head. American Express will have to get in line behind the mortgage company and the electric company. They will try and make you "feel-bad" about the way you're treating them. You need to remind them that you acknowledge the debt, but unfortunately for them, they have been placed at the low end of the priority list.

When the collections person becomes upset and threatens to cut off your card privileges...thank them. For they have just helped you take the first step in your journey; the rejection of the world's credit system. Do not be intimidated by their demands. Usually, after you break through the first tier of collection people and get to the managers of their department (if you continue to not make your payments, you'll get to the management people, I guarantee) you'll find a change in attitude. These people know you can file bankruptcy and they'll get nothing (in most cases). They understand that it's in their best interest to get in agreement with your new financial plan which leads to the eventual retirement of their debt. Once they become convinced that the "this-is-going-to-ruin-your-credit-argument" is no longer effective, they will stop using it. And just for the record, what rehabilitates your credit is going through challenging circumstances and repaying what you owe. Not starving yourself to death and having a nervous breakdown! It's ironic that when we make it through the wilderness of transition to the Promised Land of financial freedom, our credit will be stellar and we'll have no use for it then. When we've been set free we must not allow ourselves to be ensnared again, but they will offer us new credit relentlessly.

Notice that we put God number one on the priority list. We need His blessing and leadership to come through this journey. We have to adhere strictly to His Word in the area of our finances if we're going to be delivered. His Word on tithing is not negotiable and we will go into His principles of giving in succeeding chapters. But suffice it to say that He has to be on the top of our list.

The second most important area of expenses is the area of saving. We need to build a contingency fund of at least $1,500 for emergencies. If there are unexpected repairs that have to be made on our car, we need to have some money put aside for that purpose. This money needs to be accessible, but not too accessible. We don't need to be using it to pay for anything but true emergencies. Not having enough cash on you to pay your green fees at the Municipal Golf Course is not an emergency. Having to put a new transmission in the car you drive to work is. In addition, you will find that having some money laid back gives you some peace of mind, and anything we can do to reduce anxiety on our journey will be helpful.

Then, of course, the categories of housing, utilities, transportation, and food are of similar importance and are all more important than Master Card. There are steps that we can take in each category that will reduce their relative cost, but irregardless, they are expenses that are essential and cannot be reduced to zero. Perhaps if you have a large equity in a home, you might consider selling it and buying a smaller less expensive home. What you don't need to do is refinance your equity to pay off credit cards. The reason we don't advise this is that most people will keep their credit lines open or open new ones after they paid the old ones off with the proceeds from the Home Equity loan. If they haven't dealt with the truth of their financial situation and renounced consumer credit (we know they haven't since they still have credit cards), then they will run the balances back to their limits. Now they have no Home Equity to refinance because they have done that already, and as Jesus said, "*...and the last state of that man is worse than the first. So shall it also be with this wicked generation.*"" (Matthew 12:45). Moral of the story? If you're so inclined, cash in the home equity and pay off debt and move into a less expensive house. But don't refinance it.

In the category of transportation, you could sell your car and buy a cheaper used one, but I recommend that you be careful. You know the mechanical condition of your car, and if you buy another older car, many times you're just buying another man's problem. If your mechanically inclined and enjoy working and restoring old cars, then this strategy might be for you. Otherwise, take good care of the car you have and be prepared to drive it a long time. If you can trade up or across year models for something that gets better fuel mileage, then I recommend it. Fuel has become a huge portion of the transportation budget of most households, and fuel economy has become the number one consideration for most car buyers. These new "hybrid" cars are phenomenal in their fuel efficiency, and they are worthy of consideration, especially if you have to drive over a large distance to get to work. For example, if you have to drive 40 miles to work one way, and you trade a pick-up that gets 15 MPG, for a "Hybrid" that gets 60 MPG, at current gasoline prices you will save about $350 per month on fuel cost. You could buy a new "Hybrid" and you would save approximately 60% of the car payment in fuel savings each month. But if your pickup is paid for, you need to weigh out the benefits of fuel efficiency against the benefits of being free from debt. Again, the objective is to reduce the expenses in this category as much as possible, but it is impossible to reduce them to zero. Transportation is a necessary expense and one cannot function in life without it.

In the area of utilities, we recommend a programmable thermostat. They are relatively inexpensive and can be installed by almost anyone who has any aptitude for home repairs. If the husband and wife both work, there are potentially huge utility savings that can be reaped from programming the air conditioning or heat to only be active when there are people in the house. Some households can achieve up to a 24% reduction in their energy cost, depending on their lifestyles and daily schedule. Insulation and thermapane windows (insulated glass) are the other alternatives to reduce utility cost. They are extremely effective as well, but can be cost prohibitive, especially if we are struggling to build our contingency account, or meet some other financial objective. Home improvements have to be made when we have the cash. Only in extreme cases would we consider borrowing money to make these repairs and improvements. The interest on the loan will usually eat up much of the potential savings and besides it runs counter to our new philosophy of paying cash. If these improvements are critical, we will always try to save up and pay cash. In most cases, the cost of the home improvements will take years to recover through accumulative energy savings. And if we've borrowed the money to do the work, the interest we pay will greatly extend this period of recovery. Start with a programmable thermostat, and buy more insulation and thermapane windows when you can.

Food is a category that usually has huge room for improvement. Americans invented fast food, and it's killing us physically and financially. We've decided we're too busy to prepare meals anymore. Consequently, obesity and diabetes are off the charts in America. We better slow down a little and take better care of ourselves. Heart disease is more expensive than the few hours it will cost you each month to prepare your meals. Besides the health benefits, do you understand that you could become a millionaire over time just with what you can save by preparing your meals instead of eating out all the time? You think I'm kidding, right? If you and your wife both work and you eat the majority of your meals at various fast food restaurants, you're probably easily spending $20 per day on your meals. You could have prepared a lunch at home and taken it to work with you, for about $5 per day for you both ($2.50 a piece). That's a difference of $15 per working day (we'll leave the weekends out of our equation for now). There are approximately 20 working days in each month, for a total savings of $300 a month. If you took your savings from your new habit of "brown-bagging-it", and invested it in a good mutual fund which have averaged a 12% return over the last several years and you continued this habit during your whole working life of 50 years (from age 20 to age 70), you would have $11,834,000 in your account by the time you retired at age 70. Through discipline and good stewardship you've become a millionaire by investing your lunch money. You can give your money to McDonald's, or you can invest it in a Templeton Fund. The difference in the outcome is dramatic.

Remember, in the category of food, never go to the grocery store and pay for your purchase with a credit card. It doesn't matter that you pay your balances off every month. The data shows that you will spend 30% more in a grocery store when you pay with plastic. You become disconnected from the emotional pain of spending your hard-earned dollars. It's just not the same when you slide that card through the reader, as when you have to count out those Benjamin Franklins. Grocers understand that their stores are a place of great impulse buying. They will do whatever they can to get you to make an impulsive purchase. Never go to the grocery store hungry. You'll just be playing into their hands. And always make a list and try as best you can to stick to it. Remember, if you bust the grocery budget, you've got to make it up from another expense category, and that category is usually in the area of recreation or other discretionary personal spending.

Finally, you need to go to a nice restaurant and dine out occasionally. Just put it in the plan, and don't do it on impulse. The impulses of the flesh are the enemy of our freedom. We're going to take authority and responsibility over our finances. That doesn't mean we're going on a "bread and water" diet. It merely means that the purchases we make are planned, and we don't do them until we have the money to pay for them.

We have reprioritized our life and have allowed the Spirit of God to help us make new financial goals, and these goals do not include Visa and Master Card.

New Priorities Are Built Around a New Vision

God said that without a "vision" His people perish (Proverbs 29:18 KJV). If we're going to sacrifice and make dramatic changes in our lives, we have to have a vision or as this passage in the New King James Version says, *"My people will cast off restraint."* We can endure anything for a season if we're convinced we're going to a better place in the future. This is the key to our journey. We must keep our eyes on the Promised Land of financial freedom. We will never make the sacrifices necessary until we get a vision of where we're going. As a couple you need to pray and fast and seek God for your financial goals and objectives. You need to make one-year, three-year and five-year financial goals. Goal setting is a Biblical concept. The Word says, *"A man's heart plans his way, But the Lord directs his steps."* (Proverbs 16:9). Pray and set your goals, then allow God to "order your steps" toward their fulfillment.

The goals you select must be consistent with the vision that God has given you. It all starts with a vision. The vision brings order and purpose to your life, and eliminates conflict. Without it you'll cast off restraint. You won't make the hard choices and sacrifices necessary to facilitate its achievement. Your short range and intermediate goals should be steps that are ordered by God to bring you closer to your vision.

Remember that people and things may pass away, but the vision will remain. You will endure a season of adversity, but it will be well worth it if it brings us closer to the fulfillment of the vision. It is imperative that you stop reacting to life, and become "proactive". That is to say that you start standing in the authority of the Name of Jesus, and speaking to your mountains and commanding them to be cast into the sea. As John Maxwell says, "Start living your life on purpose." Not merely scrambling to deal with its surprises. Your life will be propelled in the direction of your most dominate thoughts. Think about your vision, and that is the direction your life will take. Remember, the whole world is looking to follow the man who knows where he's going.

Caleb had seen the Promised Land. He couldn't get it out of his mind. When he closed his eyes at night, that's what he saw. When he looked off into the wilderness, that's what he saw. And most importantly, he saw himself possessing it. He had to wait forty-years, but he saw the fulfillment of his vision before he died. It was because he would never let it die in his heart. He was determined to fulfill his purpose in God. He had a warrior's heart, and the vision of freedom that was worth fighting for in his estimation If we allow God to place the Spirit in us that was in this great warrior, we too will see our vision of freedom come to pass in our lives as well. There is power and potential in a vision. We'll not make it through the wilderness without one.

Step Two: Eliminate Debt

"I have learned that success is to be measured not so much by the position that one has reached in life as by the obstacles which he has overcome while trying to succeed. Out of the hard and unusual struggle through which he is compelled to pass, he gets a strength, a confidence, that one misses whose pathway is compara- tively smooth by reason of birth and race. "
-Booker T. Washington

"The first question which you will ask and which
I must try to answer is this,
What is the use of climbing Mount Everest?
and my answer must at once be, It is no use.
There is not the slightest prospect of any gain
whatsoever...So, if you cannot understand
that there is something in man which responds
to the challenge of this mountain
and goes out to meet it,
that the struggle is the struggle of life itself upward and
forever upward, then you won't see why we go.
What we get from this adventure is just sheer joy.
And joy is, after all, the end of life.
We do not live to eat and make money.
We eat and make money to be able to enjoy life.

That is what life means and what life is for."
-George Mallory

"Without a struggle, there can be no progress." — *Unknown*

"Now these are the nations which the Lord left, that He might test Israel by them, that is, all who had not known any of the wars in Canaan (<u>this was only so that the generations of the children of Israel might be taught to know war, at least those who had not formerly known it</u>)," *(Judges 3:1-2)*

And now we join the battle. It's time for talk to turn to action. The fog of our excesses has been lifted, and we've come to our senses only to realize that we're deep in enemy territory. Nevertheless, we have our bearings now…and our wits. We've *"come to our senses"*, just like the Prodigal Son in Luke Chapter 16, and we've returned to the truth of our Father's teaching. Unfortunately, the spirit of the world is still clinging to us in the form of debt. Our creditors are not interested in our spiritual awakening, they just want their money. Therefore, the first battle is the most difficult in our quest for freedom, and that is the process of debt elimination. It will test our resolve and our commitment. It will try our faith and our patience. It will strengthen us and give us a new confidence in Him and His provision for us. When we renounce debt from our hearts, and pursue its elimination just as Joshua pursued the giants of Canaan, we will progress greatly towards our goal of Financial Freedom.

The main difference between Joshua's generation and Moses' generation was their understanding of God's role in their respective struggles. Moses' generation viewed the impending contest from the perspective of their own strength. Joshua's generation understood that if they would simply engage the enemy, God would intervene on their behalf and He would bring the victory. The question was not <u>their</u> ability…it was their courage and their courage was born out of their faith. As we discussed in the last chapter, this process of learning to fight while *"resting in Him"* (Hebrews 4:10), represents a learned balance between the natural and the spiritual. We're required to engage the enemy, and at the same time understand that it is through God that we have the victory. He will bless our efforts and cause the sun to stand still so we can finish off our adversaries (Joshua 10:12-14). There is absolutely no limit to what He'll do to bring us to victory, but the essence of war is learning to fight and at the same time rest in Him for the victory.

God has always intended for His children to understand the tactics of war. In fact, the Lord raised up some enemies for Israel in Judges 3:1-2, when the generations who had succeeded Joshua became soft and lazy in their prosperity.; "...*(this was only so that the generations of the children of Israel might be taught to know war, at least those who had not formerly known it)," (Judges 3:1-2).* He is a loving and merciful God who wants us to understand that like it or not, we are at war. He has always intended for His children to know how to fight. In Canaan the war was on a natural Battlefield. In Gethsemane, the war had become spiritual, but there is always a battle.

The same principles apply to our journey. We must learn how to be as vigorous as the gazelle who is trying to deliver himself from the hunter, but in our spirit, we must be at rest. A difficult balance indeed, but an essential one for victory. We must engage the enemy. We ignore a powerful adversary at our own peril. Alas, it's not a question of our ability, but of our faith and courage. Do we believe that God wants us to be free? Really free? When we look at the Cross, do we not hear the words of Abraham Lincoln when he said..."*never has so great a sacrifice been laid on the altar of freedom."* To those of us who seek deliverance from the bondages of the enemy, Romans 8:31-32 has to become our anthem. "*What then shall we say to these things? If God is for us, who can be against us? He who did not spare His own Son, but delivered Him up for us all, how shall He not with Him also freely give us all things?"*

So we understand that God is **for** us...not against us. And He is waiting for us to enter the fight for freedom, so that He can *"show Himself strong on behalf of those whose heart is loyal to Him..."* (2 Chronicles 16:9). The fight begins with a declaration of war against personal debt. There are, however, some "rules of engagement" that must be followed if we intend for God to lead our efforts.

Be Honest with Creditors —

Number one among them is that we've got to be honest with our creditors. Remember, they didn't get us into this mess. We did! Unfortunately for them, they are going to have to be patient with us as we renegotiate the terms of our indebtedness (which we will cover in detail later). Why are we going to have to renegotiate terms you ask? Because you can never payoff debt at 21% interest. This is not spiritual revelation. It's just math. If you have $15,000 in credit card debt and you pay the minimum monthly payment every month, it will take you 30 years to pay off the balance at 21% interest if you don't charge another new purchase to your account. It may make our creditors angry, but they'll just have to get over it. We have to have a reduced interest rate to pay off these debts.

James 5:15 says, "*Confess your trespasses to one another, and pray for one another, that you may be healed. The effective, fervent prayer of a righteous man avails much.*" Just go ahead and confess to them. "*I've been living above my means and I can't continue to do it anymore.*" One of the ways that God knows you've faced the truth about your situation, is when you, "*confess your trespasses to one another*". The Greek word in the New Testament that is interpreted as "*trespasses*" is "*pasha*" (peh-shah). It is more often translated as "*transgression*". In the American Heritage Dictionary, the word "*transgression*" in its noun form is defined as: the violation of a law, command, or duty. If we have allowed ourselves to become slaves to debt, then we have committed a "*transgression*" against God's laws of freedom. We have sinned, and therefore according to the words of Jesus Christ, "*made ourselves a slave to sin*". But our confession will facilitate our healing.

There is amazing healing power in the process of confession. It's truly "good for the soul." Remember your attitude in your confession is not self-condemnation. It is spiritual revelation. "*I didn't realize it before, but now I understand that I was living a life style that was unsustainable and not good for me. I once was blind…but now I see."* Humble yourself, but don't allow yourself to receive any emotional abuse that may ensue subsequent to your confession. As we will learn later, collection practices of many companies are designed to extract an emotional response on your part that causes you to write a check to them that is not in your Financial Freedom Plan. We have taken authority over our financial lives, not them. They have to adjust to our thinking…not the other way around.

What will cause them to relent and trust us enough to renegotiate terms is our absolute honesty.

"Each time you are honest and conduct yourself with honesty, a success force will drive you toward greater success. Each time you lie, even with a little white lie, there are strong forces pushing you toward failure."
-Joseph Sugarman

It is the truth that is setting us free. Not deception. Creditors can sniff out deception like a police dog looking for drugs at a rock concert. What destroys darkness is the glaring light of the truth. As long as we're truthful with ourselves and our creditors, we've taken the enemy out. His tactics are always rooted in deception and lies. The minute we fall into the trap of deceiving our creditors, we *"give (the devil) place"* and we are propelled towards failure.

Acknowledge the Debt—

We acknowledge the debt and we intend to pay it. We're not looking to shirk our responsibility. Current circumstances just will not allow us to do what we promised them we would do when we entered into our agreement originally. Most creditors deal with people daily who are trying to "duck their responsibility", not deal with adverse financial issues. Don't get me wrong. I don't have a great deal of sympathy for credit card companies who offer credit to college students. They know full well the student will be unable to resist their offers and have no means of repaying the debt. They know that these students are going to put balances on their credit cards that their parents are going to have to pay. They don't care about the strife and discord that they cause in a family. It's just business. Nevertheless, that student signed an agreement full of fine print, and said he or she would repay the balance. That is what we must endeavor to do.

There are a few of us, however, who have been afflicted by circumstances so adverse, that bankruptcy may be our only option. Perhaps a non-insured medical problem (which can turn onto millions of dollars in a heartbeat), has destroyed you financially. Maybe an accident has kept you from being able to work. Few people have disability insurance coverage, and nearly everyone has too much life insurance. With today's medial technology, the greater risk is not that you die in an accident, but that you get severely hurt and live in an impaired state; unable to work and function as you did before. If you have debt, you need disability insurance. You need to insure your income and your life. In many cases, you can drop some life insurance and buy disability with the premium savings. In most states, you can pay your medical bills over time at nominal interest rates, but some may be so overwhelming that they have a catastrophic effect on you financially. Medical problems are the leading cause of bankruptcy in the United States, narrowly edging out credit card debt.

Many of us may have legitimate excuses, for not being able to repay our debts under the terms and conditions that we had originally agreed to. Perhaps we went through a divorce (anytime you split a household, there will be financial fallout), or loss of employment, etc. But creditors have respect for people who don't use excuses to get out of repaying debts. Most of us can eventually repay what we owe. We've just got to do it differently than we had originally intended. What we're going to need from creditors is grace.

Legal Rights of Creditors —

All debt falls into two categories. Secured and unsecured. Secured debt is debt against which collateral of some kind has been pledged. If you borrow money to buy a car, the lender will require the title to the car as collateral, for example. Furthermore, if you get behind on the payments, he will come and get the car. As we said earlier, if you owe money on it, you don't really own it. The bank does. But if you're "upside down" in a car (the car is worth less than you owe on it), you cannot voluntarily "turn it back" (allow them to repossess it), and escape the debt. They will sell the car and sue you for the deficiency. Just because it is a secured loan does not preclude us from legal action.

Whether our debts are secured or unsecured, lenders have legal remedies for default of the terms and conditions of the loan. They can sue you for the outstanding balance and the resulting legal fees (this may vary from state to state). If they do sue you, and the court rules in their favor, then the court issues a decree called a "Judgment" in favor of the lender. A judgment attaches itself to any real estate property that you might own, and your credit report. No one will loan you money for anything (which may not be all bad), if you have outstanding judgments. At the end of seven years, the judgment is released and removed from your credit (check your state laws). In many cases, judgments can be paid at discounted face amounts a year or two down the road. So if you have been sued and have a judgment outstanding against you, don' despair. You might be able to pay it off for "$0.25 cents on the dollar" sometime in the future. When a creditor has to pursue legal action that results in a judgment, he has already been required by proper accounting protocols to charge the loan off against his income. Therefore, if you show up two years after the fact and offer him 25% of the original amount for a loan that he has already written off, he's going to take it most of the time.

There is profit in negotiation. He has a "charged-off loan", you have some money, albeit, not all of it. You're in a much better negotiating position than you think. In spite of what most debtors think... everything in the world's financial system is negotiable. You just have to be patient. This is where the importance of communication and honesty are essential. Even if you do not resolve your issues initially, if you have dealt with your creditors in a "straightforward" manner, it will enhance your negotiating position later on.

The ability to negotiate, seems to be a quality that God Himself admires in His children. If you'll remember, Abraham was a man with whom God entered into an everlasting covenant of blessing.

He told him, *"I will make you a great nation; I will bless you And make your name great; And you shall be a blessing. I will bless those who bless you, And I will curse him who curses you; And in you all the families of the earth shall be blessed."* (Genesis 12:2-3). Obviously, God had seen something in Abraham He really liked. There were probably many things; none the least of which was that he was a fierce negotiator. When God had decided to destroy the city of Sodom because of its intensely evil citizenry, He told Abraham that He would spare the city if He could find fifty righteous men within its boundaries.

Abraham said, *"Far be it for me to speak to the Lord, but what if you found forty-five righteous men. Would you spare the city?"*

The Lord acknowledged that He would.

"What about forty? What if you found forty righteous men in Sodom?"

"I will spare the city if there are forty righteous men in Sodom."

And in this manner, Abraham eventually talked God down to ten righteous souls as His minimum standard of salvation for the city of Sodom. Of course as we know, it was a standard that Sodom could not meet. Surely the Lord was aware of this fact when He allowed Himself to be drawn into this negotiation with Abraham. He seemed to delight in Abraham's concern for his fellow man, no matter how depraved they were, and his negotiating skills. Abraham walked in tremendous prosperity due to the unmitigated favor of God, but also because he was a shrewd negotiator by nature. If he was bold enough to negotiate with the King of the universe for souls in Sodom, imagine what he was like to buy sheep from. Abraham had many great qualities, none the least of which were honesty, and tough negotiation skills. The Lord admired them both.

Moses is another man who had great favor with God. God called him His friend. In Numbers chapter 14, when the Israelites whom God had rescued from bondage in Egypt, refused to enter in and possess the promise of their inheritance, namely the Promised Land, God burns with fury against them.

God tells Moses, "*I will strike them with the pestilence and disinherit them, and I will make of you a nation greater and mightier than they.*"" (Numbers 14:12)

"*And Moses said to the Lord: "Then the Egyptians will hear it, for by Your might You brought these people up from among them, and they will tell it to the inhabitants of this land. They have heard that You, Lord, are among these people; that You, Lord, are seen face to face and Your cloud stands above them, and You go before them in a pillar of cloud by day and in a pillar of fire by night. Now if You kill these people as one man, then the nations which have heard of Your fame will speak, saying, 'Because the Lord was not able to bring this people to the land which He swore to give them, therefore He killed them in the wilderness.'*"" (Numbers 14:13-16).

Moses skillfully turns the issue from Israel's disobedience to Gods reputation among non-believers. "What are they going to think Lord?", he asked. And thereby negotiates for the very lives of the people. Moses was the most humble man on the face of the earth according to Numbers 12:2, and yet he was bold enough to question God's decision to execute judgment on His own people, and to negotiate a reduced sentence as it were (all those above the age of twenty were condemned to perish in the wilderness over the next forty years rather than enter into the promise of His inheritance). There was something in the character of these two men that caused God to draw them into an extraordinary relationship with Himself. Both were fearless negotiators and yet both were humble before the Lord.

Bottom line: never be afraid to negotiate with the world for a better deal. Follow the example of Moses and Abraham, and remember "*you have not because you ask not*" (James 4:3). Always remember, what your creditors want most is their money. They know that if they sue you, they can kiss their money good bye. But if they negotiate, there is a good chance that they will get a substantial portion of it back. Even though many creditors will try to undermine your negotiating position through tactics of intimidation. When they scream at you and question your character, they are trying to initiate an angry response from you that will cause you to capitulate your negotiating position and pay them at the expense of all your other creditors. Be firm, and stand on the word; *"No weapon formed against me shall prosper, and every lying tongue I shall condemn. For such is the inheritance of a servant of the Lord."*

If you are honest with creditors and negotiate skillfully, you will be successful in conquering your debt and you will avoid litigation.

Collection Practices—

All lenders are governed by the "Fair Debt and Collection Practices Act". Remember, the initial strategy of many lenders is to intimidate and stimulate an emotional response that causes you to write a check and pay them at the expense of the other creditors on your Freedom Plan list (see appendix). Whatever they do, it must not be outside the guidelines of the FDCP Act of 1996. This law contains certain protections for the debtor. Here are a few of the main ones:

1. A collector may not call you at work if they have been notified that your employer does not allow such calls.

2. They can only call you at home between the hours of 8:00 AM and 9:00 PM

3. If the collector knows that you have retained legal counsel to represent you, they must communicate with your attorney, unless he or she has given them specific authorization to communicate with you direct.

4. The collector can only communicate with "third parties" concerning you to verify information you've given to them. For example, they can verify your employment, but they are expressly prohibited from discussing your debt in any way.

5. You can insist that the collector not contact you anymore, and that they cease all communication with you. They have to honor this request, but the bad news is they will almost always initiate legal action against you.

6. They cannot harass you. They are expressly prohibited from using profanity, threats of violence, publication of a list of debtors in arrears, and use of the telephone in an annoying or abusive way, i.e. calling every fifteen minutes.

7. The collector is barred from using any false or misleading information, i.e. stating that non-payment of the debt will lead to imprisonment, etc.

The first tier of collection people, are extremely transient. The average "turn-over" rate in these departments of credit card companies, for example, is about 75%. These jobs are difficult emotionally, and we need to remember to pray for them every time we conclude a conversation with one of them. In many cases they're just trying to make extra money to pay Pharaoh themselves. As we've said, they are trained to extract an emotional response and get you to write a check, in order to get them off your back. The reason we won't do this is because _we've_ taken control of our financial future, and we no longer are allowing them to define our financial destiny by default. We are more than willing to repay the debt, but it will have to be on our terms. We're not moved by emotion any longer. We have a plan that God has given us and we're going to walk according to that plan. So be cordial to these people, and do not become angry. Tell them that you have a repayment plan that you'll submit to them in writing, or if you already have, tell then to check with their superiors. End the conversation as quickly as you can, and move on with the rest of your day. Don't become discouraged, because after a couple of these phone calls and the receipt of the debt management portion of our Financial Freedom Plan by their collection departments, you will hear from the second-tier of collection people. These people are authorized to help you. Now we can begin to implement our plan.

Four Ways to Eliminate Debt —

Our goal is to keep the commandments of the word of God, and *"Owe no one anything except to love one another, for he who loves another has fulfilled the law."* (Romans 13:8). It's hard to walk in love towards people who you owe money to. It's not that you don't love them, it's just that your debt has changed your relationship to that of a servant/master according to Proverbs 22:7. So if we're going to fulfill the law of Christ and love our neighbor as our self, we've got to eliminate debt from our lives. All debt elimination plans begin with the cutting up of your credit cards. They are no longer an acceptable way of conducting business for us, and we can get a debit card that can be used just like a credit card to make on line purchases or rent a car, etc. The difference is that the purchase will be electronically deducted out of your checking account immediately instead of charged to an account that accrues interest. This fits our new policy of "if we don't have the money, we don't buy it". We're not living on credit anymore. Then we've got to chose between one of four ways to become "debt-free".

1. Renegotiation of Terms (DMP)—

As we said earlier, if you make the minimum payment on a credit card that has a 21% interest rate, it will take you 30 years to get it paid off. Furthermore, we cannot get out of debt without a reduction in interest rate. So our first goal is to secure an interest rate reduction and a 3-5 year payoff plan. No credit card company is willing to do this without first being convinced that their principle balance is in jeopardy.

Credit counseling experts call this procedure, developing a Debt Management Plan (DMP), but we prefer to call it a Financial Freedom Plan. When you initiate your Freedom Plan, you will reorganize your monthly expenditures and most of the time the credit card companies will be required to take a back seat to your essential needs (housing, utilities, and transportation). After just two months of missed payments, they will contact you. Explain your financial dilemma and send them a copy of your debt elimination schedule (also in appendix). The process of negotiation will begin. Most of them have settlement plans that will meet your needs and probably come close to your own debt reduction schedule. At this point you will find that you and your creditor have a common goal—the repayment of your outstanding balance. They recognize that you cannot repay under the original terms and conditions, so they will place your account on a "negotiated settlement" status, which will affect your credit until you have finished the repayment program. Again, you don't need more credit, you need less debt, and there is nothing wrong with this type of trade off. "You can't borrow anymore, but we will help you get this paid off through more favorable terms." This is an equitable approach, and nearly all credit card companies will help you.

It's important that you work through the cash disbursement portion of the Freedom Plan, before entering into these negotiations. You have to know what you can pay each month, before you agree to it. Communication and honesty are the key to success of the "Renegotiation Strategy". Don't agree to something that you cannot do. It will only lead to problems later on.

If you owe multiple companies, and most of us do, as soon as you get the smallest balance paid off, close the account and apply whatever you had been paying them to the next largest outstanding balance. To determine how much you pay each company, you'll need to "prorate" the amount of your total monthly expenditure in the personal debt category in accordance with their respective balances. For example, if you have $800 available to pay on credit cards after you have worked through your Freedom Plan (reprioritization of your expenses), then you will divide the $800 in accordance with the percentage that each company represents of the total outstanding balance. Below is an example of these "Prorated Payments":

Company	Outstanding Balance	Percentage of Total	Total Payment
American Express	$4356.25	48%(4356.25/9090.81)	$384
Capitol One	$2576.52	28%(2576.52/9090.81)	$224
Visa	$1582.36	17%(1582.36/9090.81)	$136
Master Card	$575.68	7%(575.68/9090.81)	$56
Total	$9090.81	100%	$800

This is the fairest approach to the retirement of your outstanding debt. In the above example, you would apply the $56 from your Master Card to your Visa as soon as the Master Card is paid off. Then when you get the Visa paid off, you would then apply the combined $192 monthly payment ($56+$136) to your Capitol One payment for a total monthly payment to them of $416. In this manner you will eventually get all of your credit cards paid off and you won't have to starve your children to get it done. It's about fairness, purpose, and commitment. Again to make this approach work, you'll need a reduced interest rate and positively never ever will you add to those outstanding balances with additional purchases. We're paying cash now, remember? And we **ALWAYS** close the accounts as soon as they are paid off. The plan is deliverance from a "debtor's mindset" and resulting bondage. Not a "let's-get-patched-up-and-do-the-same-thing-again" mindset! We're leaving Egypt...not sticking around for a little longer since the heat's off.

I feel strongly that you can negotiate on your own behalf with as much success as the so called "Debt Consolidation Companies". Most of these companies are owned by the Credit Card Companies. They are not free, and their solutions usually include exchanging "unsecured" debt for "secured" debt with your home for collateral. There are many legitimate "Credit Counseling" services, that are truly non-profit and that have an excellent track record for helping people, however, there are many charlatans in the industry as well. You need to be careful, and understand that with a good plan, you can negotiate on your own behalf with great success. Remember, there are no quick fixes. Companies that advertise easy solutions and quick remedies are more than likely counterfeit, and most of the time the trail they lead you down will include more expense and eventual bankruptcy.

2. Negotiated Write Downs—

Debt has become such a huge problem in America, that a new phenomenon has emerged in the "debt negotiation" process called, "Negotiated Debt Reduction". There are several companies that have emerged in the market place, that actually go to your creditors and negotiate a "partial charge-off" of some of the outstanding balance. The company actually is paid by you, and not by the credit card company. Their fees are based on a percentage of the amount of debt that they are successful in getting reduced on your behalf. This is a more ethical approach in my opinion, since they are representing your interest exclusively. They receive no fees or compensation from the credit card companies.

This is a relatively new approach, and as always, you need to check these people out and make sure they're reputable. You can contact the Better Business Bureau, Federal Trade Commission, and the National Foundation of Credit Counseling. If you decide to retain one of these companies, they should be willing to collect their fees from the installments you make as you payoff the remaining balance of the credit card. Beware of any company that requires "money up front". They shouldn't be getting paid until they have done something, namely, helped you. They should provide documentation of everything they have negotiated on your behalf, and never give them a Power of Attorney. The granting of a Power of Attorney authorizes them to make binding agreements with your lenders on your behalf. You should retain the right to review and agree to the new terms and conditions, and no new agreement should be allowed to go into effect without your written consent.

You should be advised, however, that when you negotiate "write-down" type settlements, they will leave a slight blemish on your credit report. They are not nearly as bad as a default, however, and since we've disavowed the world's systems and are honoring our debts merely because the Lord commanded us to, we're not overly concerned with spotless credit. You do need good credit to be employed by some companies, however. Therefore, we need to seek the restoration of our credit rating, not so we'll use it, but so it will help document our character.

You may be wondering how we square God's commandment to repay our debts, and to actively seek a "write-down" of it? My view is this. If you add all the late fees and over limit fees and exorbitant interest rates that people are charged when they get into financial trouble, the credit card company can write off a lot of the accrued balance and still not suffer a loss on the account by the standards of the rest of the lending community.

3. Bankruptcy —

Bankruptcy should always be the choice of last resort and in fact, the new changes to the Bankruptcy Laws which went in effect in October of 2005, require that you seek credit counseling from an approved credit counselor within six months before filing for bankruptcy relief. Nearly all good credit counselors will steer you toward a Debt Management Plan instead of Bankruptcy. You can find a state-by-state approved list of these credit counseling organizations at www.usdoj.gov.ust. When you file Bankruptcy, it remains on your credit report for 10 years in most cases, and could effect your ability to secure a better job since more and more companies are checking the credit reports of job applicants. So always look into steps 1. and 2, before you consider seriously entering into Bankruptcy.

There are two main types of personal Bankruptcy; "Chapter 7" and "Chapter 13". Chapter 7 is true Bankruptcy and under its terms, your assets are sold by the court and the proceeds are distributed to your creditors. Your home, automobile, and your personal belongings are exempt assets and you may keep them. Everything else will be sold by the court. Your creditors will split up what's left, and the debt that they hold will be officially discharged. Chapter 7 filings will not discharge tax liens, court assessed fines, student loans, or child-support payments. You may have difficulty securing a home or a car loan until your Bankruptcy comes off your credit report. That's ten years.

The second form of Bankruptcy is Chapter 13. Chapter 13 is merely a reorganization of your finances and although collection procedures by your creditors will have to cease, the Court will basically take over your financial life. They will establish a DMP for you, and although none of your assets will be sold, you will be required to repay your creditors within 3-5 years under new terms and conditions as decided by the court. They will distribute payments to your creditors from your income each month, and give you an allowance to live on. They will control your spending and you will not be allowed to spend anything that is not in the plan without their approval.

In many cases, people start out in Chapter 13, and they end up defaulting on the agreed plan and have to file Chapter 7 in the end anyway. In fact, only about 1/3 of the people who enter into Chapter 13 finish the program. There are of course, attorney's fees and court cost that must be paid in a Bankruptcy proceeding. The new changes in the Bankruptcy law make it extremely difficult to qualify for Chapter 7, and most filers will be required to enter into Chapter 13. All in all, its not a very desirable alternative and usually will not meet God's commandment to "pay what we owe". Some of your circumstances may be severe enough to warrant Bankruptcy, but for most of us, there are better alternatives.

Do Nothing and Hope for the Best—

This is where Murphy's Law comes into play. *"Anything that can go wrong will go wrong if left unattended."* Edward Murphy was an aerospace engineer in the 1940's and he made this simple declaration of fact that has become part of Western Civilization folklore. He is called a pessimist by many, but in fact, he is merely stating a principle that he had observed in his work on experimental rockets. If it can go wrong, it will— eventually. He was simply making an argument for what he called "defensive design". Simply build it so it cannot fail. The same is true whether you're building rockets or handling a financial crisis...if it can go wrong, it will. You cannot leave it unattended.

I know you've got faith and you're trusting in God for your deliverance, but as you pray and believe, get ready. He's going to ask you to do something. In fact, He's probably going to ask you to do a bunch of something's. Doing nothing almost never works in the area of finances, and God is well aware of this fact. So if it's financial deliverance you're after, the "do-nothing-and-hope-for-the-best" strategy will lead you to disappointment. You defy Murphy's Law at your own peril.

Take Heart...You're Not Alone—

American's have been on a debt binge that is becoming epic in its proportions. From 1998 to 2003, we have increased our mortgage debt to 6.6 trillion dollars; an increase of 64%. In the same time period, we increased our credit card debt to 412 billion dollars; an increase of 185%. Many Federal Reserve economist state that consumer debt, as expressed as a percentage of disposable income, has not risen that much; there is nothing to worry about they say. What are these guys smokin'? The American consumer has become intoxicated on the excesses of a Babylonian credit system, and our economy has been built around their drunken stupor. U.S. consumer spending accounts for around 70% of the U.S. gross domestic product, which is a measure of the total goods and services that are produced in a year. So our economy has become heavily dependant on consumers gobbling up more goods and services than they can pay for. But the U.S. economy is not the only economy that is counting on our spending binges. Big exporting nations like China and Japan also have a vested interest in America's continued insanity. Incredibly, America's consumers actually account for about 20% of the **world's** gross domestic product. That's right! We're just 4.3% of the world's population, yet we consume 20% of the goods and services the world produces.

But never fear. Just because our government can no longer float its huge budget deficits through the sale of its financial instruments (treasury bonds, etc.) to Americans (since they've spent all their money at Dillard's and can barely make their credit card payments, much less invest in T-bills) there is no cause for alarm. Japan and China will loan us the money, since they seem to have plenty of it (we should know that since it came from us). Both countries have become the largest buyers of U.S. debt instruments. They will gladly oblige our government and it's insatiable credit needs; so long as our consumers keep chug-a-lugging their products. It pays to keep plenty of feed out for the goose that's laying your golden eggs. The problem is, the merry-go-round has got to stop some time. There is a place where the American consumer can no longer borrow any more, and we're very near that place.

What happens when we reach the point of total credit saturation, and the American consumer becomes insolvent due to their drunken spending spree? Those of us who have made the journey to freedom, will be very glad that we endured the hardship of the wilderness. We will watch from the sidelines as a world awash in insolvency, will implode, and the, *"wealth of the sinner will be laid up for the righteous."* Proverbs 13:22. Those of us who have extracted ourselves from debt and have learned to save money, will be able to buy at bargain prices. Yes...it promises to be a difficult journey, but its rewards will be abundant to those who have the courage to make it.

Step Three: Understand And Implement God's Principles Of Giving

"We who lived in concentration camps can remember the men who walked through the huts comforting others, giving away their last piece of bread. They may have been few in number, but they offer sufficient proof that everything can be taken from a man but one thing: the last of human freedoms - to choose one's attitude in any given set of circumstances - to choose one's own way."
-Victor Frankl

"No one can serve two masters; for either he will hate the one and love the other, or else he will be loyal to the one and despise the other. You cannot serve God and mammon." *(Matthew 6:24)*

"Therefore if you have not been faithful in the unrighteous mammon, who will commit to your trust the true riches?" *(Luke 16:11)*

Jesus on the subject of "Tithing"— "Woe to you, scribes and Pharisees, hypocrites! For you pay tithe of mint and anise and cummin, and have neglected the weightier

matters of the law: justice and mercy and faith. <u>These you ought to have done</u>, without leaving the others undone.*" (Matthew 23:23)*

"Jesus said to him, "If you want to be perfect, go, sell what you have and give to the poor, and you will have treasure in heaven; and come, follow Me.""*(Matthew 19:21)*

Giving is the key to everything spiritual. You cannot unlock the secrets of the Kingdom of God, unless you give. You cannot know what it is to be a disciple of Jesus Christ…unless you give. Jesus was approached by a "rich young ruler" in Matthew 19:21, who asked Him, "What good thing shall I do that I may have eternal life?" His response to the question was in essence, keep the commandments of God, since the New Covenant had not been yet established and God's people were still living under the law. The young man confidently proclaims, *"These things I have done from my youth."* Then Jesus goes on to make one more stipulation, because by now He has discerned the heart of the young man.

He says, *"If you want to be perfect, go and sell what you have and give it to the poor, and you will have treasure in heaven, and come follow Me."*

So…you want to be perfect eh! All you have to do is give your "stuff" away. I confess, I'm not their yet, but I will say that material things mean less and less to me as I progress in my walk with the Lord. As we become more spiritual in our nature, the allure of the natural-life begins to diminish. Unfortunately, the "rich young ruler" was not there yet either. The scripture says, *"…he went away sorrowful, for he had great possession."* The cost was more than he could bear. He was too attached to his "stuff", and therefore had not been perfected spiritually.

The Greek word for "perfect" is [*teleios* /tel·i·os/]. It is the root of our word telescope. It means, "1. brought to its end, finished. 2. wanting nothing necessary to completeness. 3. perfect." Or shall we say, "fully-extended". The spiritual life of most Believers seems to unfold in stages, much like the old telescopes used by mariners and early astronomers who first began to try and see the universe up close. The image produced by the instrument was distorted until the telescope became fully-extended. In like manner, we will never be transformed fully into the image of Christ, until we become "fully extended" in the Spirit of God. Until we have been, *"brought to our end or completion"*, in the Spirit.

One way to measure our spiritual growth is to examine our relationship with material things. Do we love the Lord more than we love them? And if we say we do, then how do we prove it? Simply, by giving them away. It's interesting that in the account of this encounter between Jesus and the "young ruler" in Mark Chapter Ten, after he walks away in sorrow, the disciples asked Jesus to explain His requirement that the young man surrender his wealth for the cause of the Kingdom. What about us they say? Haven't we given up farms and houses and families to follow you? Then Jesus says something that is absolutely critical to the understanding of God's doctrines of giving. He says in so many words, if he had given it away for "My sakes and the gospel's", he would have received a hundred-fold increase of those things that he had sown, in this lifetime (not in the "sweet-bye-and-bye").

Why didn't He tell the "rich young ruler" that if he would sow his possessions, that he would receive a "hundred-fold" increase on them? Wouldn't that make it much easier to do if you knew that you were essentially just trading your "stuff" in for 100 times more "stuff"? Why didn't He teach him the Spiritual Law of Reciprocity? *"Give, and it will be given to you: good measure, pressed down, shaken together, and running over will be put into your bosom. For with the same measure that you use, it will be measured back to you"* — (Luke 6:38). Whatever we do, God "reciprocates" in kind. If we give, He gives. If we extend mercy and grace, He extends mercy and grace unto us.

The reason Jesus didn't explain this important Law to the "rich young ruler" was because it only works when it is not superseded by the Spiritual Law of a Surrendered Will; or what I call the "Gethsemane Principle". It was in the Garden of Gethsemane that Jesus totally surrendered His will to the Father. It was in the Garden of Gethsemane that the miracle of the Resurrection was released. As soon as Jesus said from His heart..."*Not My will, but Thy will be done*", He authorized the heavenly release of the greatest miracle in the history of the entire universe...His own resurrection.

The angels in heaven held their breath as Jesus battled with His own flesh in the Garden that night. As with all miracles from God, this one had to be released through a submitted will and an obedient act. God will never do something miraculous in our circumstance without requiring us to get in agreement with Him, and then do something that is uncomfortable for our flesh. Many Believers sow and expect harvest, but they are unwilling to do that difficult thing that God has called them to do that will unleash the harvest. Psalms 1 says, "*...a righteous man prospers in all he does.*" God is going to bless you, but He is going to call you to do something in obedience that releases that miracle. Jesus had the final say: Would He do it or not? All of heaven anxiously awaited His answer. When He chose to act in obedience and do something that was difficult, He authorized the miracle of the Resurrection and saved mankind from an eternity in hell. It was in the Garden of Gethsemane that the fate of mankind was decided. Not on Calvary. To activate the Laws of Abundance and Blessing in your life, you must choose to harden your will in agreement with God's will, and your flesh is going to scream, "Are you crazy?" "*For Christ also suffered once for sins, the just for the unjust, that He might bring us to God, being put to death in the flesh but made alive by the Spirit*"— (1 Peter 3:18). Jesus put the flesh to death and thereby brought forth the full "release" of the Spirit. Giving by the leading of the Spirit is a "flesh-killing" act that moves the heart of God and releases miracles in the giver's life.

If the rich young ruler had demonstrated that he was willing to subject his will to the Lord's will, without the promise of rewards... just out of love for Him, the Lord would have released a great miracle of supernatural provision in "*this life*". (Mark 10:30). The Gethsemane Principle is unavoidable if we are going to appropriate the power of God in our life. It activates all the other Spiritual Laws, and qualifies us for multiplication according to the Law of Reciprocity ("*give and it will be given to you, pressed down shaken and running over...*").

Another important Principle is God's Law of Harvest. *"While the earth remains, Seedtime and harvest, Cold and heat, Winter and summer, And day and night Shall not cease."* (Genesis 8:22). This Law has an obvious natural application, but since it's in the Word of God, we know it has a Spiritual application as well. Simply put, *"To everything there is a season, A time for every purpose under heaven: A time to be born, And a time to die; A time to plant, And a time to pluck what is planted (harvest);"* (Ecclesiastes 3:1-2). The process with God is to sow a seed, and wait for a harvest. And if we wait in faith believing in God's promises and principles, we will harvest in due season. In most every instance; however, there will be a season of cultivation and growth before the harvest season arrives. We live in a "microwave" society that expects and even demands instant results. God does not operate that way. I would venture to guess that 90% of our walk with Christ will be spent on waiting for a breakthrough. *"But those who wait on the Lord Shall renew their strength; They shall mount up with wings like eagles, They shall run and not be weary, They shall walk and not faint."* (Isaiah 40:31). Waiting is a very important part of the process of "faith-building". *"My brethren, count it all joy when you fall into various trials, knowing that the testing of your faith produces patience. But let patience have its perfect work, that you may be perfect and complete, lacking nothing."* (James 1:2-4). God's plan is to perfect us, as we said earlier. We cannot be perfected or matured in the Spirit, without patience. Sowing and **waiting patiently** in faith will be required of the mature Believer by the Lord.

Furthermore, we cannot expect to harvest what we've not sown. *"But this I say: He who sows sparingly will also reap sparingly, and he who sows bountifully will also reap bountifully."* (2 Corinthians 9:6). The measure of harvest is directly proportional to the amount sown. The English word "steward" refers to the Scottish managers who took care of the Kings property in the golden age of the British Monarchy. These men were good managers and farmers, and they understood the most optimum conditions for planting and that when the conditions were favorable, the planting of much seed would yield a huge harvest. A good steward knows that if you put abundant seed in good ground, you receive big harvest. To harvest abundantly, you have to sow abundantly.

Another important principle of the Law of Harvest is that we reap "in-kind". *"Do not be deceived, God is not mocked; for whatever a man sows, that he will also reap."* (Galatians 6:7). You can't plant corn, and get cotton. If you need love, you have to sow love. If you need mercy, you have to sow mercy. If you need money, you have to sow money. The seed reproduces after its own kind. But when you sow money in a spirit of love, you receive a two-fold harvest. You harvest money and you harvest the love and affections of others and God.

It's an Issue of the Heart —

I heard a story of a young man in his late teens who was the son of a prominent minister in the South. He and a friend "cut-their-teeth" in ministry, as it were, by preaching in the little country Churches in the bayou of Louisiana. One day as they were driving down a back road on the way to one of their meetings, they passed by a scraggily, destitute little man, whose smell proceeded him everywhere he went. He asked his friend who was driving who the man was since the friend was a native of the community. The friend responded by declaring that he was the town drunk. The young "minister-to-be" asked him to stop the car and back up. The friend watched in amazement as the young minister got out of the car, ran back across the bridge to where the drunk was slumped half unconscious along side of the road, and emptied his pockets until they were literally turned inside out, and gave everything he had to the inebriated man. He placed all his money into the shaking cupped hands of this broken dismayed individual, and then he prayed over him and ran back to the car.

He jumped into the car out of breath and said, "OK…let's go!"

The friend never said a word, and the young "minister-to-be" never offered any explanation. It was forty years after the fact when the friend (now a minister himself) related this story to me, and it was still obvious that this incident had great impact on him. He never forgot this outrageous act of giving. Most of the citizenry of the community had vowed to never give the man anything. "He'll just drink it up you know", was their excuse. What this young minister-to-be saw was not the town drunk. He saw a broken life, and he gave him all he had. Exactly what Jesus would have done I suspect.

Whatever happened to the minister's son you ask. He's now the Senior Pastor of a Church with a 20 million dollar annual budget. *"Do not forget to entertain strangers, for by so doing some have unwittingly entertained angels."* (Hebrews 13:2). Was it really the town drunk, or was it a test. Either way this young man *"was found faithful"* through his giving, and demonstrated that he could be trusted with much.

The "Gethsemane Principle" overrides all other spiritual laws. The issue for the "rich-young-ruler" was a heart issue. Could he surrender his will to God's will. The young Pastor in our story simply gave everything he had, or at least everything he had in his possession at the time. And there is no doubt in my mind, that he had no expectation of increase on what he had given. He gave out of obedience and compassion. The rich young ruler had an opportunity to give it all away, and thereby gain it all back 100-fold, but he just couldn't bring himself to do it. His inability to give his possessions away demonstrated a divided allegiance.

"No one can serve two masters; for either he will hate the one and love the other, or else he will be loyal to the one and despise the other. You cannot serve God and mammon." (Matthew 6:24). Mammon is by definition, *"wealth personified and opposed to God"*. Mammon is a deceiving spirit that lies to you and tells you that the pursuit of wealth is the highest and best use of your life. Divorce court dockets are full of cases every day where the husband was drawn to the spirit of mammon. After serving it 24/7 for years and accumulating vast wealth, he comes home one day to an empty house. His wife has been emotionally abandoned and is tired of playing second fiddle to his mistress...his work. She will no longer compete with it.

God **is**, by His own admission, *"a jealous God"* who will not compete for the affections of His people either. Just like the wife who gets tired of wondering where her husband is, He will not stay in a relationship where He is of secondary importance. Our loyalty to Him must be undivided. We cannot serve Him and mammon, and the way we prove that we're not serving our wealth is through our giving. The spirit of mammon is broken off of our increase when we give.

In fact, Jesus said, *"He who finds his life will lose it, and he who loses his life for My sake will find it."* — (Matthew 10:39). We enter into the Kingdom of God not when we die, but when we become saved and born again. Therefore Kingdom principles become relevant for a Believer the minute she begins to believe. Jesus claims that for a Believer to have it, she must first give it away. The word the Lord uses for "life" in this passage is *"psuche"*. It is the root of our word psychology. It refers to the "soulish-nature"; the realm of the mind, will, and emotions. So a good interpretation of this passage would be, *"he who finds emotional contentment and satisfaction in the things of this natural life, will lose that contentment when he is judged before me. But he who lays down the things of this world and looks to me alone for peace, will find the peace he seeks, the blessing of the things he needs and eternal life besides."* There is no other way to prove to God that our allegiance is to Him…except to give all that we have to Him, and thereby authorize Him to increase us and our "stuff"..

The Condition of the Heart Governs God's Law of Increase —

We have explained how our giving is essential to activate God's Laws of Harvest and Reciprocity, and that both these Laws are superseded by the "Gethsemane Principle". There is a fourth Law which is activated through our giving that is important for us to understand; The Law of Increase. Another Biblical word for increase is "fruitfulness". God's first commandment to Adam after He had created him and Eve was for them to be *"fruitful and multiply; fill the earth and subdue it…"* — (Genesis 1:28). The last parable taught by Jesus before He went to the Cross was in John 15. He led the disciples into the Vineyard and He used the grape vine as a teaching aid. He said, *"I am the vine, you are the branches. He who abides in Me, and I in* him, bears much fruit; for without Me you can do nothing." — (John 15:5).

Then later He makes a declarative statement that should be the guiding principle for every Believer's life. *"If you abide in Me, and My words abide in you, you will ask what you desire, and it shall be done for you. By this My Father is glorified, that you bear much fruit; so you will be My disciples."* — (John 15:7-8). Bearing much fruit or increase does two things. It glorifies the Father and it demonstrates that we are His disciples. There is no other test for discipleship besides "fruitfulness". This fruitfulness must manifest in every area of our lives; in our relationships, in our Christian witness (new souls for the Kingdom), and in our finances. When we think in financial terms about "fruitfulness" it's easier to understand the concept if we use the word "increase". *"By this My Father is glorified, that you (produce much increase); so you will be My disciples."* It is God's plan for us to prosper financially, and as we have stated in earlier chapters, to be an influence on the earth through commerce. How can we be an influence in the area of commerce unless we "increase" commercially or economically? In the Parable of the Stewards in Matthew 25, it was the "unprofitable" steward that the Lord commanded be cast into the outer darkness.

So if we understand that it is God's will that we increase in every area of our life (3 John 2), including financially, then we need to understand every aspect of the Law of Increase or Fruitfulness in order to benefit from it. In Matthew 13, Jesus taught about this issue of fruitfulness in the Parable of the Sower. *"Therefore hear the parable of the sower:"* — (Matthew 13:18). This parable is not about salvation as has been taught by some. It is about "fruitfulness". Jesus gives four examples of Believers who have had a positive response to the Gospel. They all have received the word of God, but the word has produced dramatically different amounts of increase in each case. Jesus explains that the difference in the level of increase is caused by only one variable; the individual condition of their fields (or hearts).

Each individual received the same anointed word of God but each individual produced dramatically different fruit from the word and the only difference was the condition of the hearts of the four individuals. The first individual receives the seed on hard ground as on a road or hardened path. The seed is never buried deep enough to facilitate its germination. The birds snatch it up before it ever has a chance to bring increase. This is the individual who is still hardened by skepticism or unbelief. He could believe for salvation but his hardened heart will not let him believe for healing or financial provision or anything else for that matter. It's a little ironic that he has the faith to believe for the greatest miracle in human experience, that is eternal salvation, but he cannot believe for a supernatural improvement in his financial situation through the promises of God.

The second example is the seed that fell on *"stony places"* or shallow soil. It gets buried enough to rapidly sprout and pop through the surface, but when the least amount of adversity comes in the form of too much sun and not enough rain, it withers and dies. This is the Believer who receives the word with joy and quite often attempts to act the most spiritual. They praise and sing and have their arms raised the highest during worship. They seem to be having an intense spiritual experience at Church, but as soon as they have some financial adversity develop in their life or get passed over for a promotion at work, they fade fast. The first time they are rejected by their peers at work for their beliefs in supernatural deliverance from debt, they stop believing and step right back into the world. They never stick it out long enough for the Word of God to take root and to bring increase.

The third example is the most common in my opinion. It is the person who received the word among the thorns. They "receive" the truth of the word, but the *"cares of the world and the deceitfulness of riches"* choke the word out and they become unfruitful. They cannot lay their worries down and trust God for the answer to their issues. Or they succumb to the spirit of mammon, and pursue it instead of God and His righteousness. They are deceived into believing that "things" will bring them happiness, and they forsake the one thing that will bring true riches and joy into their lives. Jesus Christ.

Those who chose to turn their back on God and pursue the world, may be successful by the standards of the world and accumulate significant wealth, but wealth that has the spirit of mammon attached to it soon becomes a curse instead of a blessing. The very wealth that they were convinced would bring them happiness, soon breeds strife and discontent; especially in their closest relationships. They will reach a point where they become convinced that they are loved solely because of their money, and many times their assessment is correct. Their success will not bring contentment, but a perpetual restlessness that cannot be satisfied. Money can buy a lot of things, but it cannot buy happiness.

Another fascinating aspect of the wealth of the world is that it cannot be perpetuated through multiple generations. God's word says, *"A good man leaves an inheritance to his children's children, But the wealth of the sinner is stored up for the righteous "*— (Proverbs 13:22). People who work in Trust Departments of Banks have a saying, *"One generation makes it, the next holds it together, and the third loses it."* This is a pattern that is seen in families who have accumulated worldly wealth. People who study this phenomenon of failure to perpetuate wealth through successive generations, site several factors, none the least of which is an ever increasing number of heirs that out grow the increase in the size of the estate from generation to generation. They consumed the estate instead of increasing it.

But they have also discovered an interesting pattern in many of the wealthy families that can only have a spiritual explanation. It seems that children who have grown up competing with something for the attention of their parents, harbor a deep rooted psychological abhorrence for this competitor that stays with them even into adulthood. They can never quite forgive it or find a way to live with it. What's the name of this fierce opponent who seemed absolutely indomitable in the eyes of a child? Money! When they needed the affections of a father and a mother, they were absent from their lives. Where were they? At work, or a business meeting, or playing golf with an influential client.

When the parents die and the child inherits this enemy of joy and normalcy, the heirs will try to make peace with it. They will understand on a conscious level that they need it and that they are better off than nearly everyone else; at least financially speaking. But on an unconscious or spiritual level, they hate it and see it as their greatest enemy. This subconscious resentment will cause them to destroy this thing that stole their parents love, and they will squander and in short order, lose their inheritance.

The righteous man on the other hand has always made sure that his children understand that they are more important than the money. His actions have backed up his words, and he has taught his children that money is to serve us; we're not to serve it. His children grow up understanding that money is a useful tool in helping others and having influence in the community for the advancement of the cause of God's Kingdom. The data, therefore, bears out the fact that heirs who come from a family that places higher value on spiritual growth and love for each other rather than worldly wealth, have an ability to perpetuate that wealth from generation to generation. In fact, the size of their estates actually grows for one succeeding generation to another. Their heirs do not view money as an enemy, and due to their loving nurturing parents, they have a healthy image of themselves and usually a good relationship with their God. These factors work together to cause them to find their own way in life and to become relatively successful in their own right. Therefore they don't consume the estate to live, since they are emotionally able to do quite well on their own. *"A good man leaves an inheritance to his children's children"*, and now you understand how this is accomplished. It's by love. According to the word, it *"never fails"* (1 Corinthians 13:8), no matter what the area of life. Whether it be wealth building, estate planning, or child-rearing…it simply never fails.

The people we've just described comprise our fourth category. Jesus said, *"But he who received seed on the good ground is he who hears the word and understands it, who indeed bears fruit and produces: some a hundredfold, some sixty, some thirty"* — (Matthew 13:23). People who have *"good ground"* or a good heart, always manifest increase for the Kingdom of God. They received the same word as everybody else, so what was the difference in their lives that caused increase to manifest? It's the condition of their soil. You can sow until you are "blue in the face", but if your soil is not in good condition, you'll not produce "increase". What caused their ground to be so fruitful? It was merely their understanding of the word of God, and their effective implementation of it. So a good heart, that can perceive the truth of the word of God and subsequently apply it to life, brings "increase" to themselves and the Kingdom. It's that simple.

A heart that doesn't understand God's word, or is deceived by riches or the cares of the world, or is easily turned from God and His Kingdom by personal adversity, will never produce "increase".

The Definition of Tithing –

Another important financial truth from the word is God's principle of tithing. The Old Testament practice of tithing was initiated by Abraham in Genesis Chapter 14. After Abraham's successful campaign against four opposing Kings who had captured his nephew Lot, Abraham brought the spoils of his victory to God's priest in Salem (latter to be changed to Jerusalem). There he presented himself to the High Priest of Salem and *"gave a tithe of all"* his increase to the priest (Genesis 14:20). The Hebrew word that is translated as "tithe" literally means a tenth part. So tithe equals a tenth. Did it work for Abraham? The Bible makes the statement that, *"Abraham was very rich in livestock, silver, and gold."*

This practice was continued by Abraham's grandson, Jacob, who told the Lord at Bethel, *"And this stone which I have set as a pillar shall be God's house, and of all that You give me I will surely give a tenth to You"* — (Genesis 28:22). As far as we know, Jacob kept his end of the bargain, and he went on to incredible blessings. None the least of which was having his name changed by God to Israel, and becoming the father of twelve sons who were destined to become the Patriarchs of God's covenant people. In addition, Israel who had escaped the wrath of his brother Esau by fleeing to Syria and the household of his uncle Laben (his mother's brother), had become exceedingly rich while in exile. He came to Syria with nothing, but because of the direct intervention of the Lord, he left his uncle's house as the largest stockman in the entire region. Simply put... tithing works!!

The most quoted passage of scripture concerning tithing is the word of the Lord as spoken through His prophet Malachi. The spiritual condition of the Israelites was in serious decline during

Malachi's era which was around 450 B.C. And one of the main manifestations of their apostate condition was that they were not tithing. The Lord spoke through His prophet and admonished His people for robbing Him. *"Will a man rob God? Yet you have robbed Me! But you say, 'In what way have we robbed You?' In tithes and offerings. You are cursed with a curse, For you have robbed Me, Even this whole nation. Bring all the tithes into the storehouse, That there may be food in My house, And try Me now in this,"* Says the Lord of hosts, *"If I will not open for you the windows of heaven And pour out for you such blessing That there will not be room enough to receive it"* — (Malachi 3:8-10).

I would point out the part where He says, that if you're not tithing you are *"cursed with a curse."* That can't be good! And this sword cuts both ways. If we honor Him with tithes, He is bound by His word to pour out a blessing that is so big we can't contain it. It's sort of, "blessed if you do, but cursed if you don't" type of thing; I think I'll take blessings. What about you?

In addition, I would point out that the tithe is not an offering. The tithe is His to begin with. If you're in covenant with God, the first ten percent of your increase belongs to Him. So when you tithe, you're not giving Him an offering…you're just giving Him what already belongs to Him. The tithe of God is not the last ten percent of your increase either. It is the first ten percent. If you're paying God after you've paid everyone else, even though you're giving ten percent, you've not tithed. God requires the first of everything. He wants to be ahead of everybody in your life. Not last. *"Honor the Lord with your possessions, And with **the firstfruits of all your increase**; So your barns will be filled with plenty, And your vats will overflow with new wine "*— (Proverbs 3:9-10).

Needless to say, if you desire financial freedom and victory in your life, and you're not tithing, you can forget God's help. Not only can you forget the supernatural aid of the God who blessed Abraham, Isaac, and Jacob, but you have in fact brought a curse on your financial situation. I minister to Believers everyday who are desperate for financial deliverance and the first thing they tell me is, "I just can't tithe. There's not enough money at the end of the month to tithe." My response is always the same. God said, *"test Me in this"* (Malachi 3:10). So I tell people, test Him. Give Him the first ten percent of your increase and see if He will not make a way to get you through the rest of the month. If we're going to receive financial healing, it has to begin with tithing.

Another aspect of tithing that is not well understood I don't think is its application to Small Businesses. If you own a trucking company, for example, you don't tithe off your gross revenue or "top-line." The reason is that your gross revenue does not represent your increase. You've got fuel and overhead to pay out of those proceeds. Not only does your gross revenue not represent your increase, a lot of it doesn't even belong to you. Part of it belongs to your fuel provider, insurance company, and auto parts supplier. It's up to them to tithe on their part, not you. You need to pay your bills and whatever is left over is your increase. You tithe off of that. Now if you pay yourself a salary, you need to tithe off of it. Additionally, you need to tithe off what the business net is each month after expenses. If you're doing these things then you're in good standing with God in the area of your finances, and you need to stand on His word and expect increase in them.

There is no question that tithing was commanded by God in Leviticus 27:30, *"And all the tithe of the land, whether of the seed of the land or of the fruit of the tree, is the Lord's. It is holy to the Lord."* We're even instructed as to what to do with it. *"...to bring the firstfruits of our dough, our offerings, the fruit from all kinds of trees, the new wine and oil, to the priests, to the storerooms of the house of our God; and to bring the tithes of our land to the Levites, for the Levites should receive the tithes in all our farming communitie.—* (Nehemiah 10:37). In other words, "Bring it to Church and give it to the priest."

Some people try and claim that tithing was an Old Testament practice and does not have application to a New Covenant Believer. Jesus is on the record as having approved of the practice of tithing. He admonished the Pharisees, who were meticulous tithers when He said, *"Woe to you, scribes and Pharisees, hypocrites! For you pay tithe of mint and anise and cummin, and have neglected the weightier matters of the law: justice and mercy and faith. <u>These you ought to have done</u>, without leaving the others undone"—*

(Matthew 23:23). He was saying that they were observing the letter of the Law, but not the spirit of the Law, and that was love. They tithed even down to minute spices like anise and cumin, but still did not practice justice and mercy in their dealings with the people. *"These things you ought to have done, without leaving the others undone."* Never let anyone tell you that Jesus abolished the practice of tithing. Matthew 23, He actually endorsed it, and stated that it was an important part of spiritual discipline.

God loves a cheerful giver –

2 Corinthians 9:6-10, describes God's relationship to a giver. He loves a cheerful one. He obligates himself to provide seed to *"a sower"*. He states that those who sow sparingly will also harvest sparingly. He makes a commitment to our financial well being in 2 Corinthians 9:8 when He says:

"And God is able to make all grace abound toward you,
that you, always having all sufficiency in all things, may
have an abundance for every good work."
(2 Corinthians 9:8)

God has one plan for His people, and that is abundance and increase. Those who are not in bondage to the "unjust" through debt, and who understand the word and its application, will produce financial fruit that translates into abundance in this life and the next. When we give to His cause and Kingdom, we actually *"lay up for ourselves treasures in heaven"*. We have the ability to determine our level of paradise in the next life by the amount we give in this one. When we give, we authorize God to release financial blessing in our lives. To those who are willing givers, He will see that we have an *"abundance for every good work"* by making His grace abound toward us and producing a sufficiency in all things.

In the fourth Chapter of Luke, Jesus steps into the Temple to proclaim the beginning of His ministry. He asked for the scroll of Isaiah and reads from one of the Messianic Prophecies contained therein. Then He reads, *"The Spirit of the Lord is upon Me, because*

He has anointed Me to preach the gospel to the poor;..." The gospel means "Good News" and the Messiah has come to preach it to the poor. The Good News is that He has come to liberate us from our financial oppression, and to show us how to unlock God's Spiritual Laws of Increase and Abundance in our lives, and it begins with our giving.

Victor Frankl said the thing he remembers most about the concentration camps during World War II, were the men walking through the camp and giving away their last piece of bread to comfort others. These men chose to give all they had, but in the process they received more than they could have ever dreamed. They made an indelible impression on people who were suffering at the hands of their fellow man as to the "goodness" that still can be found in the hearts of men. The prophet Jeremiah said that the *"heart (of man) is deceitful above all things and desperately wicked. Who can know it?"*

The people of Auschwitz saw both sides. They saw the heart of a taker and the heart of a giver. They were moved and encouraged by the witness of a giving heart. The men who chose to give, received the eternal admiration of those they helped. They also received the admiration of their Father in heaven, who was moved by their self-less act. And who in turn, according to His own Laws and promises, transformed their gift into a reward in the eternal realm that *"no eye has seen, nor hear has heard, nor heart has been able to conceive..."*

He told the rich man, "*...give to the poor, and you will have treasure in heaven; and come, follow Me*"— (Matthew 19:21). There's only one way to *"lay up treasure in heaven"* and that is to give. Give of our time, give of our money, and give of ourselves.

> *"Do not lay up for yourselves treasures on earth, where*
> *moth and rust destroy and where thieves break in and steal;*
> *but lay up for yourselves treasures in heaven, where neither*
> *moth nor rust destroys and where thieves do not break in*
> *and steal. For where your treasure is, there your heart will*
> *be also." (Matthew 6:19-21)*

We have an opportunity to prove where our heart is by investing our treasure in the Kingdom of God. The return on investment is incalculable.

Step Four: Work—It's A Commandment!

"And let the beauty of the Lord our God be upon us, And establish the work of our hands for us; Yes, establish the work of our hands." **(Psalm 90:17)**

"and also that every man should eat and drink and enjoy the good of all his labor—it is the gift of God."
(Ecclesiastes 3:13)

"And whatever you do, do it heartily, as to the Lord and not to men, knowing that from the Lord you will receive the reward of the inheritance; for you serve the Lord Christ." (Colossians 3:23-24)

The master in the art of living makes little distinction between his work and his play, his labor and his leisure...He hardly knows which is which.
He simply pursues his vision of excellence at whatever he does, leaving others to decide whether he is working or playing. To him he's always doing both.
-James A. Michener

The man who wins is the average man,
Not built on any particular plan;
Not blessed with any particular luck –
Just steady and earnest and full of pluck.
The man who wins is the man who works,
Who neither labor nor trouble shirks;
Who uses his hands, his head, his eyes-
The man who wins is the man who tries.
-Conrad Hilton, from autobiography
"Be My Guest", 1957

"But if anyone does not provide for his own, and espe-
cially for those of his household, he has denied the faith
and is worse than an unbeliever." (1 Timothy 5:8)

We often think of God's commandments as instructions governing our moral and spiritual lives, but rarely do we regard His word concerning our work habits. His thoughts in this area are short and to the point. *"Six days you shall do your work, and on the seventh day you shall rest..."* (Exodus 23:12). Generally speaking, Americans don't need much lecturing on the subject of work. Studies show that Americans work more hours per week than their counterparts in Germany and France. American production per hour worked is about the same as the Europeans, but we work on average 28% more hours than the French, for example. Consequently our production per worker is about 30% higher than theirs. Americans produce more because we work more.

Wealth can only be created through increased production. The Bible refers to this increase in productivity as *"increase"* or *"multiplication"*.

"And He will love you and bless you and multiply (increase)
you; He will also bless the fruit of your womb and the fruit
of your land, your grain and your new wine and your oil,
the increase of your cattle and the offspring of your flock,
in the land of which He swore to your fathers to give you."
(Deuteronomy 7:13, NKJV)

This increase in production was very easy to measure in ancient times. The more sheep you had the wealthier you were. God blessed your flocks by causing all the ewes (female sheep) to have twins. Therefore the shepherd's wealth was drastically increased in one lambing season. The measurement of this increase is a little more difficult and sophisticated in modern times, but the underlying principle that increased wealth only comes through increased production is still true.

There was a young Christian businessman named R.G. LeTourneau who received a revelation of this principle early in his career. He was born in 1888 and passed away in 1969. He achieved many accomplishments in his life, including becoming the holder of over 300 patents relating to earthmoving equipment designs. He tells the story of how he came to understand the principle of increased wealth through increased production. One day he imagined that there were only 12 people left on the earth and so their number being so small, they were able to pass a law stipulating that they each be paid $1,200.00 per hour. One would think that this drastic increase in their wage would cause a drastic increase in their wealth, but not so. He realized that the price of the goods that they needed to live, i.e. food, housing, transportation, etc., would escalate so drastically that their actual wealth would remain the same as it was before they initiated their extravagant wage increase.

Why would the price of these necessities of life increase so dramatically you ask? Because even though their wages had increased, their capacity to produce food, housing, transportation, and other essentials of life would not. The result would be more dollars chasing the same quantity of goods and services which would result in inflated prices. The cost of these essentials would inflate to the point that they would eat up any gains made to income. Therefore there was only one way to truly build wealth, and that was through increased efficiency in the production of goods and services...not by increased wages. LaTourneau realized that the measure of wealth was not the number of dollars one held, but rather what those dollars would buy. Nothing erodes wealth like inflation, and that true *"increase"* can only come through increased production.

So he devoted his life to building machines that would make man more efficient and thereby increase his productivity. He developed the bulldozer, the Carry-all scraper, and many other types of earth-moving equipment whose designs have not changed significantly even to today. He was committed to the idea that he could enhance the wealth of all men, through the drastic production gains made by his machines in the hands of a few men. His economic theory was right on target. Increased wages without commensurate increases in productivity do not increase overall wealth.

A few years later, a group of electronic geniuses led by a man named Bill Gates, accomplished the same feat except on a much greater scale. Bill Gates and his contemporaries were successful in harnessing the mysterious power of the electron moving at the speed of light through an intricate circuit called a microchip, to create the Personal Computer. Perhaps even they were dismayed at the magnitude of the impact of their vision. Nothing in history has increased productivity and thereby increased the wealth of all men, like advances in computer technology. The formula is simple; labor cost divided by decreased production = decreased wealth, while conversely, labor cost divided by increased production equals increased wealth.

In other words, fruitful efficient work produces increased wealth. The Bible clearly teaches that a righteous man prospers in all he does. "(A righteous man) *shall be like a tree Planted by the rivers of water, That brings forth its fruit in its season, Whose leaf also shall not wither; And whatever he <u>does</u> shall prosper* "- (Psalm 1:3). It's obvious that we have to **<u>"do"</u>** something so that God can bless it. We have to produce something, so God can "increase" it. God cannot bless the book we never wrote, or the business we never started, or the idea we never developed and patented.

The word of God says, *"(See) If I will not open for you the windows of heaven And pour out for you such blessing That there will not be room enough to receive it"*- (Malachi 3:10). What do you think a "poured out blessing" looks like? Maybe dollar bills floating down from heaven, or an armored truck turned over in your front yard? Maybe Ed McMahon knocking on your front door? None of these is a likely scenario of God's blessing.

When God opens the portals of heaven and pours out blessings, they will more than likely come in the form of concepts, ideas, opportunities and uncommon favor. Notice that all of these instruments of blessing will require action on your part. A concept or an idea has got to be developed into a product or service. I'm sure that many of R.G. Le Tourneau's ideas were divine inspiration, but they all required that he invest some human perspiration in their implementation. I'm not sure the revelation that Bill Gates received concerning computer operating systems was divine or not, but he makes for a fascinating study in how the process of "being blessed" financially works. Bill Gates made a perfect score on the math section of his SAT Test prior to entry into Harvard University. It would be a fair assumption that he had a natural gift in the area of mathematics. He then developed a vision for the future. He became fascinated with micro-computers and he was able to see their potential impact on the world. To put it plainly, he saw something that few people could see.

He then pursued his vision with a vengeance. He quit Harvard... he simply didn't have time for it, and he and his childhood friend, among others started Microsoft. They then developed an operating system called "DOS" (disc operating system), and had extraordinary favor with the major producer of Personal Computers at the time, IBM. He used this favor with IBM to become established as the "standard" for operating systems in a world that was struggling to develop some consistency and uniformity. The rest is history. Microsoft became the dominant software provider in a market that literally exploded worldwide, and even out lasted their first customer, IBM, in an business environment that was hostile to those who stood still. He created a company that was lean and mean and knew how to think on its feet. In his own words they created a "culture of adaptability".

So let's review. Bill Gates took his natural gift (math) and developed it to it's maximum potential. Then he had a vision of a new and dynamic industry that was totally foreign to anything anyone had dreamed of before. He then pursued this vision which required faith, diligence, and the astute application of his natural gifting, and refused to be deterred. Then after mixing the right proportion of perspiration and inspiration, he harvested the largest fortune ever to be amassed by any individual...ever! And now he is using his wealth to help the poor around the world. His foundation, the *Bill and Melinda Gates Foundation*, has committed around 6.6 Billion dollars to causes around the world.

Basically, Bill Gates conducted his financial affairs exactly as the Bible prescribes. I can make no guarantees concerning his personal life, but as to the way he has developed what he has been given to its maximum potential, he is without peer. Christians need to study his business principles and apply them since they were not his originally anyway. They were God's. Most can be discovered in the Book of Proverbs. It is precisely in this manner that God blesses His people; through inspiration and favor. They are still required to supply the effort.

-God's People Have Always Had a Diligent Nature-

In fact, one of God's requirements for financial blessing is that we develop a diligent nature.

"The hand of the diligent will rule, But the lazy man will be put to forced labor." (Proverbs 12:24)

There is nowhere in the Word of God where He makes a promise to reward laziness or wastefulness. There are many places where He commits to reward the work of the diligent hand. What does the Bible mean by diligence? A diligent person has a "chip-away-at-the-problem" attitude. They don't expect instant success, nor do they expect failure. They are prepared for setbacks on the way to their destination. They're never frantic or upset...they're just committed. They know what they're called to do, and they refuse to be deterred from their objective. They understand that you eat an elephant one bite at a time.

A diligent person has a disciplined nature. The root of the word "disciple" is discipline. To be a disciple of Jesus Christ you must do more than adhere to His teachings. You must develop a disciplined life style in every area. In our eating habits, our use of time, in the media we ingest, the way we handle money, and our work habits. The Word of God has a clear commandment concerning effort:

> *"And whatever you do, do it heartily, as to the Lord and not to men, knowing that from the Lord you will receive the reward of the inheritance; for you serve the Lord Christ."*
> (Colossians 3:23-24)

Our attitude concerning our work should be a witness for Jesus Christ. We should remember that He will be our ultimate rewarder and we will stand before Him one day and give an account of our witness while we were on earth. An important part of our diligence is our work ethic. If we work as *"unto the Lord, and not men"*, then we have tremendous motivation to pursue a standard of excellence.

One of the things that disheartens me at times, is when I see a Casino in Las Vegas that has an immaculate lobby, with first rate service from management to the bar maids. And although scantily clad, their physical appearance is well-groomed and reflects the benefits of the physical disciplines of diet and exercise. There is not one scrap piece of paper lying about in their lobbies, nor one discarded cigarette butt on their sidewalk. Their level of excellence is very high.

In the mornings I come to my own Church office which is in varying degrees of disarray, after having worked up the courage to weigh myself earlier, which usually causes me to become somewhat depressed. What I lack that Caesar's Palace has is in a word...discipline. I'm disheartened by the fact that I have true motivation to be diligent and disciplined; a desire to be excellent for Him who gave Himself for me. The one who paid for my sins.

Their motivation...money. That's right. They can stay trim and fit, and keep their hotels and Casino's immaculate, provide the highest level of service on the globe, and maintain the highest standard of excellence to be found; all of which require discipline and hard work, and diligence. And their sole motivation is profit. We on the other hand are representing the King of the Universe, the Lord of Hosts, the Alpha and the Omega, the Creator of everything seen and unseen, and Vegas shouldn't be able to touch our standard of excellence because of who we serve. They not only touch it, most of the time they exceed it.

No matter what it is we do from painting a house to painting a great work of art through skillfully laying brush strokes on canvas, we should do it so as to glorify Christ. Our work should be an expression of the joy, peace, and satisfaction that we have in Him. People who are in a place of emotional rest and peacefulness are at their creative best. Our life's work should reflect this creativity that is a by product of being at peace. Isaiah 26:3 says, *"You will keep him in perfect peace, Whose mind is stayed on You, Because he trusts in You."* A peaceful spirit can hear the voice of God and receive creative inspiration from Him. R.G. LaTourneau and many others like him have proven that creativity leads to increased production which in turn leads to wealth. Therefore it follows that Christians should be the most creative, productive, and wealthiest people in the world. This was His promise in Deuteronomy 8:18 says, *"And you shall remember the Lord your God, for it is He who gives you power to get wealth, that He may establish His covenant which He swore to your fathers, as it is this day."* The power we have to get wealth is a byproduct of inspired creativity that is facilitated by a soul that is "Resting in Him". We will have more of this subject later.

The modern workplace is, by and large, not conducive to creativity. Pharaoh has turned God's people into robots that perform tasks on command and with precision. There is no room in the cubicle that we call an office, to do something radically different; to take a risk. It's hard to dream while you stare at the blank white wall that partitions you off from life. We pursue increased production through soul-killing schemes we call efficiency enhancements. We easily forget that vast strides in production were accomplished through the creative genius of men like Gates and LaTourneau; not by squeezing two-hundred people into an office space that was designed to hold one-hundred. Many of the things that management does in the name of efficiency, actually snuff-out creativity, which is the only real way to accomplish increased production.

Nevertheless, Christians have always been the most productive, diligent, and creative people on earth, regardless of the environment they work in. Diligent people are neither frantic nor are they lazy.

They're simply committed to excellence, and they take whatever time it takes to do the job well. They don't really view it as their "job". They view it as their "work", and their "work" is part of their witness. The moment we begin to view our "job" as our life's "work", our attitude changes concerning it. The great author James Michener said,

> *"The master in the art of living makes little distinction between his work and his play, his labor and his leisure... He hardly knows which is which. He simply pursues his vision of excellence at whatever he does, leaving others to decide whether he is working or playing. To him he's always doing both."*

Our work should be a source of great satisfaction to us, not just a paycheck. What makes our work satisfying is our attitude about it. If you have a boss that is impossible to please, then quit trying to please him and start trying to please the Lord. If he or she just makes your workplace intolerable, then find another job, but before you quit you better be sure that the boss is the problem and not you. Ask the Holy Spirit to reveal to you any habits that you need to change and to show you how you can improve your work witness. Are you chronically late? Do you complete the tasks you've been given to do? Are you submitted to those God has placed in authority over you? This doesn't mean that you tolerate abuse, but it means you don't rebel every time they ask you to do something differently that you think it ought to be done.

> *"and also that every man should eat and drink and enjoy the good of all his labor—it is the gift of God."*
> (Ecclesiastes 3:13)

Satisfying work is a gift from God, and it is born out of a diligent spirit. My grandmother was an avid "Quilter". In West Texas where I was raised, many of the women of my grandmother's generation engaged in this social activity that required the skilled use of needle and thread simply know as "Quilting". This process involved the cutting, arranging, and sowing together pieces of scrap cloth into amazing patterns so as to form a large bedspread or blanket referred to as a Quilt. These women were diligent by nature; taking care of the house, preparing three hot meals a day for their families, tending to many of the chores like milking the cow and gathering the eggs from the hen house. They lived a pretty difficult life, but you never heard them complain. There were no trips to the big city to see a Broadway show or even go to a movie for the women of the Texas plains in those days.

In the eyes of a child, this "quilting" seemed rather too bland and unexciting to be the source of such passion and social importance. I still remember the huge room in my great grandmother's house that contained the ominous looking "Quilting frame" that was suspended from the high sealing. This was a sacred room where the male of the specie was not allowed to go. Primarily, I assume, because the women that were gathered around this mass of cloth hand sowing the fabric together, were entertaining themselves by gossiping about the men whose access they had forbidden. Even though I was a little boy and innocent in most things, I still remember thinking there was just a little too much laughter coming from behind the closed doors of the quilting room.

Exactly what these women talked about in there I cannot say, but what they created out of various scraps of fabric was nothing short of a masterpiece. To this day, some of my most prized possessions are the quilts that my grandmother made for me over the years. They were an incredible amount of work, and I was a grown man before I realized what great satisfaction they brought her. My grandmother lost my grandfather at the tender age of 56, and she was left alone to attend to my uncle Leon who had Cerebral Palsy and was an invalid. Although my mother (her daughter) and my other uncle helped her and were there for her, she never would allow herself and my uncle Leon to be a burden on them. It was some 18 years after my grandfather passed away until my uncle Leon followed him into heaven, and I never heard my grandmother complain one time. Looking back I see that her relationship with Jesus Christ and the satisfaction she got from creating with her hands is what got her through those very trying days. If she felt depressed, she just started another quilt. She was made in her Lord's image and He was a compulsive Creator. He just Created the earth because it pleased Him. Then just like my grandmother, He took what He had so lovingly created, and He gave it away. He told Adam, *"Here, take the earth and subdue it and have dominion over it..."*

It wasn't a job to my grandmother...it was her life's work, and she sowed a piece of herself into every scrap of cloth. Then it pleased her to give it away in an act of love. She didn't do it for the money... she *"did it as unto the Lord"*. Vegas had nothing on her when it came to excellence, and they could never match her motivation. She was motivated by the love she felt for the person she was creating each work of art for. She would try and capture some of the personality of the recipient in each quilt. In the process she left some of her own character. Paul said;

> *"...what may be known of God is manifest in...the creation of the world His invisible attributes are clearly seen, being understood by the things that are made, even His eternal power and Godhead, so that they are without excuse,"*
> (Romans 1:19-20)

Just as many of the attributes of God are discerned through what He made, namely the Creation itself, so the quilts that drape across my bed reflect the strength of character of their creator...my Grandmother. Her work brought her great satisfaction and scratched an itch that cropped up from deep within her heart; her compulsion to create with her hands. *"She simply pursues her vision of excellence at whatever she does, leaving others to decide whether she is working or playing. To her she's always doing both."*

♦ Resting in Him —

Now that we've spent several pages of this chapter illuminating the word of God in the area of hardy effort, diligence, and the lack of laziness as being key ingredients to God's financial blessing, we come to Hebrews Chapter Four which speaks about resting in God. So how do we reconcile "working hard" with "resting"? Hebrews

3:7-4:10 concerns "entering into" the "Promised Land" of God's provision. This was a geographic place in the Old Covenant where God had set aside financial blessing for His people. It was their destiny in Him. It is still the destiny of God's people; only now, for those of us under the New Covenant (the Blood Covenant of Christ), it has become a spiritual place. Just as the Kingdom of God that Jesus preached to the incredulous Jews was not a place that could be identified on a map, but a Kingdom that would spring-up within the hearts of men. He was talking about a spiritual place. And to those who *"believed on His name"*, to them was given the right to become *"children of God"* (John 1:12). Not in the "sweet-by-and -by" of the after life, but in the difficult days of the "here and now". We stepped into this invisible Kingdom the minute we accepted Jesus Christ as our savior. Just as the Kingdom of God is not yet physical (John 18:36), entering into a place of *"rest in Him"*, is not a physical place but a spiritual state. It's a state of emotional and spiritual rest; a spiritual condition exemplified by a work-life that is not filled with anxiety and trepidation, but with joy and creativity.

I would remind you again, during the Exodus while God's children were in the wilderness, they only received "manna" from heaven (Exodus 16:31). This was God's provision. Its purpose was to keep them alive...not to prosper them. God had no intention of prospering the Israelites in the wilderness. They had to get in the right place to be blessed financially, and the place was their Promised Land. It was their inheritance. There are many of us who are not blessed financially because we've not entered into the right land, and until we enter the right land we'll not *"enter His rest"*.

One of the amazing attributes of Abraham was that he would pack up and go wherever God instructed him to go without a second thought. He *"moved his tent"* regularly, and he pursued a land that he had only seen in a vision. When he got to the Promised Land it was in a drought. What did he do? He built an altar and offered a sacrifice of thanksgiving to God (Genesis 12:7), then he proceeded south with his flocks to Egypt where there was pasture for his livestock. But he didn't remain in Egypt. He returned as soon as the drought was broken and he prospered in the Land of God's promise.

Many of us have tried a business that we thought God had led us to, only to experience drought. Don't give up on the dream, but wait for the drought to pass and take it up again. Continue to thank Him for that business even though you're compelled to dwell in Egypt for a season to sustain yourself and your flock. Remember, the test is always a test of faith. Abraham heard the word of God and he always believed the word of God. He was never moved by circumstances in the natural. He built his future on his faith in the promises of God, and he became the wealthiest man in the history of the earth. Abraham understood how to move where God wanted him to move, and to "rest in His promises".

Many of us are eating manna, when God wants us to enjoy the fruit of abundance. How do we get to the fruit? Come out of the wilderness. How do we come out of the wilderness? Through faith and obedience. There is no other way. The Israelites left Egypt on their financial Exodus, and they failed to enter in. *"So we see that they could not enter in because of unbelief."* (Hebrews 3:19)

What exactly was it that they could not believe? It certainly was not in the provision. Their scouts had gone into the Land and searched it out and found tremendous fruit. Grapes so big that they had to carry a cluster on a pole between two men (Numbers 13:23). They reported that the land, *"truly flows with milk and honey. And this is its fruit. Nevertheless, the people who dwell in the land are strong; the cities are fortified and very large; moreover we saw the descendants of Anak there"—* (Numbers 13:27-28). "The descendants of Anak", were a race of giants. They were the ancestors of Goliath of Gath whom David killed before the armies of Israel which propelled him to international fame. This man Goliath held the entire army of Israel at bay because they were intimidated by his size and ferocity. His ancestors literally scared the Israelites out of their inheritance, because they could not believe that God would give them victory over such a fierce and imposing enemy.

They had been slaves for so long in Egypt, they did not see themselves worthy of God's protection and provision. *"There we saw the giants (the descendants of Anak came from the giants); and we were like grasshoppers in our own sight, and so we were in their sight"—* (Numbers 13:33). When you've been making bricks for

Pharaoh for 435 years, it's hard to picture yourself as anything but a *"grasshopper"*. Especially when you're confronted with a giant for an adversary! It's hard to see yourself as a successful businessman or woman, when your credit card company is calling you every five minutes about your past due account. If this is your circumstance then you must not do what they did. They refused to believe that God would give them victory over such an imposing obstacle, therefore they failed to "enter is Promise, and His rest".

Lest we judge the Israelites of Moses' generation too harshly, we should heed the Holy Spirit who proclaims in the book of Hebrews that if we examine scripture we see that we are in the same dilemma today. Psalms 95: 7-11 says:

7 ...__Today__, if you will hear His voice:
8 "Do not harden your hearts, as in the rebellion,
As in the day of trial in the wilderness,
9 When your fathers tested Me;
They tried Me, though they saw My work.
10 For forty years I was grieved with that generation,
And said, 'It is a people who go astray in their hearts, And
they do not know My ways.'
11 So I swore in My wrath, 'They shall not enter My rest.' "

The word *"Today"* means...today. You and I can make the exact same mistake through a hardened heart that the Israelites made in the wilderness thousands of years ago. The Lord was grieved because they did not *"know My ways."* They had been hearing about the Promised Land since before they left Egypt. They had even been told that it was currently inhabited by *"...the Canaanites and the Hittites and the Amorites and the Hivites and the Jebusites..."* (Exodus 13:5). Still no one said anything about the giants.

Somehow they had concluded that they would be given this land on a silver platter; that they would not be required to fight. If they had known His ways they would have known that nothing could be further from the truth. God has always required that His people face their enemies or perish. We're told to have faith and believe for God's provision, yet we're genuinely shocked when we discover that a giant is squatting on our inheritance. Many times God allows adversity to come into our lives so that we can learn how to wield the sword of the Spirit which is the Word of God. Trials teach us how to stand on the doctrines of grace. We learn to conquer not by our own strength, but through His grace and provision.

"For though we walk in the flesh, we do not war according to the flesh. For the weapons of our warfare are not carnal but mighty in God for pulling down strongholds, casting down arguments and every high thing that exalts itself against the knowledge of God, bringing every thought into captivity to the obedience of Christ," (2 Corinthians 10:3-5)

What we **do not** do is run from the obstacles to success. We take a stand on the Word, and we fight according to the Spirit and not the flesh. The devil will always *"argue"* against what God has called you to do. He will present giants to stir up a spirit of fear in you. He doesn't want you to have the faith of Abraham and willingly "move your tent" into the land of your financial provision. He wants you to remain in the wilderness and die there. He doesn't want you to start that business that God has placed in your spirit because he knows that it will mean that you've moved into the Promise of God's blessing. So we must learn to *"cast down arguments"* that are contrary to the Word of God. We must not allow our hearts to become hardened through unbelief, and we must call on Him to bring us the victory. But most of all we must enter into His promised rest. Hebrews 4:9-10— *"There remains therefore a rest for the people of God. For he who has entered His rest has himself also ceased from his works as God did from His."*

So again we ask the question, "How is being required to work (Exodus 23:12) consistent with 'ceasing from our works'?" The answer lies in the difference between the meaning of the words "work" and "works". In Exodus when God proclaims the Laws regulating the Sabbath He said, *"Six days you shall do your work...."* The implication was that we are commanded to take care of things; that we are to "do", in order to have. But the word "works" in Hebrews 4:10 is referring to the creative act of God. *"For he who has entered*

His rest has himself also ceased <u>from his works</u> as God did from His." After the six days of creation the scripture says, "*And on the seventh day God ended His work which He had done, and <u>He rested</u> on the seventh day from all His work which He had done. Then God blessed the seventh day and sanctified it, because in it He rested from all His work which God had created and made.*" (Genesis 2:2-3)

God created the earth for man to inhabit, and when He created it He placed all of man's provision within it. Everything we need has already been placed here on the earth, and for those who have reached the Land of God's promise, it has been placed within our hearts as well. Adam was required to "tend to" the garden…not create it. One of my greatest weaknesses is that I'm always trying to do things my way. I have had many excellent ideas in my life, and I have tried to implement several of them, but most of the time I forgot to ask God what He desired for me to do. I was trying to "create" my own opportunities, and thereby missing most of the ones that God had ordained for me. I have spent years trying to manufacture my own provision instead of merely cultivating the seed that God had placed in my heart. I was trying to replant the garden instead of just tending to it. Therefore I was not "resting in God". I was "in the flesh" which only leads to frustration.

I've always enjoyed writing and have admired the works of the great authors of our time. But instead of cultivating the gift to write and communicate that I've been given, I've spent most of my life following after schemes to bring me riches. It never dawned on me that God would bless me through something that I really liked doing. I thought I had to hit an oil well or something to prosper financially. I entered into "works" instead of "rest". Don't misunderstand… writing is work, but it's what I love. I try and pursue my personal vision of excellence in writing and I leave others to speculate as to whether I'm working or playing. To me, I'm always doing both.

The work God has given us to do is supported by the natural gifts that He has instilled in us. I can paint pictures in the imagination with words, but give me a canvas and paintbrush, and I'll create something that no one can figure out…no matter how imaginative they might be. If I tried to appropriate God's provision through the art of painting, I would be walking in "works"—not work; because

I'm not called to be an artist. I've tried to recreate the provision that God had already created for me, and thereby I've failed to "enter His rest".

I believe that there are millions of Believers staring at computer screens doing something that is killing their soul because it is not what they have been called and equipped to do. They are afraid to step out and take on the obstacles to their prosperity, because they just can't see themselves overcoming the giants that are between them and their inheritance. Or perhaps they got to their Promised Land only to find that it was in a drought, and they had to return to Egypt for a season, but they never made the trip back because of discouragement.

The bottom line is simple. Are we *"dwelling in the land and feeding on His faithfulness"* or are we *"perishing in the wilderness?"* Are we nurturing and developing the seed (natural talents) that God has placed in us, or are we trying to replant the garden? The choice is ours. Possessing the Promised Land of our financial blessing requires work and it requires rest. We must diligently pursue the natural gifts that God has placed within us. We must realize that they are the seed of our prosperity. Then we must remain in a state of emotional and spiritual rest. Work hard but don't "sweat it". It's going to be fine. *"What then shall we say to these things? If God is for us, who can be against us?"* (Romans 8:31)

Resting Means Not Worrying—

The greatest enemy to fruitful, productive work, is depression. People who are depressed do not have the emotional capacity to do anything *"heartily as unto the Lord"*. They want to. They just can't. They have a spirit of despair and hopelessness. There can be many reasons for this darkness that falls on many of us. Psychologist acknowledge that "serotonin" enhancing drugs (SSRI'S) are little more effective than placebos[2], and that people who have developed

---

[2] **Antidepressants Versus Placebos: Meaningful Advantages Are Lacking,"** *Psychiatric Times* 2004, 19:9.

the spiritual aspect of their lives have less problems with depression[3]. Many people who are depressed (even though they may be middle aged) are experiencing the effects of childhood emotional trauma caused by various forms of abuse. They experience a setback years later in the form of a loss, i.e., lost job, or divorce, or health issue, and the anger they have repressed from their childhood pushes them into emotional darkness. It's not within the scope of this book to deal with this subject in depth, but it is important to discuss the implications of a depressed state of mind on your work performance.

Depressive disorders affect approximately 18.8 million American adults or about 9.5% of the U.S. population age 18 and older in a given year. This includes major depressive disorder, dysthymic disorder, and bipolar disorder.[4] People who are at "rest in Him", are not just people who go to Church. They are people who have dealt with the spiritual issues in their own lives and have been healed of the emotional traumas from their past. Clearly even secular psychologist agree that drugs are not the long-term answer for most people. The "issues of the heart" can only be healed through the power of the Spirit of the Living God. Often people try to literally "buy happiness". They will charge things on a credit card that they don't really need, because they get a temporary rush from the psychological processes of buying something they want. It makes them happy for awhile, and then the remorse for spending money they don't really have sinks in. Their emotional condition becomes worse than it was when they began their shopping spree.

Their depression deepens, absenteeism from work increases, until finally they lose their job. Then a real sense of hopelessness ensues. They feel worthless and unable to cope with life. The Bible says, "*Hope deferred makes the heart sick, But when the desire comes, it is a tree of life –*" (Proverbs 13:12). All everybody wants in life is happiness. And when we've tried to find it in things, we will always be disappointed. When we have experienced continuous disappointment in people or things, and their failure to make us

---

[3] **Handbook of Religion and Health • The Link Between Religion and Health: Psychoneuroimmunology... Milstein** *Am. J. Geriatr. Psychiatry.*2004; 12: 332-334

[4] **According to a 2004 Rand Corporation report.**

happy…we become *"heart sick"*. We become depressed. Many of us are not lazy, we just have not learned how to deal with the disappointments of life. Therefore our ability to work fruitfully has been consumed by darkness and worry.

> *"But seek first the kingdom of God and His righteousness,*
> *and all these things shall be added to you. Therefore do*
> *not worry about tomorrow, for tomorrow will worry about*
> *its own things. Sufficient for the day is its own trouble."*
> *(Matthew 6:33-34)*

If we're not careful we will waste our time living in regret of a past that we cannot change, or in worry about our future over which we honestly have little control, and in the process we'll squander the present which is the only thing we truly have any control over that can make a difference in our lives. Jesus said, "Seek God and stop worrying." The subject of this book is financial freedom. I'm convinced, however, that financial freedom can only occur after spiritual freedom has been achieved. Spiritual freedom does not come through an improvement in our "natural" circumstance…it comes from deep within. When we have accepted that God loves us and is not mad at us. When we acknowledge that we've made some mistakes, but that doesn't make us a bad person. When we realize that everyone will experience setbacks in life, and these trials (as the Bible calls them) are what facilitate spiritual growth and refinement. When we have dealt with the wounds and the disappointments of the past, and have been healed from their emotional trauma; then we are free. It has little to do with the amount of money we have in our bank account.

To *"Rest in Him"* means to be in a place of Spiritual freedom. A place where we love our work and are in bondage to no man. A place where we work *"heartily as unto the Lord and not men"*. A place where life is satisfying and fulfilling and money serves us instead of us serving it. Get free spiritually, and you will soon be free financially. Furthermore, we know financial freedom comes through "fruits of our labors", not from winning the lottery. *"Six days you shall work…"*; and what we do with the seventh will determine the amount of blessing that comes from the previous six. The miracle of God's provision comes through opened doors and opportunities in the workplace. If we're not working, we'll simply miss Him and His provision.

God chose a trade to master before He proclaimed Himself as the Master. He was a carpenter…a craftsman without peer. What would a piece of furniture be like that had been created by the hands that created the universe? Don't you know that His compulsive desire to create wrought some incredible works of art in His father's wood-shop? He probably just couldn't help Himself. He would see a hunk of wood and He just couldn't leave it alone until He had transformed it into an ornate table.

The mission of the Christ of God was for God to become man. For Him to walk in our shoes as it were. For Him to manifest in a form that we could relate to and that would perhaps, make it easier for Him to relate to us. Also for His atoning sacrifice to qualify Him as a *"kinsman redeemer"* as spoken by the Lord by the mouth of His prophets. The price for man's sin would have to be paid by someone who was the *"Son of Man"* as he often referred to Himself.

Work was an important part of this process of becoming familiar and relative. He chose to excel in the workplace before He tried to get people to follow His spiritual path. Most of God's leaders have been shepherds. Moses, David, and several of the prophets of God earned their living in the beginning as men who excelled in the care of livestock. Abraham was a skilled shepherd and herdsman, becoming vastly wealthy through the increase in his flocks and herds. *"Abram was very rich in livestock, in silver, and in gold"* — (Genesis 13:2). Jesus even described Himself as a shepherd in John 10:11 —*"I am the good shepherd. The good shepherd gives His life for the sheep."* The whole point being that the attributes of their character that made them leaders for God were the aspects of their personalities that they developed in the workplace. The lessons they learned at work, in the sheepfold, qualified them for spiritual leadership of God's people.

Peter, John, James, and Andrew were fisherman. Their experi-ence catching fish would make them uniquely qualified to become *"fishers of men"* as Christ would put it. Matthew was a tax-collector; skilled in the recording of accurate records. His work skills made him perfect for the writing of the first Gospel of the New Testament. Luke was a physician; an expert in diseases and their treatment. Who more qualified to document the miraculous healings by the hands of the Apostles which he recorded in the Book of Acts. Paul was a "tentmaker" which gave him instant employment in every city that God called him to in his missionary travels. His trade provided him with a unique frame of reference to describe the natural body as a *"tent that is being destroyed"* in his letter to the Church at Corinth (2 Corinthians 5:1). God uses our work to mold and shape us into useable vessels that have relevance to the natural world. The work-place is the intersection point of the world and the Kingdom of God. Work not only constitutes a route of God's financial blessing, but it also builds our character, and provides us with a venue in which we can be a witness for Christ. Our work is nearly as important as anything we will do. And so we say:

"... let the beauty of the Lord our God be upon us, And establish the work of our hands for us; Yes, establish the work of our hands" — (Psalm 90:17).

Step Five: Do Not Hasten To Be Rich (Or Entering Into Godly Contentment)

"And the Lord your God will drive out those nations (enemies) before you little by little; you will be unable to destroy them at once, lest the beasts of the field become too numerous for you." (Deuteronomy 7:22)

"People who look for easy money invariable pay for the privilege of proving conclusively that it cannot be found on this earth."
—Famous Stock Speculator Jesse Livermore

"A man with an evil eye hastens after riches, And does not consider that poverty will come upon him." (Proverbs 28:22)

"Do not despise these small beginnings, for the Lord rejoices to see the work begin…" (Zechariah 4:10, NLT)

That man is the richest whose pleasures are the cheapest.—Henry David Thoreau (1817 - 1862)

To be content with what one has
is the greatest and truest of riches.
— Cicero (106 BC - 43 BC)

"Now godliness with contentment is great gain. For we
brought nothing into this world, and it is certain we can
carry nothing out." (1 Timothy 6:6-7)

"There's no reason to be the richest man in the cemetery.
You can't do any business from there."
-Colonel Harland Sanders

The Word of God clearly warns us against the trap of *"hastening after riches"*. It says:

"A man with an evil eye hastens after riches, And does
not consider that poverty will come upon him." (Proverbs 28:22)

According to the American Heritage Dictionary, the definition of the word *"hasten"* is: To cause to hurry; to speed up; to accelerate. There is only one result that can come from hurrying to get rich. Poverty. In fact, quick riches actually violate God's principles of Harvest which state:

"But this I say: He who sows sparingly will also reap spar-
ingly, and he who sows bountifully will also reap bounti-
fully." (2 Corinthians 9:6)

"Do not be deceived, God is not mocked; for whatever a
man sows, that he will also reap." (Galatians 6:7)

"While the earth remains, Seedtime and harvest... Shall not
cease." (Genesis 8:22)

Get-rich schemes are built on the premise of reaping without sowing. It's just not consistent with the nature of the Kingdom of God that you could sow a $5.00 lottery ticket, and harvest a $1,000,000 jackpot. This is the quintessential illustration of the antithesis of God's Principles of Harvest; namely the act of sowing sparingly and reaping abundantly; hitting the "jackpot" as it were. It is the very character of the spirit of the world that has financed the construction of the Babylonian cities like Las Vegas, Nevada and Atlantic City, New Jersey. Their lavish hotels and casinos were built and paid for through a very universal lust found in the heart of the unregenerate (those not "born again" in the Spirit of God). It can be best described as the desire to become rich without effort; through luck…not by diligently sowing *"the work of the hands"* as well as resources, in faith.

"Luck" is not a Biblical concept. Luck is the product of the law of statistical probability. For example, if you bet on the same football team enough times, sooner or later they're going to win. This is a statistical certainty. The question is how many times will you have to bet on them before they do, and what could you have done with the money you lost on their losing games? Meanwhile the Casinos promote the benefits of *"luck"* by celebrating the winners who have *"held the hot hand"* at their dice and card tables. They show them standing between two beautiful women with the cash they've won piled up on the poker table before them. They encourage the rest of us to follow this person to the "pot of gold" at the end of the rainbow. I've noticed, however, they seem to show no remorse for this pile of cash that they've just lost.

That's because the Casinos who herald the excitement of these games of chance, don't play them. They understand the Laws of Probability, and they "take the odds" as it were. They know that with one big winner properly promoted, they can generate thousands of losers in their establishment. The allure of harvesting where you have not sown is powerful and profitable for them so they sell it continuously. Yet they don't operate their businesses on chance; they operated them on the certainties of the Law of Probability and human heart's lust for easy wealth. They promote "luck", but they refuse to bet their own future on it. They know that leaning on luck will lead you to the poorhouse, but betting the certainty of statistical probability will pay for a new wing on their lavish hotel. Depend on luck for your retirement and you'll be dining on ALPO.

For the Believer, blessing not "luck", is the Kingdom route to financial prosperity and it comes from only one place…God Himself. The same God, who magnifies His Word even above His own Name (Psalm 138:2), is not likely to violate that Word or the principles outlined therein, in order to bring financial blessing into the lives of His people. He will not permit harvest where there has been no sowing, and the harvest that will occur where there has been seed sown, will be directly proportional to the amount of seed sown. In other words a "jackpot-mentality", is not consistent with God or His Word. God says that he who sows a little, can only harvest a little.

He goes even further than that and says that quick riches will bring poverty. I call it the lottery curse. In an article in *MSN Money Central* entitled *8 Lottery Winners who Lost Their Millions*, the lives of eight different lottery winners were examined after their *"lucky-breaks"*.

1. Evelyn Adams—won the New Jersey Lottery not once but twice (1985 and 1986), to the tune of $5.4 million. Today the money is all gone and Adams lives in a trailer. "I won the American dream but I lost it all too. It was a very hard fall. It's called rock bottom," says Adams.
2. William "Bud" Post won $16.2 million in the Pennsylvania lottery in 1988 but now lives on his Social Security. "I wish it never happened. It was totally a nightmare," says Post.
3. Suzanne Mullins won $4.2 million in the Virginia lottery in 1993. Now she is deeply in debt to a company that lent her money using the winnings as collateral. She borrowed $197,746, which she agreed to pay back with her yearly checks from the Virginia lottery through 2006. When the rules changed allowing her to collect her winnings in a lump sum, she cashed in the remaining amount. But she stopped making payments on the loan. She blamed the debt on the lengthy illness of her uninsured son-in-law, who needed $1 million for medical bills.

4. Ken Proxmire was a machinist when he won $1 million in the Michigan lottery. He moved to California and went into the car business with his brothers. Within five years, he had filed for bankruptcy.

5. William Hurt of Lansing, Michigan won $3.1 million in 1989. Two years later he was broke and charged with murder. His lawyer says Hurt spent his fortune on a divorce and crack cocaine.

6. Charles Riddle of Belleville, Michigan won $1 million in 1975. Afterward, he got divorced, faced several lawsuits and was indicted for selling cocaine.

7. Missourian Janite Lee won $18 million in 1993. Lee was generous to a variety of causes, giving to politics, education and the community. But according to published reports, eight years after winning, Lee had filed for bankruptcy with only $700 left in two bank accounts and no cash on hand.

8. One *Southeastern* family won $4.2 million in the early '90s. They bought a huge house and succumbed to repeated family requests for help in paying off debts. The house, the cars, and the relatives ate the whole pot. Eleven years later, the couple is divorcing, the house is sold and they have to split what is left of the lottery proceeds. The wife got a very small house. The husband has moved in with the kids. Even the life insurance they bought ended up getting cashed in.

These are just a few documented examples of Proverbs 28:22 in action. The lottery curse brings poverty and great heartache in the end, and is totally consistent with the word of God. Believers who are hoping to win big in order to be set free financially do not understand the very nature of the King they serve. If we believe that God's method of financial deliverance would be a "rags to riches" scheme of sudden wealth, then we clearly do not know Him, or His Word.

In the Parable of the Talents in Matthew 25:14-30 the Lord explains the financial side of the Kingdom of God. A "talent" was a measure of weight used to measure gold and other precious metals. It was equivalent to about 66 lbs. A talent of gold would be worth about 950,000 today. The Lord starts out by saying that the *Kingdom of Heaven* is like a man who calls his servants together and entrusts His property to them to take care of while He is away. To one He gives five talents, to another two talents, and to a third He gave one talent. Then He leaves on a journey. Notice the scripture says He gives to each one *"according to his own ability"* (Matthew 25:15). The observation of my friend about stewardship that I mentioned earlier is thus validated by scripture. He says, "If I could steward $10 million then I would have $10 million dollars." In other words, if we want more financial blessing, we have to work on *"our own ability"* to steward (we will discuss the concept of stewardship in more detail in subsequent chapters).

Then the Lord comes back to *"settle accounts"* with the stewards. Sure enough the one to whom He had entrusted five talents had earned five more. The one to whom He had entrusted two talents has gained two more as well. To both of them His response is the same:

> *"...Well done, good and faithful servant; you were faithful over a few things, I will make you ruler over many things. Enter into the joy of your lord."* (Matthew 25:21)

Because they had demonstrated their trustworthiness on earth, they would be made stewards and rulers in the Kingdom of God.

Notice the reward they received in heaven was not commensurate with the amount of gain they had produced through their investments, but was the same for them both. Although their abilities were unequal, the attribute of their character that won them equal rewards in heaven, was their faithfulness. *"You were faithful over a few things, I will make you ruler over many things."* What the Lord was impressed with was the fact that they each did as well as they could with what they had been given, and they never forgot that it was not theirs but was indeed His. It was not the brilliance of their gifts that mattered to the Lord. He understood their relative abilities better than they did. That's why He only gave to them what He knew they could handle. It was the trueness of their hearts that mattered and led to their ultimate reward. *"Moreover it is required in stewards that one be found faithful,"* (1 Corinthians 4:2). They did not lust after the things that they had been given charge over. They always understood that it all belonged to Him anyway, and that He had given them authorization to use His "stuff" until He returned.

The third steward, the one to whom He gave only one talent, is an interesting study, in that he did not receive a reward from the Lord; in fact, what he received was punishment. The Lord referred to him as the *"unprofitable servant"*, and God took what he had and gave it to the servant who had five talents. As we discussed earlier, all that this servant would have had to do to be given authority over much in the Kingdom of heaven, was to have done the best that he could with the talent that God had given him. He would not be expected to produce the same amount of increase that the "five-talent" servant had produced.

But instead he hid his talent in the ground. He understood that the talent belonged to the Lord. This was not the issue. What the "one-talent" servant did not understand was the nature of God. On the day of accounting, *"…he who had received the one talent came and said, 'Lord, I knew you to be a hard man, reaping where you have not sown, and gathering where you have not scattered see,"* (Matthew 25:24). This statement clearly illustrated that the "one-talent" steward did not know the Lord at all. He did not know that the Lord lived by His own Laws and Principles. He thought of the Lord as a harsh taskmaster, not a loving nurturing Father who wanted to encourage us to be all that we could be. He didn't understand that the sin that God admonished was not "trying and failing, but failing to try." He did not understand that one could not harvest where he had not sown; be it the Lord or one of His subjects.

The root of the problem for the "one-talent" servant was that He basically failed to comprehend who God was and how He worked. In other words he was unfamiliar with God's nature. This led him to several errors in judgment, which wrought disastrous consequences in his life. The Lord said, *"And cast the unprofitable servant into the outer darkness. There will be weeping and gnashing of teeth,"* (Matthew 25:30). No steward can expect to do well and prosper when they don't know and understand the character and personality of the Boss. Get rich quick schemes and devices are not consistent with the nature and character of God. Get rich schemes rely on *"luck"*, not the skillful development of a persons God-given talents.

They are contrary to the nature of God. He doesn't endorse them and neither should those who work for Him.

The history of America's lottery winners exemplifies the fact the *"he who hastens after riches, does not consider that poverty will come upon him."* The "one-talent" steward did not know the Lord intimately, and therefore his ignorance led him to disastrous mistakes. Quit buying lottery tickets, and start investing in a mutual fund. Commit to a consistent approach that requires diligent effort and watch what God will do for you. And to those who are in covenant with Christ and therefore *"partakers of the promise (of wealth and prosperity)"*, just remember what financial guru Dave Ramsey says, "Ed McMahon is not coming!!"

If it's too good to be true...it usually isn't!

> *"The world wants to be deceived."*
> —Sebastian Brant (1457 - 1521),
> *The Ship of Fools*

One of the most dominant fraud schemes in American today is the "Nigerian Letter Fraud". Just imagine. You're behind on your bills and the credit card companies are hounding you all day wanting their money which you do not have. You feel your stomach draw into a knot everytime the telephone rings. You lay awake at night trying to figure a way to pay your utility bills and mortgage payment this month. "What can I sell," you ask yourself? Finally you give up on trying to sleep. You're just too tense. This is becoming a recurring pattern. You go into your home office and you boot up the computer to take your mind off your problems. You decide to check for e-mails, even though it's 3:00 AM. An e-mail catches your eye. It's from a guy in Nigeria who has apparently fallen on bad times (you already feel better...misery loves company). This guy, it seems, has suffered a political setback.

There has been a coup in his country (you've been too upset with your own problems to pay attention to the evening news), and he is evidently on the losing team. He says he has vast wealth that he needs to get moved out of the country and he's willing to pay handsomely to accomplish this process. His plan is intriguing. He cannot make large transactions through conventional financial institutions because his assets are being watched by his political enemies. They think they have confiscated most of them, but there is a stash of cash they know nothing about. They watch diligently to see if our friend makes any significant deposits or large cash acquisitions. He has millions of dollars socked away, but cannot use it for anything in his own country nor can he send it to himself in another. Hence the plan! You send him your banking information and he will send his money, in the form of money orders, to your bank account in chunks of less than $10,000. Then when he escapes Nigeria, he will meet up with you and give you half for helping illegally smuggle his money out of the country. By the way, what he's asking you to do is actually illegal. It is in violation of Nigeria's penal code section "419".

"This is what I've been praying for", you think to yourself. In desperation you've never bothered to check on the legality of these transactions.

"After all, this government is trying to steal this guy's inheritance", you convince yourself. It seems your judgment of what's right or wrong has been impaired by the desperation of your financial circumstance.

"I've been praying for a breakthrough. This has to be it", you decide. You never bother to pray and ask the Spirit of God to show you if this is of Him. You never test the Spirits as John recommended in 1 John 4:1.

You send your bank information to a foreign country to a guy you don't even know. So does he send you the millions in illegal transactions? No. You guessed it. He drains your bank account and uses your other financial information to steal your identity and "max" your credit cards out.

You fell embarrassed as you finally breakdown and call the FBI. You're about to confess that you were willing to conspire to transfer money illegally out of a foreign country, but you discovered that your partner was a "crook". You wonder how you're going to sell them on the idea that you were just a freedom fighter who was trying to right a political injustice. It occurs to you that if they are dumb enough to believe in the innocence of your motives, they're not probably smart enough to get any of your money back. Your embar-rassment is compounded by your grief over the fact that you now are certainly not able to pay your utilities or your mortgage payment. You wonder if the mortgage company will have sympathy for your campaign on the behalf of the oppressed peoples of Nigeria.

Your embarrassment turns into anger when the FBI agent cuts you off half way through your story (just as you were getting to the part about how righteous your cause was), and says abruptly, "There's nothing we can do."

"What…what do you mean there's nothing you can do?!"

"We receive thousands of calls on this very scam everyday, and I'm telling you there's nothing we can do about it. Look, since 9/11 we've been preoccupied with homeland security, and we don't have the available agents or resources to investigate these cases. We don't even look at fraud cases that are less than $150,000. We just don't have the time. And even if we did track the guy down, we have no jurisdiction in Nigeria and we would be unable to arrest him," the agent elaborates.

"What about my money?"

"It's G-O-N-E…gone. I'm very sorry, but I've got another appointment," the agent says feigning sincerity as he hangs up.

You stare into space as your emotions alternate between shame and hopelessness. Sure enough, what was too good to be true… wasn't. Famed stock speculator Jesse Livermore once said:

"People who look for easy money invariable pay
for the privilege of proving conclusively that it cannot be
found on this earth."

If this has happened to you, don't think you're alone. This specific con was perpetrated on the American public last year to the tune of 4.94 million dollars, and I'm sure some of the victims were Christians who had become desperate for financial relief. Suffice it to say, God will never bless you through a "get-rich" scheme that doesn't require sowing on your part, or that is possibly illegal. The "one-talent" servant in Matthew 25 made major mistakes because he didn't understand the Lord or how he worked. We must not do the same.

The internet has proven an effective venue from which to perpetrate these fraud schemes. In fact, internet fraud has risen from 17.8 million in 2001 to 183.12 million in 2005[5]. 62.7% of overall internet fraud is "auction fraud". If it's so cheap that it's too good to be true… it isn't. The scheme is as follows: You buy it on the internet and forward a partial payment, then you never here from the seller again. 15.7% is non-delivery and 9.4% is credit card/check fraud (never give your financial information to a stranger, i.e. a company that you've never heard of who has no history with the Better Business Bureau). Just remember, "get rich quick" equals poverty (Proverbs 28:22).

Success too soon is suicide—

Success in your new journey towards financial freedom will come in degrees or as the Bible says, "Little by little". God's *motisoperandi* is not sudden wealth. It is clearly gradual and sustained progress over time. He told His people who were about to be called to go in and possess their inheritance in the Promised Land:

> *"And the Lord your God will drive out those nations*
> *(enemies) before you little by little; you will be unable to*
> *destroy them at once, lest the beasts of the field become too*
> *numerous for you."* (Deuteronomy 7:22)

The Lord is saying, "If I give you sudden and complete victory over your enemies, the *"beasts of the field"* will rush in to consume the fallen bodies of your dead enemy, and they themselves will become a problem." In other words, sudden success merely creates a new set of problems. This illustration may be graphic, but the Principle of "Sudden Success is Suicide" is one of life's universal truths. If God delivers you from your financial bondage too quickly, you're destined to repeat your mistakes and your growth as a person will be stifled.

---

[5] **IC3 2005 Internet Crime Report (FBI)**

Another Biblical example of the Principle of Sudden Success is Suicide is the life of King Saul. Saul was selected by God to be King of Israel. He had immediate success as King dealing decisively with the Philistines. However his sudden success led him to become arrogant and independent. No longer did he seek God and His word for guidance. He became too self-confident. He rebelled against the Commandments of God and lost the anointing. God anointed a young boy named David as King, and even though Saul had lost the anointing, he remained in the office of King; continuing to rely on his natural gifts to perform his office. To the natural eye he was relatively successful, but spiritually he was in quicksand. He began to struggle internally knowing that he was merely acting out the part of King, not walking in the anointing and calling of God.

Meanwhile the young David had slain the giant Goliath, and become extremely popular with the people. Saul knew that he was anointed by God to become his successor. He tries desperately to kill David, and thereby eliminate his competition. He persecutes David for ten years, and becomes literally consumed with his mission to maintain the appearance of success of his monarchy. He becomes so paranoid that he murders eighty-five priests in the city of Nob who had innocently given David bread thinking he was on a mission of the King. He literally goes insane until he finally commits suicide on the battlefield.

David on the other hand endured ten years of persecution and wilderness living, all the while being anointed King of Israel. Although he had been called and anointed, he did not take the office of King until he had endured a season of struggle. It was in the wilderness that David's personality and character were shaped. Not in the throne room of the Palace. David also had some success, but it was mixed with trial. This kept him from making the same mistakes his predecessor had made. He was humble and looked to God for guidance and leadership. He knew better than to have confidence in the strength of his flesh.

Saul had early success...David had trials early. One committed suicide; the other became the greatest King in the history of Israel. For every ten people who can handle adversity, there is only one in that same group who can withstand prosperity. Prosperity is much more lethal spiritually than struggle. God has to be careful not to bring it too soon, *"least the beasts of the field become too numerous for you."* God's M.O. is *"little by little"*.

I'm not saying it will take ten years for you to become free financially, but I am saying that you didn't get in this mess overnight and you won't get out overnight. God will use your journey to freedom to mold and shape you into a vessel that he can pour anointing and prosperity into.

The proper investment approach is discipline over time

We learn from the Parable of the Talents in Matthew 25, God intends for us to invest what He has given us; not just spend it. He told the "one-talent" steward who buried his talent, you at least should have, *"deposited My money with the bankers, and at My coming I would have received back My own with interest."* God expects us to develop an "investor" mindset. Furthermore, as we learned earlier, *"the hand of the diligent makes rich"* – (Proverbs 10:4). Remember the definition of diligence is: *1. Earnest and persistent application to an undertaking; steady effort; assiduity. 2. Attentive care; heedfulness.* We will apply the same diligence we used to eliminate debt, to our investment approach. Discipline over time; this is the key to successful investing. This is consistent with God's nature. He is not a gambler. He is an investor. When Adam fell in the garden and introduced sin into His spectacular creation, God could have dealt with it immediately by eliminating Adam and Eve before this evil seed had a chance to spread. But instead He chose to invest in mankind, by sending His Son to redeem them. This may seem more like a gamble than an investment, but God knew that He would be able to build His vision of an earth populated by men and women who were led by the Spirit and not the flesh. He knew that those who demonstrated their faithfulness on earth and followed Christ to redemption, would be the foundation on which He would build His Kingdom here on earth. Christ would be the Chief Cornerstone, and we are the *"living stones"* out of which God is building a *"spiritual house"* (1 Peter 2:4-5). God chose to invest in us in the belief that we would be willing to be transformed into something out of which He could build His Kingdom. He was patient and when Christ returns to establish His Millennial Kingdom on earth, God's patience will be rewarded. This process has taken thousands of years. God doesn't sow a seed and expect harvest immediately. Neither should we.

Three Cardinal Rules of Investing —

Rule #1: The shorter the time-line of the investment, the riskier the outcome.

Investments are "long-term" in nature. Gambling is a short-term proposition. You place a bet and you deal the cards. In a very short period of time you will know the outcome. As we discussed earlier, it's speculation based on the Law of Probabilities. Investment on the other hand is about holding something long enough to eliminate all the chance involved. In other words, you may buy a stock and it may go down initially, but if it is a viable company at all, in time it will go higher. The key is to not "jump in and jump out" of investments. No one can time the entry and exit of an investment position perfectly. The key to successful investing is to learn to think in terms of ten's of years and not days. In other words, put it in the market and leave it.

Warren Buffet is the most successful investor in the world today, and the second richest man. He is considered one of the most sophisticated and wisest investors in history. When asked what the optimum time period for holding an investment was, he responded, "Our favorite holding period is forever." Smart investors understand that successful investment strategies are long-term. Jumping in and out of markets is dangerous. Remember, the shorter the term (time period) of the investment, the higher the chance of loss.

Rule #2: Never put all your eggs in one basket. Diversification is key in economic downturns.

Or in other words, don't try and "pick stocks". This is the way it usually goes. You go to the new neighborhood Target and are very impressed with the store. They had a huge crowd for their grand opening. Merchandise was flying out of there like crazy. You go home and you get to thinking, "I've got some money lying around from that rental property I sold last month. I think I'll buy some shares of Target."

Now let's examine your decision making process. There are over 1300 stores in the Target Corporation around the world. As a company they have $13 billion in capitalization. You've made your investment decision based on an emotional experience in one of their newest stores on Grand Opening Day. Surely the best day any store will ever have. What do you know about the overall debt load of the company (it's actually quite low)? What about the stock price as it relates to earnings (price to earnings ratio)? What about their management? Are there any sudden shifts in their marketing philosophy? You don't know the answers to any of these questions yet you've made a decision to spend your hard-earned money on their stock, based on an emotion stirred in you by a courteous employee in the Sporting Goods Department.

The issue here is perspective... you don't have any. You've judged the condition of the entire forest based on the wonderful shade provided by one tree on a hot summer's day. I know a guy who was bullish on Enron the day before it collapsed. It seems his brother-in-law worked in the maintenance department and was putting out a buy order to his family and friends based on the fact that a roughneck had brought his truck in for repairs and it had oil all over it; must have been a wildcat well that had just come in. If the people who worked for Enron were clueless as to the problems in management, how do you expect to have insight? It is foolish to try and "pick winners" on a hunch (or your brother-in-laws inside information).

The best approach to investing is through Funds or Fund Families. The Mutual Fund Company was created by a great Christian businessman, Sir John Templeton. We use the prefix "Sir" because he was "Knighted" by the Queen of England for his investment innovation and philanthropic endeavors in 1987; a considerable accomplishment in view of the fact that he was American born and bred. He has long been an Elder in the Presbyterian Church USA, as well as a former trustee of the Princeton Theological Seminary. You may agree or disagree with the intricacies of his theology, but a cursory examination of his biography will cause you to understand that he has revelation knowledge of the art of investing. If you had invested $100,000 in his original Fund Company, Templeton Growth, Ltd., in 1954 when it was started, your investment would have been worth $55 million dollars by 1999.

The key significance of Mr. Templeton's approach which was radically innovative, was he provided, through the "Mutual Fund" company, a way for the small investor to utilize Rule #2—diversification in investing. The philosophy of these fund managers is to "bet sectors" of the overall economy, not individual companies. Our economy has evolved to the point that it rarely experiences downturns across the board. In other words, one sector, say energy, may be in a severe downturn, but cheap energy prices will stimulate rapid expansion in another sector, say manufacturing or travel. The CEO of Exxon may be stocking up on Rolaids, but the CEO of American Airlines will be basking in the sun in Cozumel, Mexico savoring their record profits due to cheap jet fuel. It would take a cataclysmic event to cause the whole US economy to crash across the board today as it did in 1929. The most recent test of this resiliency brought on by overall economic diversification, was of course on September 11, 2001.

While the airlines and travel industries reeled in the aftermath as the emotion of fear kept people off America's airlines, the Security Industry experienced an expansion like had never been seen before. Terrorism virtually created an entire new segment of the economy in the US. The government began investing billions in new security devices and services, and the companies who had the goods prospered beyond their wildest dreams. They couldn't produce enough surveillance cameras and bomb detectors. Their salesmen used to get the cold shoulder when they called on the human resource people at most large corporations, but now they got the royal treatment. Security was on everyone's mind. They had to begin hiring and training new people. They had to order more products and the manufacturing segments had to quit making aircraft parts and start producing security equipment.

One sector of the economy went into a tailspin, while the other went to the Penthouse. This has become the reality of the modern diversified US economy. In spite of the setback in the US, brought on by the events of 9/11, the economy has grown 23.48 % since that terrible day[6]. To help put this figure in perspective for you, the amount of growth in the US economy since September 11, 2001, is larger than the entire aggregate of the Chinese Economy. While China has been hailed as the fastest growing economy in the world (over 10% per year compared to the US last year of 6.7%), their average GDP per person is still low at $14,200, while the US stands at $43,500. Ten percent growth in a $1000 base is not nearly as much as five percent growth in a $100,000 base. Not only is the American economy the largest in the world, it has also become the most diversified. This is bad news for Al Queda. Imagine their frustration to discover that instead of crippling the US economy, they merely energized it into producing a whole new line of goods and services. This diversity has created immense resiliency.

What's responsible for these positive developments in the character and nature of the US economy besides the character and nature of its citizens? The revelation in investing given to a devout businessman from Tennessee named John Templeton. His innovation called the "Mutual Fund Company", provided an investment vehicle for the small investor to diversify. If you have $500 to invest in the market, you'll never be able to buy enough different stocks with it to own several different sectors of the economy. That's just not enough money to buy shares of 100 different companies. But you can buy shares of a Mutual Fund, and the Mutual Fund owns billions of dollars of shares in several segments of the economy. The value of your shares in the mutual fund are calculated at the end of each trading day and reflect the aggregate value of all the shares held by the fund divided by the total number of shares outstanding in the mutual fund (your shares plus everybody else's who owns shares of the fund). The term for this valuation is called Net Asset Value or NAV.

These funds are managed by people who are well paid to study trends and economic data and to determine what sectors of the economy are going to do well. If they buy Target it won't be based on emotion...it will be based on in-depth knowledge of their finan-

---

[6] **Bureau of Analysis—US Dept. of Commerce (GDP: Percent Change Form Preceding Period)**

cial condition. Many of these funds have produced returns in excess of 15% over the last ten years. With a 4% average inflation rate, this means a retirement account with these funds is getting somewhere. If you contributed $250 per month to one of these funds, from ages 20 to the new retirement age of 70, and the overall return was 15%, you would have $22.5 million dollars in your retirement account after a management fee of 1% per year was deducted by the time you retire.

Mutual Funds have opened the equity markets up to the realm of the small investor and have thereby caused billions in new capital to flood onto the balance sheets of America's Corporations, giving them the equity they need to grow and prosper. Just as debt is the enemy's strategy for bondage of God's people, the shared risk and diversification of investing "mutually" or communally, is God's plan for wealth building. He wants us all to prosper, not just those who already have wealth. Get your debts paid, then open a retirement account with any reputable fund. Seek to diversify. Don't just buy stock in the company you work for. It may be a great company but you cannot predict events that might occur that will have a negative effect on your employer or its economic sector. Always employ Rule #2 in your investment strategy.

There are many different types of investments that you can make including real estate, corporate bonds, government bonds, etc. All of these can be made through mutual holding companies which provide diversity to the investor that is essential to security. Even in real estate, diversification is important. For example, if you had large holdings of real estate in New Orleans prior to hurricane Katrina, you're more than likely currently insolvent. In contrast, a person holding real estate in Houston, Texas prior to Katrina has experienced a substantial increase in her net worth post Katrina. Both are real estate investors, and the fortunes of each were dramatically impacted by the same event; one positively…one negatively. Smart investors should hold companies that have investments in several large American cities (known as Real Estate Investment Trust or REIT's), thereby dampening the impact of a cataclysmic event like a hurricane or an earthquake. This can only be accomplished through the "mutual holding" concept. And it doesn't matter if you've got

$500 invested or $500,000, the beneficial effects of diversification work equally well for both investors.

Rule # 3: Never invest borrowed money. The primary cause of the great stock crash of 1929 was a practice called "buying-stock-on-margin." This means that if you could rake together 20% of the stock price, the Banks would loan you the remaining 80%. By "leveraging" their cash they could boost their return on equity. In other words, if you have $5,000 to buy stock with, rather than buy $5,000 worth of stock, a "leveraged investor" would buy $25,000 dollars worth. He would put up $5,000 (20%) and a lender would loan him $20,000 (80%) to make the purchase. Say the share price was $100 per share then the leveraged investor would buy 250 shares, while the un-leveraged investor ($5,000 of his own money and no borrowed money) would only purchase 50 shares of stock.

If the stock were to increase in value by $10 per share within a year, the leveraged investor would have made a total of $2,500 and the un-leveraged would have made $500. Keep in mind they started out with the same amount to invest...$5,000. The leveraged investor has thus earned an "Annualized (based on one year) Return on Equity" of 50% ($2500/$5,000 = 50%). The un-leveraged investor has earned a Return on Equity of 10% ($500/$5000 = 10%). "Why wouldn't you go for the leveraged deal every time", you asked?

Well before we hock the kids and charge into the stock market, we better look at our example in a down-trending market. Say the stock price loses $10 per share. The leveraged investor will have then lost $2,500 and the un-leveraged investor will have lost $500. The Annualized Return on Equity for the leveraged guy would be minus 50% and the un-leveraged guy would be minus 10%. The thing to remember about leveraged investments is this; the numbers look terrific going up, but you can very easily turn those numbers into negatives going down, and no market has ever gone up continuously. All markets have "correction phases" and a leveraged investor can go completely broke in one. The un-leveraged investor, on the other hand, will live to fight another day.

But the true damage to the market occurs when most of its participants are leveraged. This is what happened in 1929. Remember the bank that loaned us the money to buy the stock. There's some fine print in the lending agreement that says we will maintain that 20% margin in the stock we've pledged against the loan. So as the stock heads south, we will enter into a wonderful financial state known as "being on call". In simple language, "being on call" means we've got 12 hours to put additional money in the stock by paying down the outstanding loan balance until the magic 20% margin level has been achieved once again. So using our example above, the value of our stock dropped $10 per share to $90. We own 250 shares, and the bank will not finance more than 80% of the value (now $72). The new loan value of the stock has become $18,000 ($72 X 250 shares). We currently owe $20,000 and now we've got until the end of the day to come up with $2,000 to get the loan back within its "covenants" as they say. Not a big deal…unless of course we don't have the $2,000.

In this case the bank exercises their right (it's in the fine print also) to sell our shares and pay the loan balance down arbitrarily to bring us back within covenant. This act of arbitrarily selling shares has no impact on a market unless it becomes pandemic in nature. Let's say that everyone who "owns" stocks are leveraged investors and the market takes a pretty good correction; perhaps 15% or greater. This means that everyone in the market will become suddenly "on call". There will certainly be many who are unable to "make margin" (cough up the cash to pay their credit lines down to a level of compliance with their lending covenants). Stock holders or their Banks, it makes little difference which the effect is the same, will begin to systematically sell stocks in a desperate attempt to raise cash. Remember, in our "perfect storm" example virtually everyone is "on call" so there are no buyers for the shares being forced onto the market.

What impact to price might we expect from a forced sale of anything in a market where there are no buyers? I believe the appropriate term is "Crash". In 1929, the stock market lost 77% of its value in a matter of months. Oh!…one more thing we forgot to mention concerning our beloved lending agreement; if they can't sell the stock for enough to recover the principle balance of the note along with accrued interest, they'll come after us personally. They get our cars and our mansions and our kitchen sinks. A guy could go from the Penthouse to the Outhouse in less time than it took that ink to dry on that 14 page document we signed to buy this stupid stock in the first place.

To our knowledge, there are few lenders who will loan money to people to buy stock "on margin". This is one of the reasons that I believe that the prospects for another 1929esk "Crash" seem remote. Although stocks seem somewhat overpriced to me at the time of this writing, when held for a long-term (see Rule #1), they should perform well. There will not be forced liquidations during corrections due to the fact that the money in the market is not, by and large, borrowed.

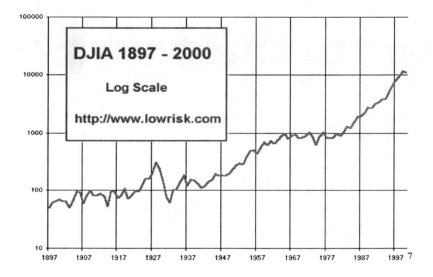

It should be noted as well, that men who had cash available to buy stocks right after the '29 Crash, built fortunes that are still intact today. Families like the Rockefellers, and Kennedys, etc. It should also be noted that there has never been a ten-year period in the history of the Stock Market, where the Dow Jones Industrial Average has not ended higher. This includes any ten year period

---

[7] **This is a logarithmic yearly chart that clearly shows the overall up trend that stocks have maintained throughout their one hundred year history. Notice how profitable the market was to those who invested right after the "Crash".**

even including 1929. So the key to being successful in the Stock Market is holding for a long-term, diversifying your holdings, and never using borrowed money that might lead to you being forced to liquidate your position in the market.

From another practical standpoint, any investment that can return enough to pay interest to a lender and profit for the investor is too speculative. Now there are many fortunes that have been made by borrowing to invest. Perhaps in a small business or a piece of real estate, etc., but as a general rule we're looking only at investments that will yield us between 8 to 15%. These are solid growth investments in either stocks or corporate bonds. They are infinitely safer than either real estate or starting your own business (85% of new small businesses fail within the first five years). This is not to say that we're never going to start our own business, because a large majority of small businesses are owned by Christians and I don't want to discourage anyone from following after the vision that God has given them for their life. But we're talking about our retirement and our security in our old age here. We have to look at the risk realistically and choose accordingly.

I Thought We Were Going To Forsake The World And It's Systems?

In our chapter on debt we explained that the world's credit system is the precursor to the Babylonian System of prophecy, and that God is calling, "*...Come out of her, my people, lest you share in her sins, and lest you receive of her plagues.*" (Revelation 18:4). The world borrows money and lives beyond their means and calls it prosperity. Many of the people who are acting like they're millionaires, merely have a large credit line. They don't have wealth, they have an over abundance of credit. They are acting out a part that comes replete with props, such as expensive automobiles and huge houses, and costumes complete with jewelry. All for which they have gone into hock up to their eyeballs.

Those who are truly wealthy may not have an overt appearance of wealth. They drive a car that is three years old, but they paid cash for it. The actors on the other hand drive a new Mercedes and they're two months behind on the payments. Looks good in the driveway, but look in their mailbox and you'll find past due notices and threats of repossession. Which of these two people is truly wealthy?

The truly wealthy live in a nice house that is comfortable and well kept, but it too is paid for. They have a huge equity in an older home that is increasing in value every year. The actor lives in a huge and opulent home that is financed with an "interest-only-mortgage" (a very loose use of the term "mortgage") that is basically renegotiated every five years. He doesn't own the home, the mortgage company does. Technically they are just letting him live there as long as he keeps the interest paid. It never occurs to them that the value of the house can actually go down. At the time of this writing, many of them currently are doing just that.

These are the deceptions of the world we are turning from. We will, *"...not be conformed to this world, but be transformed by the renewing of (our) minds, that(we) may prove what is that good and acceptable and perfect will of God"* — (**Romans 12:2**). A mind that has been renewed in the Word of God, can <u>prove</u> what the will of God is and is not caught up in appearances. We must never forget that it is God's will for His covenant people to, *"...prosper in all things and be in health, just as your soul prospers"* — (**3 John 2**); to have an abundance for every good work, and to be free financially. Not to live an opulent and materialistic lifestyle.

As we have stated earlier, the world's system of investing and shared risk is actually quite Biblical. Obviously the spirit of greed and fear can overtake these systems, and they must be regulated by people like the SEC in order to prevent abuses, but this is true of anything of the world. It is not perfect, and we must rely on an imperfect government to regulate it. This is a disquieting notion of course, and of little consolation to the holders of Enron and other companies managed in a fraudulent way, but this merely reinforces the importance of Rule # 2 (never put all your eggs in one basket).

In truth we are commanded by the Lord to invest. He spoke in a parable of the time when He would return and demand an accounting from His stewards: *"And so it was that when he returned, having received the kingdom, he then commanded these servants, to <u>whom he had given the money</u>, to be called to him, that he might know* *how much every man had gained by trading"—* (Luke 19:15). So by this parable we can discern that we're going to give an account for our stewardship. And that the Lord wants us to show him what we've *"gained by trading"*. This is a sobering thought for some of us who have made some poor investment decisions. But we need to remember that we have a merciful God who gives us many new chances to become what He has ordained us to become. He's pulling for us, and wants us to be successful. All He requires is that we learn the lessons we need to learn and employ our new-found knowledge to become successful in the future.

Isn't investing in the stockmarket (equities) really risky? This is why we adhere to our investing rules. They are designed to minimize risk. But if the Fortune 500 companies (the 500 largest companies listed on the exchange) all go broke, what will a US Government Bond be worth? Answer: Not Much!! The truth is the real threat to wealth building is not a crash of the markets; it's a monetary condition known as "hyper-inflation." Markets will always rebound from crashes, but high inflation over an extended period of time, will eat away at our wealth building strategy in a more permanent fashion.

The *"inflation rate"* by definition is the measure of the cost of goods and services. It defines the value of money in a literal sense. Since we measure wealth in the terms of dollars and cents, to truly know the measure of wealth we need to understand the effects of the rate of inflation on it. In other words, the money is not important…it is what the money will purchase that's important. For example what $1.00 would buy in 1931, takes $13.24 to buy in 2006. The annual inflation rate in the US from 1929 to 2006 has been 3.25%. Doesn't seem like much except when you consider there have been a few years along the way when the inflation rate was 17+%. If you were invested in an investment like a Treasury Bond that was yielding 4%, your inflation adjusted net-worth was losing 13% per year. If you're in the stock market via your 401-K or IRA taking risk and losing 7% or 8% due to inflation, you're not walking in good stewardship practices. In inflationary times like these, you should park your savings in a money market instrument (CD's, etc.) of some kind. Their rates will be very high, and the risk much lower than stock in a company trying to make a profit in a hostile environment like hyper-inflation; then when inflation moderates, move back into the equities markets.

For retirement planning, we recommend that you use 4.5% as an annual inflation rate estimates. For example, if you're currently making $50,000 per year, and you want to continue in that lifestyle when you retire, first look at your debt and make it your objective to be "debt-free" at retirement age...let's say 70. Remove your current mortgage payments from you needed income for retirement. If you're making $800 per month in mortgage payments now, you can reduce your needed retirement income by this amount which is $9600/year. Be sure and remove the taxes and insurance from your payment amount since you'll still have to pay these after the mortgage is paid off. So $50,000 less $9600 is $40,400 as your target retirement income in today's dollars. In other words, it's what you're making now without the mortgage payments. You also would need to remove your income tax liability from your income estimates since a properly structured retirement plan will be distributed back to you essentially tax-free. But for simplicity sake we'll just deal with the mortgage in our example.

Let's say you're 40 years old currently and are planning for your retirement in 30 years. So we would take the desired income of $40,400 per year and inflate it at 4.5% per annum (annually) over 30 years. To do this calculation we will treat it just like an interest bearing savings account, and compound the 4.5% annually to the principle amount. So at the end of the day we see we will need an annual income in thirty years of $151,000 to equal today's income of $40,400. That's a little sobering isn't it! "Well, I'll have social security to fall back on, you say. Don't count on it. The social security system is broke. In thirty years it may not even exist.

"So how can I accomplish a retirement plan that is viable at all", you ask. By investing and understanding the effects of inflation on your wealth. If your 40 and you start from scratch right now, you can put $500 per month in a Mutual Fund through a Roth IRA (always go with "Roth" type IRA since you're contribution is not tax deductible but your gains and your distributions back to you after retirement are not taxable), by the time you retire at age 70 you will have accumulated $1,500,000 in your retirement account if you have an average yield of 12% (many mutual funds have produced higher returns). At retirement you'll be able to live off the interest your account earns annually and leave the balance to your children whom have hopefully learned stewardship from you and will perpetuate this seed down your family line.

Most importantly we see by our example, it is not possible to "out-run" inflation by putting your savings in a savings account in a Bank that yields 3%. You're losing 1.5% a year. The best plan for your future is to invest mutually in equities or metals or real estate. All these can be accomplished through numerous reputable firms like T.Rowe Price, Vanguard, The American Funds, Fidelity, etc. We recommend that you go to www.morningstar.com and they can give you a breakdown on the track record and administrative cost of all the Mutual Fund Companies. It is a quite useful website for investors on any scale. And remember, one place you can get an immediate 20%+ rate of return on is your credit cards. BY PAYING THEM OFF!! They're charging you 20%+, so by paying them off your earning 20% on your money. You cannot build wealth and service consumer debt, so get started with our debt reduction plan (see appendix).

Remember, your investment strategy should reflect how close you are to retirement. For example, if you have 15 years to your retirement date, keep your portfolio heavily invested in Equity Mutual Funds (stocks). They have the highest return potential, but the highest risk as well. As you get closer to retirement, move more of your account out of stocks and into Bond Funds. Corporate and government bonds present less risk, but the tradeoff is a lower return. The risk is less because a bond holder is "upstream" financially from a stock holder in the same company. For example, if Ford Motor Co.'s troubles continue, they may be forced to take their equity (value of outstanding shares) and pay off their outstanding bonds (short-term promissory notes) since the claim of bondholders supersedes the claim of shareholders. So in this case the bondholder will always get his money before the shareholder since the shareholders are owners of the company but the bondholder is a creditor to the same company. Ford has an obligation to pay its creditors before disbursing anything to its shareholders. This, of course, is an extreme example and is certainly unlikely to happen to a good company like Ford, but you never know.

The better Bond Funds have yielded around 8-10% annualized over the last ten years, while the better Equity Funds have yielded from 14-18% over the same time period. The Bond Fund yields are much more stable with fewer ups and downs, therefore they are more suited to people who are nearing retirement. Both investments should be approached through good Mutual Fund Companies.

Godly Contentment Is Great Gain—

People who are hastening after riches are never content with what they have. I have found that before God will move us higher, we've got to get content where we are. Joyce Meyers says, "Be happy with where you are while you're on the way to where you're going." Don't let your ambition to better yourself and change the financial future of your family tree get the better of you. These are good goals, and we all need to be focused on them, but as soon as God's position in your life falls to number two you're in trouble. It doesn't matter if He's running a close second...second place is never good enough for God. He is a jealous God and a consuming fire and He is more than able to "toast" your financial schemes to get wealth when you've made them number one.

The socio/economic group that wins the top prize for the category of suicide is the people with the most wealth. They commit more suicides that any other group. You see true happiness comes from relationships, not money. When you seek a close relationship with the Lord Jesus Christ, it will lead you to close relationships with the other people in your life. If you get your "self-worth" from your "net-worth", you'll trash all the relationships in your life trying to get the money that you think will give you value as a person and enhance your self-esteem. Unfortunately, what you'll discover after you've made all the money, is that it has no capacity to love you back or make you fell better about yourself. The relationships with the people in your life that you neglected and let wither and die were the source of love in your life. You could have drawn love from them and that would cause you to love yourself and that would greatly enhance your self-esteem.

God knows that success too soon is suicide. The test for Him is to see if we can get content with where we are, while we're on the way to where we're going. *"Now godliness with contentment is great gain"* — (1 Timothy 6:6). It's alright to desire to have a new car but when we're cursing under our breath because we're having to drive the one we've got instead of thanking God for it, He's not likely to bless us with a new one. Ambition to be more and have more is a good thing, but covetousness is a sin. If you feel bad about yourself because your car is four years old and your neighbor is driving a new one then you've got a problem. Furthermore, this problem will stop God from bringing increase into your life until you deal with it. Cicero said, *"To be content with what one has is the greatest and truest of riches."* The Apostle Paul said, *"Be anxious for nothing, but in everything by prayer and supplication, with thanksgiving, let your requests be made known to God;"* (Philippians 4:6).

The heart that God can bless is the one that wants more for themselves and their family, but is thankful for what they have. They don't feel bad about themselves because they're not rich, and they don't covet the success of others. They can truly *"rejoice when a brother rejoices"*.

Colonel Harland Sanders of Kentucky Fried Chicken fame said, *"There's no reason to be the richest man in the cemetery. You can't do any business from there."* People who lust after material wealth spend their health chasing after money…then they spend their money trying to regain their health. It's our pursuit of God and the honing of our stewardship skills and natural giftings that bring us prosperity. Not an "inner vow" that we've made to ourselves that says, "I'll be rich no matter what it takes." Wealth comes naturally to a steward who walks in the blessings of God. Our only motivation for material wealth should be to help build His Kingdom, because if we'll dedicate our lives to building His Kingdom, He will in turn build us up. And we'll know what it really means to *"prosper as our souls prosper."*

John D. Rockefeller was the founder of Standard Oil Co. and the richest man in the world in the early 1900's. He has the historical distinction of being a faithful "tither" and philanthropist as well as the world's first billionaire. When he died, a reporter asked a close associate, "I wonder how much he left behind?"

The associate answered simply, "...all of it." And so will we.

"And He said to them, 'Take heed and beware of covetousness, for one's life does not consist in the abundance of the things he possesses.'" **(Luke 12:15)**

Step Six: Deal With Your Idols (Before God Does)

"We see many who are struggling against adversity who are happy, and more although abounding in wealth, who are wretched." -Tacitus

"Professing to be wise, they became fools, and changed the glory of the incorruptible God into an image made like corruptible man—and birds and four-footed animals and creeping things." (Romans 1:22-23)

"And God spoke all these words, saying: "I am the Lord your God, who brought you out of the land of Egypt, out of the house of bondage. "You shall have no other gods before Me. "You shall not make for yourself a carved image—any likeness of anything that is in heaven above, or that is in the earth beneath, or that is in the water under the earth;" (Exodus 20:1-4)

"but the Lord, who brought you up from the land of Egypt with great power and an outstretched arm, Him you shall fear, Him you shall worship, and to Him you shall offer sacrifice." (2 Kings 17:36)

"Therefore, my beloved, flee from idolatry." (1 Corinthians 10:14)

"Set priorities for your goals. A major part of successful living lies in the ability to put first things first. Indeed, the reason most major goals are not achieved is that we spend our time doing second things first."—Robert J. McKain

God's Word is very clear on the issue of financial prosperity. If you're in covenant with Him, you shall have it, and He shall be the source of it. Period. No exceptions:

"That I may cause those who love me to inherit wealth, That I may fill their treasuries." (Proverbs 8:21)

"...Let the Lord be magnified, Who has pleasure in the prosperity of His servant." (Psalm 35:27)

"And you shall remember the Lord your God, for it is He who gives you power to get wealth, that He may establish His covenant which He swore to your fathers, as it is this day." (Deuteronomy 8:18)

The covenant He *"swore to your fathers"* was the Abrahamic Covenant. The fifth dispensation of God to man (we will have more on this in the next chapter). It is foundational to the other covenants or dispensations. God is a covenant maker and a covenant keeper. In the words of the Psalmist:

"... For You have magnified Your Word above all Your name." (Psalm 138:2)

God cares more about honoring His Word than He does about His own reputation. He doesn't care who it offends, He is going to do what He said He would do. The premise of this book is not that God will not bless you financially, but that He is waiting for you to make the necessary changes in your life so that He can move your blessing from a state of trusteeship (Galatians 4:1) to full manifestation. God's Word, which He esteems even more than His name, clearly calls for financial blessing upon His people.

And yet God finds Himself in a particularly sticky dilemma in His relationship with man and His promises to him. This dilemma I'm sure did not catch Him by surprise since He acknowledges that, *"The heart (of man) is deceitful above all things, And desperately wicked; Who can know it? I, the Lord, search the heart, I test the mind, Even to give every man according to his ways, According to the fruit of his doings."* (Jeremiah 17:9-10). God surely was not stunned by the darkness within men. He knows the capacity of evil of the heart, and yet He has given His Word that He would prosper those who *"diligently seek Him"*. The dilemma lies not in the blessing of His children whom He loves, but in the fact that due to their rebellious condition, the very blessing He has made covenant with them to provide is the thing that will compete for their affection. In other words, what He has bound Himself to give them through His Word, is the exact thing that, in many cases, will draw them away from Him.

Did He make a mistake? Is God fallible? These are deep theological questions which I cannot answer. But a cursory examination of the history of His covenant people leads one to conclude that God has a problem when it comes to financial blessing. The more God's people have prospered, the more their possessions have captured their hearts and have in fact become their idols. Thomas Carlyle said, *"Adversity is sometimes hard upon a man; but for one man who can stand prosperity there are a hundred that will stand adversity."* Truer words were never spoken. In my experience in ministry I have found that nothing destroys the Spiritual Life the way prosperity does. Prosperity turns our hearts to the self-nature, and away from a dependence on the Spirit of God.

As Moses led the children of Israel to the Promised Land after spending forty years living in the wilderness, I believe he had a vision in the middle of the night. In this vision he saw the future of Israel and he was horrified. What he saw did not line up with what he had dedicated his life to. What he saw in the vision was not the devotion and reverential fear he had taught the people to maintain towards God. What he saw was a people who had become enchanted with the wealth of the Promised Land and who had forgotten the source of the provision. Moses had delivered God's people from the spiritual and financial bondage of slavery, into the prosperity and blessing of the covenant. He is about to end his ministry and be *"gathered to his fathers"*, as the Old Testament puts it so eloquently. The Book of Deuteronomy is his last impassioned plea with the children of Israel who had fought so hard in the wilderness to get there, not to allow the impending wealth of the Promised Land to ruin them spiritually. The eighth Chapter of Deuteronomy is known as the great prosperity chapter. I see it as the great prophetic warning chapter. In it Moses said,

"For the Lord your God is bringing you into a good land, a land of brooks of water, of fountains and springs, that flow out of valleys and hills; a land of wheat and barley, of vines and fig trees and pomegranates, a land of olive oil and honey; a land in which you will eat bread without scarcity, in which you will lack nothing; a land whose stones are iron and out of whose hills you can dig copper." *(Deuteronomy 8:7-9)*

Then towards the end of the chapter he goes on to give a warning to those who were about to be blessed:

"Then it shall be, if you by any means forget the Lord your God, and follow other gods, and serve them and worship them, I testify against you this day that you shall surely perish." *(Deuteronomy 8:19)*

I feel compelled to deliver the same warning today that Moses delivered on the high plains of Moab overlooking Jericho some 3500 years ago. It was good advice then, it's great advice now. Do not let the prosperity you're about to enter into become your idol.

God has "jealousy" issues—

A complicating factor for us in God's great dilemma is His personality. Yes…that's right, even God has some "quirks". It seems He's jealous...and He even admits to it!

> *"You shall have no other gods before Me. "You shall not make for yourself a carved image—any likeness of anything that is in heaven above, or that is in the earth beneath, or that is in the water under the earth; you shall not bow down to them nor serve them. For I, the Lord your God, am a jealous God…" (Exodus 20:3-5)*

God will not compete with your business for the number one spot in your heart. He will not compete with your bass boat or your mountain cabin or anything else for that matter. Furthermore, He has warned you of His jealous nature toward you and you best heed the warning.

In the Old Testament there was a prophet named Balaam. He lived in the Mesopotamian region in a town called Pethor. He was it seems, a *"soothsayer"* and magician and had obviously become known for his prophetic acumen. In addition, he seemed to have a rather bizarre relationship with the Lord, in that while he is a non-Israelite he still calls on the Name of the Lord and the Lord apparently responds. When the nation of Israel began to approach the region of Moab in the beginning days of the Canaanite military campaign, Balak the King of Moab was sufficiently alarmed to summon the Prophet Balaam. He sent the Elders of Midian to him who offered him the customary diviner's fee, in exchange for his cursing the approaching armies of Israel. Amazingly, he inquired of the Lord to seek His permission. Perhaps Balaam was not "in the loop" as they say concerning the restoration of Covenant lands to the descendants of Israel that was in the process of being accomplished. Surely if he had had a sense of the epic magnitude of the event he was being called upon to curse, he would have never been foolish enough to think that God would allow him to curse it.

Nevertheless, inquire of the Lord he did. The response was predictable. He was forbidden to go. The Elders of Midian returned to the King and reported their failure to enlist the aid of the sooth-sayer. Balak sends princes who were *"more numerous and honorable"* than the previous ones. This time they offered whatever Balaam wanted. Again this corrupt man of inexplicable spiritual ability goes to the Lord and inquires again. This time, amazingly, God relents and instructs him to go with them with one admonition;

"And God came to Balaam at night and said to him, "If the men come to call you, rise and go with them; but only the Word which I speak to you—that you shall do." (Numbers 22:20)

We can all predict where this is headed. God intends to use the mouth of Balaam to release prophetic blessing on the very people that King Balak of Moab wants to curse; namely the Israelites. Balaam better not spend the money yet.

So in verse 21:

"So Balaam rose in the morning, saddled his donkey, and went with the princes of Moab."

God's response to Balaam's willingness to go under His authorization with the princes of Moab tells us much about God's personality in verse 22.

"Then God's anger was aroused because he went, and the Angel of the Lord took His stand in the way as an adversary against him…" (Numbers 22:22)

He became angry at Balaam for doing the very thing that He had given Him permission to do. To understand this somewhat illogical response, we have to refer back to Exodus 20:4, *"I am a jealous God"*. If you are a happily married man who has asked his wife if you can go fishing with your buddies rather than attend her sister's birthday party, and she has amazingly said "yes"…perhaps you can relate to Balaam. Because when you did the very thing that she gave you permission to do, she became very upset. What's that about?!! It's about love and devotion that goes beyond mere obedience. God surely had a desire to have a sustained relationship with this man Balaam, yet Balaam kept making bad choices. Much in the same way you decided to run to the lake not noticing your wife looking through the window with disappointment in her heart as you disappear down the road. You've just communicated to her that a large-mouth bass is more important than she is.

Obedience to the commandments of God is the most basic level of devotion. Pursuing His heart is what got David the throne of Israel. David went beyond obedience into the realm of devoted pursuit. God noticed and He told Samuel the prophet to tell the rebellious King Saul, "... *The Lord has sought for Himself a man after His own heart, and the Lord has commanded him to be commander over His people, because you have not kept what the Lord commanded you*" (1 Samuel 13:14). David was a fourteen year old shepherd boy who had learned to pursue God through praise while he watched over his sheep in the fields. He was not a warrior at the age of fourteen. He was a kid. He didn't earn his way onto the throne of Israel with his sword or his sling shot. He did it with his harp. David made a discovery as a young boy in the sheep folds. God was drawn to praise. So he sought the presence of God through his praise and worship. David was not merely obedient to God. He was *"after His...heart"*. His devotion went past obedience into pursuit.

Balaam was not after God, he was after what God could do for him. If God helped him fulfill this big contract with the King of Moab, he would be very grateful I'm sure. Perhaps Balaam would say, "Thanks for your help. I couldn't have done it without you. Maybe we'll hook up together and do it again some time. See you the next time I need a big score, but for now I've got a little vacation planned." And this would be the last time God would see or hear from him until the money was gone.

David didn't care about the money. He cared about God and His presence in his life. David received an eternal covenant. Balaam, on the other hand, was slain by the army he tried to curse for money (Joshua 13:22) as they advanced into the territory of Moab in the early days of the Canaanite campaign. One pursued God for what He could do for him, the other pursued Him because he loved Him. The Lord can tell the difference.

Moses has another take on the personality of God that we ought to heed as well. He describes Him this way, "*...the Lord your God is a consuming fire, a jealous God*" (Deuteronomy 4:24). The combination of jealousy and being a consuming fire does not bode well for the thing that is competing for our devotion. This combination can be lethal for your business if you have begun to worship it. People in covenant with God need to realize that God will destroy whatever you have exalted over Him. Maybe you're believing God for the restoration of your marriage. My best advice to you would be to keep your spouse off of the pedestal if you want God's help. It's true God *"hates divorce"*, but your best strategy is to pursue Him first. Then He will move on the heart of your spouse and intervene on your behalf for healing of the relationship. If you want your husband back, begin to offer the sacrifice of praise unto the Lord and He will draw him back to you.

God has an unnerving habit of vaporizing His competition. He will give you permission to do many things that He would prefer that you didn't. He will test the heart to know what is in it and the financial blessings that He pours into your life is part of the test. Are you going to worship Him, or are you going to make the blessing into the image of something else.

The Golden Calf

When Moses led the people of God out of Egypt, they didn't leave empty-handed. In fact the scripture says

> *"And the Lord had given the people favor in the sight of the Egyptians, so that they granted them what they requested. Thus they plundered the Egyptians." (Exodus 12:36)*

After the first born of the Egyptians had perished in the Passover, the people of Egypt were more than glad to give the Israelites everything they asked for just to get rid of them. They literally *"plun-*

dered" their oppressors. I believe that a time is at hand when the people of God will literally plunder their oppressors once more. So as they looked back to see the pursuing Egyptian Army drowning in the Red Sea, they shouted no doubt—but they also feared. They trembled at the awesome power of Jehovah their God.

"Thus Israel saw the great work which the Lord had done in Egypt; so the people feared the Lord, and believed the Lord and His servant Moses." (Exodus 14:31)

They had never seen anything like it and they would never doubt God or Moses again. At least that's what they said. In fact no generation has ever seen the manifest power of God like Moses generation. When Moses is confused and discouraged after making his initial entreaty to Pharaoh on the behalf of the Israelites, He asks God why it didn't work. Not only did Pharaoh refuse to release the people, but he added to their work load. Their condition was not better but had actually deteriorated. Moses was serious when he asked, "...*Lord, why have You brought trouble on this people? Why is it You have sent me? For since I came to Pharaoh to speak in Your name, he has done evil to this people; neither have You delivered Your people at all.*" (Exodus 5:22-23). God's response was interesting and if were not careful we'll miss its significance:

"I appeared to Abraham, to Isaac, and to Jacob, as God Almighty, but by My name Lord I was not known to them." (Exodus 6:3)

He was about to reveal to Moses a new Name. Now a name in the Old Testament was more than a means of identification. It was a description of who you are; a one word description of your character, and your destiny in God. For example Jacob (means "Trickster") was named prophetically at birth to describe the defining moment of the first part of his life; the tricking of his older brother Esau into trading his inheritance for a bowl of beans then subsequently tricking his father into conveying that inheritance to him thinking he was his older brother. You know the story. Jacob flees the rage of his brother who has vowed to kill him. He escapes to the lands of his uncle Laban, where he eventually marries his two daughters and has twelve sons. Then after suffering from similar misrepresentation by the hand of his uncle Laban, he elects to leave after some fourteen years had passed. He takes his two wives, twelve sons, thousands of sheep, and various livestock he has accumulated because of the blessing and he endeavors to return to the lands of his fathers. The night before his fearful reunion with Esau, the brother he swindled, he has an encounter with God where he holds tightly to Him and begs Him to bless him. God blesses him and then He changes his name to Israel ("Prince of God"). This new name reflects a new destiny and prophecys the place that Jacob will rise to in the Kingdom of God; the position of a Prince. Such is the role of a name in the Old Testament. It defines your character and your destiny.

Moses was about to see a new Name of God that no one else had ever seen. To Abraham, Isaac, and Jacob, He had been known as "El Shaddai", or God Almighty. They had known Him through the Word (spoken rather than written since they had no Bibles). But Moses was about to know God as Jehovah (the powerful covenant-making God), and he would see the manifest power of the Spirit of God. Abraham knew God through the word, Moses knew Him through the Word and the Spirit. Abraham had "heard" the Word of God, and had been obedient to the Word; so much so that it was *"accounted to him as righteousness"* (Genesis 15:6). The spoken Word of God was Abraham's basis of revelation of God.

Moses, on the other hand, would get a new revelation of the Name of God. Moses would hear the Word, speak the Word; then the Spirit of God would bear witness to the Word. Moses would usher in the dispensation known as the "Law and the Prophets". This was a new aspect of God and His relationship with man. God's Word is written and the Spirit of God bears witness to it wherever it is proclaimed by the prophet. He bears witness through manifest power by the Spirit. Moses spoke and there were frogs everywhere. Again he spoke and the water turned to blood. Again he spoke and the first-born of Egypt died. You get the idea. This generation would see the power of God bearing witness to the word of the Prophet.

The previous generations had known only the Word; not the power coupled with the Word.

And yet just some fifty days after witnessing God's power and provision at the Red Sea and the plundering of the Egyptians, the people melted down the provision (gold and silver), and made for themselves an idol in the image of a golden calf. Now cattle and livestock were their measurement of wealth. They had no currency system. Although gold and silver were of universal value, sheep and goats were a much more convenient medium of barter and exchange. If you had been able to apply for a credit card back then, the application would ask not how much money you had but how many sheep and cattle you owned. So the people made an image of the medium through which God's provision came; namely a calf. They began to worship the provision instead of the provider. Down through the generations, God's people have been doing the same thing. Paul said of the people of his era:

"Professing to be wise, they became fools, and changed the glory of the incorruptible God into an image made like corruptible man—and birds and four-footed animals and creeping things." (Romans 1:22-23)

The Greek word that is interpreted as "incorruptible" is: [*aphthartos* /af·thar·tos/], which means "imperishable". Men have been exchanging the "imperishable" glory of God for the "perishable" image of something else ever since the incident of the golden calf in the wilderness during the Exodus. Modern Christians tend to think of the golden calf incident as the irrational act of a primitive and uneducated people who were obviously a bunch of fools. "How could they turn from the God who had just delivered them from the bondage of Egypt and start worshipping the image of a stupid calf?", they say. Yet there are many images that modern man has exalted over the image of God. *"Professing to be wise, they have become fools."* I saw an interview of a prominent oil tycoon on a business news channel. He had a huge scale model of an offshore drilling platform on the credenza behind his desk. After watching a little of the interview it was obvious that his golden calf took the image of a drilling rig. God would get no credit for the financial blessing in his life. He had begun to worship the medium through which the provision was channeled rather than the source of the provision. I've seen idols made in the image of footballs, baseballs, music instruments, bank buildings, stock exchanges, the Capitol Building, and the White House. I've even seen idols made in the image of the created things like spotted owls, Redwood trees, and mountain streams. And believe it or not I've seen idols made in the image of Churches.

Modern idolatry is every bit as prevalent as it was during the age of the Exodus. It has just taken on a more sophisticated and subtle form, but idol worship it is to be sure. Paul the Apostle had good advice for those tempted to engage in idolatry. *"Therefore, my beloved, flee from idolatry"* (1 Corinthians 10:14). Just as standing too close to a missile target in a war zone is not conducive to long life, worshipping an idol is not helpful to your financial future.

Remember God judges a sinner but, He chastens a son.

"You should know in your heart that as a man chastens his son, so the Lord your God chastens you." (Deuteronomy 8:5)

"Chasten" is not an everyday word so its meaning needs to be investigated. It means to "subject somebody to discipline". In other words, the lost can worship their idols but the consequences will not manifest until the Day of Judgment. But those of the covenant will be chastened (subjected to discipline) in this life time. The jealous God of the Exodus will consume whatever needs consuming to protect His relationship with His people. Jeremiah asked, *"Why do the ways of the wicked prosper?"* God's response was that they would only prosper for a season. Eventually their deeds would catch up to them. But to those who are of the covenant, God will not wait until eternity knocks upon their door to deal with the idols which they have set up. Paul's suggestion…run from them as fast as you can.

A Life Well-Lived is a Life Lived with Purpose:

Every "success coach" in the history of the science of success, will tell you that the secret to achievement is goal setting. A life that is unfocused cannot accomplish much. So we are encouraged to set goals and accomplish them, and I certainly agree with the value of living a life of purpose and focus. But the truth is, we usually set goals that are very selfish in nature. In fact we have a tendency to measure goals in the terms of "things"; to have a nice car or a house or a business or something else that is shinny and new. There is absolutely nothing wrong with having "things". But in ministry I've had the opportunity to minister to several wealthy men on their death bed. As death draws near, a man will begin to make inventory of his life. To date, I've not had a single one list the banks, or real estate property, or businesses they've owned in these poignant moments of reflection. In fact to a man, they all talk about their families, their friends, their fishing trips with their grandchildren. These great men who have achieved so much by the world's standards, in effect, count it all rubbish in their last days and universally regret that they didn't spend more time with their families. If these accomplished men, masters of the art of achievement, could speak to the masses of humanity from the edge of eternity, they would not disparage the value of setting goals and living a focused life. They would, however, counsel us to be extremely careful in choosing our goals and priorities in life.

Helen Keller said, "Many persons have a wrong idea of what constitutes true happiness. It is not attained through self-gratification, but through fidelity to a worthy purpose." FIDELITY TO A WORTHY PURPOSE. She says this is the path to happiness and fulfillment. Not stuff. Everyone wants to be happy. This is the universal pursuit of man-kind. And yet very few of us are. America is the most prosperous nation on earth and yet we're the leading consumer of anti-depressants. We virtually created an industry to produce mood enhancing drugs. Having stuff has not made us happy. Only being true to "worthy purpose" can make us happy.

Jesus had an observation or two on this subject. His definition of success is service.

"But Jesus called them to Himself and said, "You know that the rulers of the Gentiles lord it over (people), and those who are great exercise authority over them. Yet it shall not be so among you; but whoever desires to become great among you, let him be your servant." (Matthew 20:25-26)

Jesus said that the one who will be exalted in the Kingdom of God will be the one who chooses to serve others. There is another byproduct of service besides rank and esteem in the Kingdom of Heaven, and that is happiness. When we serve others in obedience to the teachings of Christ, we find true happiness and purpose. Isn't that amazing! A life well lived is a life that has been true to "worthy purpose" and the most worthy purpose that we can devote ourselves to is service to others; not self-gratification.

The most miserable people on the planet are people who have climbed their ladder of success all the way to the top, only to discover that it was leaning against the wrong wall. These are goal-driven people who are stunned when they find they've spent their life in pursuit of "things", and in the process squandered their relationships. You cannot have a relationship with "things". You can love them, but they cannot love you back. The only thing that can bring you a sense of real joy and accomplishment in life are the close relationships that you've built. And these relationships are built through love and service. Nothing else.

Successful people invest wisely. Jesus said, *"For where your treasure is, there your heart will be also"* — (Matthew 6:21). In other words, wherever you're investing is where you're heart will be turned. Successful people also understand that you measure you're commitment to an investment in two ways...time and money. Not idle words. *"Therefore the Lord said: "Inasmuch as these people draw near with their mouths And honor Me with their lips, But have removed their hearts far from Me... "*(Isaiah 29:13). So your heart is going to be wherever you're investing your time and you're money. If your marriage has gone south, it's because you've not been investing in it. Not because you married the wrong person. You have to invest in a marriage to get any return on it and the more you invest the more your heart will turn toward it. Your loved ones spell love "t-i-m-e". God spells love "t-i-m-e". How much time are you spending with Him and them?

Successful people not only invest wisely, they put first things first. Robert J. McKain said, "Set priorities for your goals. A major part of successful living lies in the ability to put first things first. Indeed, the reason most major goals are not achieved is that we spend our time doing second things first." Goals must be born out of "worthy purpose" and not selfish gratification if their achievement and pursuit are to bring us happiness. In addition, they must also be prioritized. A great structure like a skyscraper can only be built after a sure foundation has been laid. You wouldn't do the landscaping before you've poured the foundation, even though the landscaping is an important part of the overall project. So a successful life must also be one of priorities. God teaches us that He is to be the number one priority; then our family and then our career. A shrewd investor invests in the foundational things first; then she moves on to the other parts of her plan. God has to be the foundation on which our lives are built if we're to *"prosper just as our soul prospers"* 3 John 2.

Relationships bring true happiness…nothing else can. And all relationships begin with our relationship with Jesus Christ. *"Now all things are of God, who has reconciled us to Himself through Jesus Christ, and has given us the ministry of reconciliation,"* (2 Corinthians 5:18). Through Christ, our relationship with God has been restored, and when our relationship has been restored with God…we've become restored to *"all things"*. Earlier we talked about how God created everything we will ever need then He rested (Genesis 2:1). In Hebrews Chapter 4, His Word makes it clear that He has invited us to enter *"His rest"*. When we've become reconciled to God, we've become reconciled to our provision. It's here; all around us. We appropriate it by faith in His Son. If we're not careful, we will spend our lives chasing after something that has already been provided, and in the process destroy the relationships in life that were intended to bring us joy and happiness. We destroy them through neglect and misguided goals.

But when we make Jesus number one, then everything else works. *"But seek first the kingdom of God and His righteousness, and all these things shall be added to you"* (Matthew 6:33). In fact, Jesus will become the foundation that bears all our relationships. *"But if we walk in the light as He is in the light, we have fellowship with one another..."* (1 John 1:7). Fellowship with Him facilitates fellowship with everyone else. He becomes the mediator of all our relationships. When we have a problem in an important relationship, if we'll take it to Him in prayer, He will restore it and just as importantly guide us to its restoration. The key is to stay out of the flesh, and walk by the leading of the Holy Spirit. This process of "Spirit-led" guidance to success in all relationships can only be accomplished through an intimate relationship with Christ. This will only happen when we have chosen to make Him our top priority. The key to prosperity is Christ. The key to peace is Christ. The key to a successful marriage is Christ. The key to deliverance is Christ. The key to happiness and joy is Christ. Seek Him first, and all things will come to Him who waits. *"For evildoers shall be cut off; But those who wait on the Lord, They shall inherit the earth"* (Psalm 37:9).

In summary, misplaced priorities and lack of focus are the number one cause of failure in life. The great business consultant Peter Drucker says, "Doing everything right is the definition of *efficiency*, but doing the right things is the definition of *effectiveness*." This principle of living effectively and with purpose applies to everything we do, and Job #1 is to worship Him. When we bow a knee to idols, we are killing God's plan for our lives...including His plans to prosper us.

After the Assyrian king Shalmaneser over ran Israel in the days of king Hoshea and took all of God's people captive back to Assyria. He then ordered the territory to be repopulated with an ethnic mixture of people from many regions. These people who reoccupied the covenant lands of Israel were know as Samaritans (named after the region of Samaria they occupied) and the Book of 2 Kings makes an interesting observation about them. The Lord apparently sent much travail against them because they brought the idols of their previous cultural with them into His covenant land. Their afflictions were sufficient to cause the conquering Assyrian king to inquire of the captured Jewish priests as to the problem causing these maladies.

They advised the king that the worship of their idols in the covenant lands of the Lord of Israel were the cause of their woes. He promptly dispatched a priest to teach them the proper way to worship.

The results of the efforts of these priests to teach and inform these people as to the dangers of idol worship, were mixed at best. The scripture says, *"They feared the Lord, yet served their own gods—according to the rituals of the nations from among whom they were carried away."* (2 Kings 17:33). So in the immortal words of Dr. Phil, "How did that work for them?" The answer; not very well. The Samaritans were placed of the most fertile part of the covenant lands of Israel, and yet they rank as barely a footnote to history. Their greatest historical legacy remains an honorable mention in the parable of the "good Samaritan" that was taught by Jesus in the New Testament. In it He used a Samaritan as an example of caring for others to show the religious Pharisees of His day that even a "back-slidden-idol-worshipping" Samaritan who would help someone, could fulfill God's purposes of serving others. Their feeble spiritual state served as a hyperbolic contrast to drive home the point that religion never helped anyone; actions from a heart of love is what is hurting people need. But the truth is, the Samaritans never amounted to much because they would not lay down their idols even though they "feared the Lord".

We too can fear God and still worship idols if we're not careful. As God begins to deliver us from the oppression of the world's financial system we need to hear the instructions of the Prophet:

> "but the Lord, who brought you up from the land of Egypt with great power and an outstretched arm, Him you shall fear, Him you shall worship, and to Him you shall offer sacrifice." (2 Kings 17:36)

Step Seven: Understanding The Essence Of Stewardship

"Lots of folks confuse bad management with destiny."
Unknown

"Command those who are rich in this present age not to be haughty, nor to trust in uncertain riches but in the living God, who gives us richly all things to enjoy."
(1 Timothy 6:17)

"Management by objectives works if you first think through your objectives. Ninety percent of the time you haven't." **Peter Drucker (1909 - 2005)**

"Destiny is no matter of chance. It is a matter of choice: It is not a thing to be waited for, it is a thing to be achieved." **William Jennings Bryan**

"Management is doing things right; leadership is doing the right things."
Peter Drucker (1909 - 2005)

"Moreover it is required in stewards that one be found faithful." **(1 Corinthians 4:2)**

**"What we do in life echoes in eternity." Maximus from
the movie *Gladiator***

*"And cast the unprofitable servant into the outer dark-
ness. There will be weeping and gnashing of teeth.'"*
(Matthew 25:30, NKJV)

John Nelson Darby was an Anglo-Irish evangelist who lived from
1800-1882. He was a devout man. In 1825 he became a Deacon of
the Church of Ireland, then an ordained priest in the following year.
In 1827 Mr. Darby fell from a horse and broke his leg. He chose to
"redeem the time" of his recuperation by giving himself to the study
of the scriptures. As happens many times when we have nothing to
compete for our time or attention, he received a new level of understanding from his study of the Word of God. What Darby discovered was a pattern of revelation he came to call "Dispensations".
Ephesians 1:10 says, *"having made known to us the mystery of His
will, according to His good pleasure which He purposed in Himself,
that in the dispensation of the fullness of the times He might gather
together in one all things in Christ, both which are in heaven and
which are on earth—in Him."*

The word dispensation is defined in the American Heritage
Dictionary as: *(a) the divine ordering of worldly affairs (b) a religious system or code of commands considered to have been divinely
revealed or appointed.* These "dispensations" can be viewed as
"phases of revelation". God's relationship with man would evolve
around a series of seven of these "phases" over time. Furthermore,
it appears that God has a very precise plan in these revelations that
revolves around a preordained time table, which will culminate in
the gathering of all things back to Him…in Christ; similar to the way
a landlord lets a tenant manage and live off of an estate, then returns
to reclaim His legal right of ownership at some future date. In other
words, God has a plan to reorder and reestablish His dominion of the
earth. And the plan is built around these seven preordained revelations (dispensations) of Himself to the men and women He created
who inhabit it.

Five of these Dispensations included the establishment of a Covenant with man. With the exception of the first covenant with Adam, they were actually modifications of a preexisting Covenant. A Covenant is an agreement between two parties that spells out their relationship and what each party is to do for the other in order to maintain the relationship. God is by nature a covenant maker and a covenant keeper. Since God makes His covenants from a dimension that is timeless (eternity), His covenant agreements are not subject to the effects of time. They never expire—they are eternal in nature. Man's record is not as illustrious however. He has broken every one he has ever made. His track record was so abysmal that God had to become man to make an everlasting Covenant with man. In Jesus Christ He came as the *Son of Man*, since there was no man with which He could depend, to make Covenant on the behalf of man. Christ was our *"kinsman redeemer"*, and the Cornerstone of the "New Covenant" under which we currently live. So it is helpful to think of these Dispensations as new Covenants or agreements between man and God.

It's also interesting to note that the Greek word interpreted as "dispensation" in Ephesians 1:10 is *"oikonomia"*. This word is interpreted "dispensation" four times in the New Testament, but three times it is interpreted as "stewardship", and literally means the oversight or management of another's property. What does a "divine ordering of world affairs" and their subsequent revelation to mankind have to do with "stewardship" you asked? We will endeavor to explain. The Holy Spirit chose to use the word *"oikonomia"* instead of *"apocalypse"* (which means revelation) intentionally in Ephesians 1:10. The principle He was trying to illustrate through this passage was that with new revelation comes more responsibility. There are seven dispensations of God scheduled for seven specific times in man's history that require seven ever increasing levels of stewardship.

Furthermore, these dispensations that John Darby identified in scripture, do not preclude one another, but instead expand on and build on each other. Just as when you construct a building, there is a prescribed order in the construction process. Remember, you do not do the landscaping before you have even poured the foundation.

God has used each of these "phases of revelation" as a foundation for the next phase. The Dispensation of the Age of Grace (in which we currently live) did not eliminate the preceding Age of the Law and the Prophets (God's covenant with Moses); it built on the Law as its foundation. In other words, if you didn't have the Law you wouldn't know that you needed grace. Jesus said in Matthew 5:17-18, *"Do not think that I came to destroy the Law or the Prophets. I did not come to destroy but to fulfill. For assuredly, I say to you, till heaven and earth pass away, one jot or one tittle will by no means pass from the law till all is fulfilled."* Even though He had come to usher in the next dispensation called the *"Age of Grace"* (salvation through faith in Him), He is careful to emphasize that it will not abolish the previous one; it will expand on it by providing a remedy for the Law of God since by now man had proven that he could not live within His boundaries. That remedy is the Atoning Blood of the perfect sacrifice from the veins of the *"Son of Man"* our *"Kinsman Redeemer"*.

The theological implications of all of this are deep and profound and outside of the scope of this book. Suffice it to say that one need not break a leg and spend your recuperative time seeking these revelations since Brother Darby has already accomplished this for us. When the Word of God is studied from the perspective of these evolving "dispensations" it makes all of it make more sense. Also remember that with revelation comes responsibility (James 4:17). The seven levels of revelation bring ever increasing levels of responsibility of stewardship.

The Seven Dispensations of Man:

The Dispensation of Innocence (Genesis 1:1-3:7). Adam and Eve were innocent in their original state. They had no "self-awareness" and were led purely by their spiritual nature. Man's relationship with God was innocent and uncontaminated by the forces of sin and evil. Stewardship responsibilities: Be led by the Spirit and do not rely on human reasoning which is of the flesh-nature. (Note: After Adam ate of the tree of knowledge, his spiritual nature died and he nor his descendants could be "Spirit-led" thereafter. This "spiritual-nature" was not restored to man until the first Pentecost after the Resurrection of Christ.) Adam was to populate the earth and exercise dominion over it.

The Dispensation of Conscience (Genesis 3:8-8:22). Adam to Noah. Man has become self aware and his conscience is allowed to develop and determine his behavior. He is no longer led by his spiritual nature which died in the Garden. Stewardship responsibility: Do what is right and understand that man has an innate understanding of what is right and wrong.

The Dispensation of Human Government (Genesis 9-11). Noah to Abraham. Man is given authority to exercise capital punishment and to govern himself using his developed conscience. Stewardship responsibility: Do what was right and establish self-government that was based on "good conscience", and to repopulate the earth and exercise dominion over it.

The Dispensation of the Promise (Genesis 12:1-Exodus 12:36). Abraham to Moses. God promises to bless the people of a specific genealogical bloodline; more specifically the descendants of Abraham and his progeny through his son Isaac, commonly referred to as the Jews. He also promises to bless those who bless them, and to curse those who curse them. These blessings are predominantly financial. Stewardship responsibility: Do what was right and establish self-government that is based on "good-conscience". To fruitfully populate the earth and exercise dominion over it, and to believe in His Promise and thereby see prosperity manifest in your life. Righteousness is defined by faith in the Word of God... not works. The scripture says, *"just as Abraham believed God, and it was accounted to him for righteousness."* (Galatians 3:6)

The Dispensation of the Law and the Prophets (Exodus 12:37-Matthew 3). Moses to Jesus Christ. Justification before God is determined by our ability to keep His commandments. Moses is given the Law on Mount Sinai, and God speaks to His people through His prophets. Stewardship responsibilities: Do what is right, govern out of "good conscience", populate and be fruitful in the Promised Land, walk in financial blessing as an heir to the Promise, keep God's Law and His commandments which included certain stewardship practices concerning the Land itself. (Leviticus 25).

231

The Dispensation of the Age of Grace or the Church Age (Matthew 3:1-Revelation 19:21). Jesus Christ's first-advent to Jesus Christ's second-advent. Justification before God and entry into the Promise is based on faith in Christ and not works of righteousness. By now man has figured out that without the Spirit to lead him, he has no ability to be righteous and to keep the Laws of God. The work of the Cross of Christ that marks the beginning of this age is two-fold. The Blood of Christ meets God's absolute standards of justice and provides a remedy for the sins to all who believe. The Cross itself produces a transforming work where the flesh-nature is severely pruned, thus allowing the "spiritual-nature" to become dominant in the Believer's life. As the Believer begins to mature and to enter into the condition of spiritual-dominance, otherwise known as being "spirit-led", the spiritual-nature enables him to keep the commandments of God. Thus a Believer in Jesus Christ has come full circle, and the spiritual nature of man that was lost in the Garden of Eden has become fully restored through the Cross of Christ.

Stewardship responsibilities: Be led by the Spirit, which will in turn cause you to do right, govern in "good-conscience", reproduce other "spirit-filled" Believer's, walk in the Promise of God's blessing since the scripture clearly says, *"And if you are Christ's, then you are Abraham's seed, and heirs according to the promise"* (Galatians 3:29), and keep God's Law and Commandments.

The Dispensation of Divine Government or the Millennial Reign of Christ (Revelation 20:1-15). Christ returns to take full dominion over the earth. Evil is dealt with and the devil is placed in chains. Christ lives on the earth and His followers reign and rule with Him. Stewardship Responsibilities: Authority is given to the Believer based solely on his or her record of stewardship and faithfulness. All rewards are based on the works of the Believer in the previous dispensation. "Salvation is a free gift to the sinner, but for the Believer, rewards come only by works"—*Watchman Nee*

As we understand more of the nature of God and our relationship with Him, the more we realize that all we have and all we do is not really ours…it is His, and He intends to *"gather together in one all things in Christ"*. Intelligent analysis of these "dispensations" can lead us to only one conclusion: every thing that has been created belongs to Him, and He's coming back for it. It has merely been loaned to us as a source of provision for a season. Furthermore, our place in the final Dispensation is determined by how well we took care of these things in this one. Remember we're not talking about salvation…we're talking about rewards in the eternal realm— as in *forever!!* It is a sobering thought for me to realize that not only is my salvation dependant on the choices that I make in this life, but my eternal rewards are dependant exclusively on the works that I do for Him— in this life.

The Parable That Nobody Wants to Remember—

In Matthew chapter 24 the Disciples asked Jesus a pointed question. "When are you coming back and what will be the sign of your coming?" The rest of the Chapter is known as the Olivet Discourse and is devoted to an explanation of the "Signs of His Coming". Let it be duly noted that according to his own prophetic description of these signs, His Second Coming is very close. Chapter Twenty-four is speaking to the Pre- Millennial period or the last days of the church Age. Chapter Twenty-five occurs immediately after the end of the Great Tribulation and at the very beginning of the final dispensation—the Millennial Reign of Christ. He has dealt with His enemies and is in the process of establishing His government here on the earth. According to scripture, Jesus will at this time judge the brethren based on their works done in His name:

> *"Therefore we make it our aim, whether present or absent, to be well pleasing to Him. For we must all appear before the judgment seat of Christ, that each one may receive the things done in the body, according to what he has done, whether good or bad."* (2 Corinthians 5:9-10)

God establishes His government on earth and resides in His capital city of Jerusalem; the same city in which He was crucified. The first order of business in the installation of the government of Christ will be the assignment of positions in His Kingdom based on our performance in the previous Dispensation. One of the primary judgment criteria is explained in verses 14-30:

"For the kingdom of heaven is like a man traveling to a far country, who called his own servants and delivered his goods to them. And to one he gave five talents, to another two, and to another one, to each according to his own ability; and immediately he went on a journey. Then he who had received the five talents went and traded with them, and made another five talents. And likewise he who had received two gained two more also. But he who had received one went and dug in the ground, and hid his lord's money. After a long time the lord of those servants came and settled accounts with them. "So he who had received five talents came and brought five other talents, saying, 'Lord, you delivered to me five talents; look, I have gained five more talents besides them.' His lord said to him, 'Well done, good and faithful servant; you were faithful over a few things, I will make you ruler over many things. Enter into the joy of your lord.' He also who had received two talents came and said, 'Lord, you delivered to me two talents; look, I have gained two more talents besides them.' His lord said to him, 'Well done, good and faithful servant; you have been faithful over a few things, I will make you ruler over many things. Enter into the joy of your lord.' "Then he who had received the one talent came and said, 'Lord, I knew you to be a hard man, reaping where you have not sown, and gathering where you have not scattered seed. And I was afraid, and went and hid your talent in the ground. Look, there you have what is yours.' "But his lord answered and said to him, 'You wicked and lazy servant, you knew that I reap where I have not sown, and gather where I have not scattered seed. So you ought to have deposited my money with the bankers, and at my coming I would have received back my own with interest. So take the talent from him, and give it to him who has ten talents. 'For to everyone who has, more will be given, and he will have abundance; but from him who does not have, even what he has will be taken away.

And cast the unprofitable servant into the outer darkness. There will be weeping and gnashing of teeth.'" (Matthew 25:14-30)

A *"talent"* is an ancient measure of weight that was around 66 pounds. Five talents of gold would be worth $4,750,000 in today's dollars at $900 per ounce. Two talents would be $1,900,000, and one talent would be the equivalent of $950,000. So we can see that even the *"one-talent"* steward had quite a lot to start with. It should be clearly understood that this parable is not about singing talent or playing professional sports or other ability. It is about money and investing, and it clearly states that we will be judged by how we've handled our money. Not as an issue of heaven or hell, but as an issue of where in the Kingdom of Heaven we're ranked and what eternal rewards we enjoy as a result of our stewardship.

There are several important facets of this teaching that are vital to understanding the essence of stewardship.

No. 1: God gives to each according to their ability!!

Verse fifteen clearly states the amount of ***money*** that God gives every Believer is determined by one and only one factor—their ability to steward it. This is a widely understood practice in the economy of the world. You're not given the Chief Executive position of a major corporation until you've proven that you can run one of the divisions within the Corporation. Even though God's economy and the world's economy are direct opposites in most respects, in the area of tested stewardship ability they are identical (Galatians 4:1-2). For a Believer to purchase a lottery ticket is a fruitless enterprise, since God's economic principles clearly state that if you could steward a million dollars— He would have already given it to you.

The key therefore to financial increase is not luck (a concept that does not exist in the Kingdom of God), nor is it the act of giving exclusively; but is in the increase of our stewardship abilities. For example, a Kingdom steward must demonstrate that she is unwilling to allow the world and it's systems to steal from God's provision through exorbitant interest payment on "stuff" that was not necessary to the mission that she had been called to in the first place. She may have needed the new couch, but more than likely she wanted it. Wants are usually of the flesh and this is the domain of the devil. If he can create enough desire he can coax someone into paying 30% interest to get it now, and thereby steal their financial seed. This is not the character of a "Five-Talent" steward who has demonstrated discipline over her flesh nature.

She must also demonstrate that she has not confused abundance of credit with prosperity. God loves to give good gifts to His children (Matthew 7:11), but God does not spell His name *GMAC*. There are exceptions of course, but for the most part, if you had to finance it—it's not a blessing but a curse. I've known ministers who have bought new cars, and when I would congratulate them on their purchase they would respond, *"God really blessed me because I couldn't have bought it if GMAC hadn't given me seven years to pay it out!!"* God didn't bless him— GMAC did and they're going to want to take their blessing back if he misses two consecutive payments, which is likely since he couldn't even save any money for a down-payment. If he couldn't save money without a car payment, he certainly isn't going to *with* one.

I'm not implying that GMAC is inherently evil. I'm merely trying to point out that the best interest of the borrower is not their concern. Moving vehicles and collecting interest is their concern and this is as it should be. For the Believer, however, there is no one as concerned for their welfare as the one who died for them on the Cross. He has earned the right to instruct them in financial matters or any issue of the heart for that matter, and He has proven by His sacrifice that He loves and cares for them. GMAC or Ford Motor Credit or any other financial institution gets paid to care for their shareholders and no one else. The "Five-Talent" steward understands the reality of the world's financial systems and the dangers of debt.

No. 2: The amount we gain is not important to God. It's the faithfulness of the steward that He judges!!

After a *"long time"*, Jesus comes to settle accounts with the stewards. The Five-Talent steward shows Him he has gained five more for a 100 percent increase on what he was entrusted with. The Lord then replies, *"Well done good and faithful servant; you were faithful over a few things, I will make you ruler over many things. Enter into the joy of the Lord."* Then He checks on the "Two-Talent" steward. He also has doubled his investment and has gained two more talents. One steward has gained five talents and the other one has gained only two. Yet Jesus' response to both was identical. *"Well done good and faithful servant; you were faithful over a few things, I will make you ruler over many things. Enter into the joy of the Lord."* It seems that Jesus was not concerned with the dollar amounts; only with faithfulness. Even though one steward gained three talents more than the other their reward was identical. He chose to make them both *"rulers over much"*.

So God would rather give you what you can handle and see you earn rewards in heaven than give you more than you can handle and see you suffer loss in heaven due to poor stewardship. God uses gold for paving material in heaven. It has little value there. He understands it has great value in the world however. How we use it and the nature of our relationship with it will provide God with a great deal of information concerning the condition of our heart. This is the essential issue as far as God is concerned. It was their faithfulness. Their ability was only important to him as a quantifying factor that determined what they were given to start on. Moral: We can give and we can pray, but the key to the equation of having more is moving up from a "One-talent" steward to a "Five-Talent" steward.

*No.3: In God's economic system, He is the one who brings the increase. The primary quality that defines the "Five-Talent" steward is **faithfulness and an ability to follow His leading**..*

If the steward will merely do what God has instructed him to do, God will bring increase to the investment. We should not be overly worried about economic data, but we should be worried about the diligence we have employed in our pursuit of Him. Are we praying and staying in His Word? We need knowledge alright, but the knowledge we need is His knowledge, not man's wisdom which is highly unreliable! Will Rogers said, *"The only thing absolutely certain about an economist is that they are always wrong!"* Although the science of economics has certainly made advances as all the natural sciences have, it is still inexact at best and is no match for the knowledge that comes from God.

How do we get this knowledge from God? By the Spirit! *"For what man knows the things of a man except the spirit of the man which is in him? Even so no one knows the things of God except the Spirit of God. Now we have received, not the spirit of the world, but the Spirit who is from God, that we might know the things that have been freely given to us by God. These things we also speak, not in words which man's wisdom teaches but which the Holy Spirit teaches, comparing spiritual things with spiritual. But the natural man does not receive the things of the Spirit of God, for they are foolishness to him; nor can he know them, because they are spiritually discerned. But he who is spiritual judges all things, yet he himself is rightly judged by no one. For "who has known the mind of the Lord that he may instruct Him?" But we have the mind of Christ."* (1 Corinthians 2:11-16).

God's system of communication is spirit to Spirit. Believers will have had an experience with the Spirit of God that He referred to as being "born again" (John 3:3-8). In this instant God places His Spirit inside a receptive heart and from that day forward communication between the Spirit of God and the spirit of the person receiving, begins to develop. The level of this development is entirely contingent upon the condition of the receiving heart. By the Spirit the Word is implanted and the amount of fruitfulness can range from none to *"some 30, 60, or 100-fold"* (Matthew 13: 8). Some hearts allow the devil to pluck up the seed before it can take root. Some allow the deceitfulness of riches and the cares of the natural-life choke out the Word. Others receive the word with gladness and they worship and serve Him as long as it is *"cool"* as it were, but the moment that persecution comes because of the Word (and it surely shall) they fall away because they have no *"root in themselves"* and they dry up spiritually. None of these three categories of hearts that have had the spiritual rebirth experience will develop an ability to really hear the voice of God from deep within themselves. They never become truly "spiritual" in their nature.

Jesus made a rash statement that must be taken seriously by anyone who wishes to become a true disciple. He said, *"If anyone comes to Me and does not hate his father and mother, wife and children, brothers and sisters, yes, and his own life also, he cannot be My disciple"* (Luke 14:26). He was not encouraging people to hate their parents. What He was saying was that if you did not value your relationship with Him above everything of the "natural-world", you have little chance of bearing fruit *"some 30, 60 and 100-fold"*. If you do not crucify the natural life, the spiritual life will never become dominant (Luke 14:27). So if you came to Christ in the search for riches and gold, you're barking up the wrong tree, as they say. But by His own words, if you came to Him because you realized that the natural-life was worthless compared to the *"excellence of the knowledge of Christ"* (Philippians 3:8), then you may very well be given riches to steward for Him before all is said and done. The key to financial fruitfulness is spiritual development.

The Spiritual-man (one who has developed his Spiritual nature and become a true apprentice to Jesus Christ), judges all things correctly (1 Corinthians 2;16). How you ask? By the Spirit. The Spirit of God reveals all things to him and bears witness to the truth (John 16:13). The trick is to stay in a condition spiritually where we are hearing from God clearly. He will guide us and direct us and by the Spirit we will acquire intuitive knowledge. Spiritual knowledge is intuitive in nature. Intuitive knowledge is knowledge without understanding or more precisely, with the absence of reasoning. You don't know how you know—you just know. We know by the Spirit according to 1 Corinthians 2:11. That is to say that our knowledge does not come to us by way of our reasoning ability (which is of the realm of the flesh-nature), but it comes via the Spirit of God. A true disciple or apprentice to Jesus Christ has been given an ability to know intuitively what to do in any situation through spiritual revelation that can only come by the Spirit of God.

Each of these stewards was given according to *"their ability"*. What ability was that? It was their ability to be disciplined and to hear the voice of God. The "Five-Talent" and the "Two-Talent" stewards had a much closer relationship with Christ than the "One-Talent" steward. We know this by the "One-Talent" steward's allegation that the Lord was *"...a hard man, reaping where (He had) not sown, and gathering where (He had) not scattered seed."* He obviously was a Believer since the Lord would not have dispersed seed to a Non-Believer. The problem was he was not a *true* disciple of Christ. If he had been, he would have known that the Lord never harvests where He has not sown—He is in fact the quintessential sower since He had to sow His own Son for our freedom and deliverance from death. So we have a hint in this parable that a key difference between the "Five-Talent" and the "One-Talent" steward lies in their level of discipleship—not necessarily in their training and education in the field of Business Administration. One certainly does not preclude the other, but business acumen without spiritual maturity is not a prescription for blessing in the Age to come. A faithful heart is one that has disavowed the natural-life and the materialism that it represents, to the point of being willing to choose a relationship with Jesus Christ over that of say, a "worldy" parent.

No.4: To him who has— more will be given

The "One-Talent" steward buried his talent rather than lose it. The consequence of his action was that he was sternly rebuked by the Lord for his lack of faith, and his talent was taken from him and given to the one who had ten talents, then he was cast into the outer-darkness.. This seems harsh on the initial reading. After all, wasn't this an example of taking from the poor and giving to the rich?! How could this man be held accountable when he was just trying to refrain from losing what was not his? It was the Lord's and he was afraid of having to answer for losing it. Wasn't this somewhat sensible? Was the Lord just having a bad day? Is He that unstable emotionally?

When we view these actions from the Lord's perspective, perhaps we begin to understand His response a little better. The Lord is the one who brings the increase—not us. What releases this increase in a steward's life is his faithfulness. Therefore if the "One-Talent" steward had prayerfully invested the talent, the Lord would have made it profitable. Instead he was ruled by fear instead of faith, and he squandered an opportunity for the Lord to multiply the seed. It was never an issue of the "One-talent" steward's ability—it was an issue of his faith. Furthermore, he could have had the same reward as the "Five-Talent" steward if he had only sown what he had been given.

The Lord referred to him as a lazy and unprofitable steward. Lazy because he was unwilling to invest effort in the pursuit of financial gain; it's the hands of the diligent that are blessed. Unprofitable because an opportunity for increase was missed because he would not try; this is the greatest sin in the area of stewardship. The sin that the Lord admonished was not that he tried and failed, but that he failed to try. If he had trusted the Lord and followed His leading, he would have been profitable. It's apparent from this passage that God is going to insist that His people be *profitable*! And there are no excuses for failure whenever the Lord is in control, and He will not accept any excuses for a lack of effort. He's more than willing to accept the responsibility for bringing the increase, but He cannot increase what has never been sown. He will simply take what an unprofitable servant has and give it to one who is profitable.

The Day of Reckoning is at Hand

The King James Version of Matthew 25: 19 says, *"After a long time the lord of those servants cometh, and reckoneth with them."* Then the Believer will stand before the *Bema Seat of Christ* and give an account for their works. The Word says that Christ is the foundation and that *"... if anyone builds on this foundation with gold, silver, precious stones, wood, hay, straw, each one's work will become clear; for the Day will declare it, because it will be revealed by fire; and the fire will test each one's work, of what sort it is. If anyone's work which he has built on it endures, he will receive a reward. If anyone's work is burned, he will suffer loss; but he himself will be saved, yet so as through fire."* (1 Corinthians 3:12-15). Again, the great Apostle to the nation of China, Watchmen Nee said, "Salvation is a free gift to the sinner, but for the Believer rewards can only come by works." At the Day of Reckoning Christ will insist on an accounting of what He has given us to steward. Our rewards in heaven will be determined by our stewardship.

Luke's version of the parable of the stewards says, *"So he called ten of his servants, delivered to them ten minas, and said to them,*

'Do business till I come.'" (Luke 19:13). Then in verse 15, *"And so it was that when he returned, having received the kingdom, he then commanded these servants, to whom he had given the money, to be called to him, that he might know how much every man had "gained by trading."* It's obvious that God has always intended for His people to be engaged in commerce — not consumerism. God's people should be business leaders and owners. They have been ordained by the Word of God to succeed in the commercial realm. The key to success of a Believer in the financial arena depends on their understanding the six principles of Biblical stewardship.

Six Principles of Stewardship:

Rule #1: A Good Steward Never Forgets Whose It Is.

The English word "steward" comes from the 12th century England and refers to a manager who was given the responsibility of caring for vast portions of the Kingdom of the ruling monarchs. The steward had abilities perhaps in the area of farming or livestock management that made them particularly effective in the care of the estates which belonged to their lord. They lived on the estates of course and they basically treated them as their own. They made all the decisions concerning what crops would be planted — what types and quantities of livestock would be pastured. They lived in the estate mansion and they had servants who helped care for and manage the households. They might go several years between visits from the lord of the estate. When he came to inspect the estate, they would give an account for their management and settle the accounts of the king. These men not only possessed extraordinary ability as managers, but also strength of character which warranted this extreme level of trust from the king.

The basic factor that kept these managers in good stead with the kings they served was that they never forgot who really owned the estate. They used the estate like it was their own, but they never got what was theirs and what was the lord's confused. The scriptures say, *"Moreover it is required in stewards that one be found faithful."* (1 Corinthians 4:2). Ability was certainly a factor, but the overwhelming character traits that were crucial to being selected for the position of steward, was faithfulness and honesty. The King did not want to return to find that the steward had consumed the estate on extravagant living. He expected to find that the wealth of the estate had increased due to the diligence and skillful management of the steward. This was essential to the holding onto the position. It is essential to staying in good stead with our Lord. Remember, it doesn't belong to us—it's His.

Rule #2: A Good Steward Can Never Be Ruled by a Spirit of Fear

World renown management expert Peter Drucker said, "Management is doing things right; leadership is doing the right things." When we're right with the Lord of the estate, we have no reason to be anxious about the outcome of our management. If we're allowing Him to lead us and guide us, we're going to be successful. If we stay close to Him and listen for His voice, we will "do right things", and by definition we will be leaders in business or in any field of endeavor we've been given stewardship responsibility in. As we've said, there are great difficulties ahead for the world's economy, and yet the Kingdom Steward will prosper in the chaos. How? By being led by the Spirit. It's God's will that we *"prosper just as our soul prospers"* (3 John 2). The Spiritual-man *"judges rightly"* (1 Corinthians 2:15), because he is led by the Spirit of God which leads him into all truth. Even truth about economic trends and problems.

The root of the "One-Talent" steward's error was that he allowed fear to keep him for investing his talent and he buried it instead. Because he didn't have an intimate relationship with the Lord, he didn't understand the principle of multiplication (see Rule #3). Good stewards do not spend time worrying about markets—they let the Lord do that. They just make sure that they don't consume what is His and they *"cast their bread upon the waters"*. *"There is no fear in love; but perfect love casts out fear, because fear involves torment. But he who fears has not been made perfect in love."* (1 John 4:18). There is no fear in those who have been perfected in His love. He loves us and He has plans for us to be successful as His stewards. He's not trying to trip us up. He's trying to lift us up— on wings as eagles. We know He has not given us a spirit of fear (2 Tim. 1:7). We have nothing to fear. If we know and trust Him, He will bring the increase. There is only one failure that we should be afraid of and that is the failure to try!

Rule #3: Good stewards operate their business and their lives on the Law of Reciprocity and/or Multiplication.

The root of our scriptural claim to prosperity is the fifth Dispensation called the Abrahamic Covenant or *"Promise"*. You will remember that even though we're currently living under the Sixth Dispensation or Covenant, the Dispensations don't nullify the each other, but instead they build on each other. Each one is a modification or an improvement of the previous one. In the Abrahamic Covenant God's promise to the children of Abraham is, "… *I will make My covenant between Me and you, and will multiply you exceedingly*" (Genesis 17:2). The descendants of Abraham that were partakers of this Covenant were by the seed of his son Isaac. Isaac was the product of a supernatural miracle that allowed Abraham's wife Sarah to become pregnant at the ripe old age of ninety. No covenant of God can be fulfilled by a natural act. They are all established through a super-natural event— such as a supernatural pregnancy of a barren woman.

As any student of the Bible knows, Abraham had two sons. After God tells him he will be the father of an entire nation and that this nation will walk in financial blessing, he and his barren wife Sarah decide to take matters into their own hands. They have no children and are in their eighties. Then, through her own reasoning, Sarah decides that if Abraham is to have an heir as promised, they will have to act quickly. After all, Abraham is eighty-six and she was barren. He may not be able to father a child if they wait much longer. So in her haste, she decides that her husband needs to father an heir by her own handmaiden Hagar. It was a bad plan, because when the product of this union, Ishmael, is 13 years old the Lord instructs Abraham that he is not his heir and that the heir will be produced by his wife Sarah. Sarah becomes pregnant at the age of ninety and has another son named Isaac. Ishmael is sent out of the camp with his mother Hagar due to the intense jealousy that ensues between his mother and her master (who would have guessed), and thus grows up to become an angry rejected young man who becomes the progenitor of the Arab race. The Lord promises to bless Ishmael and his descendants for Abraham's sake, but emphasizes that Isaac will be the *"seed of the promise"*. Jacob, whose name was later changed by the Lord to Israel, was the blessed son of Isaac and further progenitor of the *"Promise"*.

Furthermore, as we stated earlier, the work of the Cross of Christ did more than save us from eternal judgment—it grafted us into the Covenant of Abraham. *"And if you are Christ's, then you are Abraham's seed, and heirs according to the promise"* (Galatians 3:29). "What does this mean exactly?" you asked. It means that if you're in Christ He has grafted you into an eternal covenant that was made with Abraham and his descendants, and that the key word of this covenant is "multiplication". If you're in Christ then God wants to multiply you in every aspect of your life. Through your children, your influence, and your finances.

Jesus further expounded on the Principle of Multiplication in Luke 6:38 when He said, *"Give, and it will be given to you: good measure, pressed down, shaken together, and running over will be put into your bosom. For with the same measure that you use, it will be measured back to you"* (Luke 6:38). When we sow in the Spiritual realm, God increases what was sown and gives it back to us. Smart stewards understand that they must sow in the natural as well as the Spiritual. In other words, when we sow in the natural through an investment, if we will also sow a Spiritual seed we invoke the supernatural principles of increase or multiplication. Too many of us are sowing in the Spiritual only. We give to the Kingdom of God through tithes and offerings, but we do not sow a seed in the natural that God can increase. He cannot increase an investment you never made, or a book you never wrote, or a business you never started.

Good stewards understand that the increase doesn't come overnight. *"While the earth remains, Seedtime and harvest... Shall not cease."* (Genesis 8:22). We must sow then wait patiently for our harvest. While we're waiting we stand on the word of God for our increase. Faith will always be a requirement to unlock the keys to

God's Kingdom. Patience is a virtue of a perfected faith (James 1:3).

Good stewards understand that the amount of increase is determined by the condition of the soil into which the seed is planted. For example, if you're investing in a company that has a hidden agenda to persecute Jewish people, you're never going to harvest increase from such an investment (remember they are the vine of blessing into which Christians are grafted—Romans 11). But if you're investing in a company that is helping God's covenant people and providing employment opportunity for them—the increase will always come (Genesis 12:3). The ability of the steward comes in her discernment of the type of soil she is sowing into. Either way, she knows that she has to sow into both the natural and the spiritual to unlock God's potential for increase.

Rule #4: Good stewards are free from the bondages of debt.

A good steward never confuses debt with prosperity. At the time of this writing the US economy is being inundated with bad news about emerging default rates in the so called "sub-prime sector" of the home mortgage market. Just as there is more of the iceberg under the water than what is visible above the water, this problem runs much deeper than just the "sub-prime sector". As outlined earlier, we have become a nation that has become too tolerant of the dangers of debt. The world economy is about to be shaken by the ramifications of this cavalier attitude on the part of American consumers. As we stated earlier, the expansion of the world's economy has largely been based on the insanity of American consumers, who have taken on debt at a terrifying rate in order to satisfy their insatiable appetite for "stuff".

Those who have been filled with the Spirit of Truth understand that it is God's plan in the last days to transfer the wealth of the wicked into the hands of the righteous (Proverbs 13:22). Practically speaking how is this transfer to take place? I believe that God's plan is for His people to *"judge rightly"* concerning the dangers of credit, and to become delivered from the bondage of debt through a disciplined lifestyle that does not thrive on consumption. With His supernatural help, they are delivered from the bondages of the world's

Babylonian System, after they repent of living like the world. The result is they have cash to spend and as the world has to cough-up assets to try and unleverage itself, God's people will be in a place to buy cheap. The subsequent profits that are derived from these fire-sale purchases will fund a huge campaign to bring people to the knowledge of Jesus Christ through international evangelism that will have by then become extremely well funded.

The key to good stewardship is to stay away from all consumer debt. If you can't pay for it—**_DON'T BUY IT!!_**. This is the fundamental mindset of a good steward. They may use credit moderately to finance business inventories or income properties where the property produces enough revenue to make the mortgage payments, etc., but they refuse to borrow money to consume. They live on what the Lord provides and ask Him to help them become better stewards so as to increase what they are given.

Never think that you can stand on the covenant of Abraham and not repent of the bondage to debt and expect to be blessed. Jesus said, *"Therefore bear fruits worthy of repentance, and do not begin to say to yourselves, 'We have Abraham as our father.' For I say to you that God is able to raise up children to Abraham from these stones."* (Luke 3:8). These warnings were to the religious leaders of His day and they echo through eternity. Jesus warned them that it would be futile to stand on the Abrahamic Covenant if they did not repent and bear fruits of their repentance as well. It had to be more than lip service. He had to be able to see by their actions that they meant it. The same is true for Christians today who have brought bondage on themselves through debt. Repent and bear the fruits of repentance—and then your claim to the covenant will be valid. Cutting up your credit cards would be a good *"fruit of repentance"*. You get the idea. Deliverance begins with you. Good stewards are free from the encumbrances of excessive debt and they live a modest and simple lifestyle of service and dedication to Christ. And if they are truly *"good"* stewards, they manage great amounts of wealth.

Rule #5: Good stewards are not in love with the opposing Kingdom.

The problem, I'm told, with many very effective undercover narcotics agents, is that they become so good at what they do they forget who they really are. They become taken in by the very world that they have come to defeat. This seems to be a similar problem for the Christian businessman. They become so good at what they do and so successful at the world's system that they often forget who and what they are. The scripture warns us to, "*love not the world or the things in the world. If anyone loves the world, the love of the Father is not in him.*" (1 John 2:15). It further warns us that to fall for the world is a fatal mistake because, "*...the world is passing away, and the lust of it; but he who does the will of God abides forever.*" (1 John 2:17). The world and its systems have already been judged, and if we become entangled in it we will suffer like judgment.

Good stewards are committed to a life of service and simplicity. They have seen the damage the "soulish" pursuit of pleasure can incur. They know that true happiness can only come from within—never from our circumstances or from earthly pleasures. They know that the happiest people are usually the people that are fully engaged in struggle. That life is not a destination, but a journey. And that true satisfaction is derived from helping others along its path, not accumulating wealth. Bill Gates remarked publically that his wealth was his biggest encumbrance. He loved the development of technology and witnessing its impact on people's lives. His wealth was the biproduct of this pursuit, not the object of it. And since he had become famous for his money, it had stifled the freedom he felt when he was a young entrepreneur who could come and go as he pleased and make mistakes without criticism (failure being an essential part of success). The things of the world bring with them bondage, therefore good stewards are in the world, but not of the world. They love the Kingdom of God—not the world.

Rule #6: Good stewards understand how to impact eternity

Good stewards have a close relationship with Christ, and therefore understand that our *"works"* cannot produce salvation, but do dictate our rewards in heaven. I had a very successful business partner who used to say, "Always think long-term. Never fall into the trap of short-term thinking." It's a good business philosophy and as is so often the case, it's a good spiritual philosophy as well. Jesus warned us to, "*...lay up for yourselves treasures in heaven, where neither moth nor rust destroys and where thieves do not break in and steal.*" (Matthew 6:20). How do we do that exactly? One good way is by modeling Biblical stewardship. Remember He gave rewards to the stewards in accordance with their faithfulness. The ones who had been faithful doubled what they had been given, because they had relied on the Principles of Multiplication and trusted the Lord for the increase.

At the Day of Reckoning, the Lord said to them, "*Well done, good and faithful servant; you were faithful over a few things, I will make you ruler over many things. Enter into the joy of your lord.*" These stewards had used earthly opportunity and taken the ultimate "long-term view". They had converted them into eternal rewards through faithfulness. In the movie *Gladiator* the main character Maximus makes a statement that every believer in Jesus Christ should live by. He said, "*What we do in life echoes in eternity.*" Everything we do in this life, dictates our position in the eternal realm, not the least of these things is the way we handle our money. Good stewards see business and investing as a responsibility, but also as an opportunity to lay up treasure in heaven.

Summary:

The problem for the deceived person is that he doesn't know he is deceived. Therefore it takes a major shaking in his life to cause him to see the truth about himself and his situation. He cannot become free until he acknowledges he is in bondage. The children of Israel were in bondage to Pharaoh for 430 years. God finally came to Moses in a burning bush and commissioned him to bring them out of their slavery. He declared, "*...I have surely seen the oppression of My people who are in Egypt, and have heard their cry because of their taskmasters, for I know their sorrows.*" (Exodus 3:7). The question we asked earlier was simply, "What took Him so long?" They had been in oppression and bondage for 430 years, and the

Lord confessed that He had heard their cry. Why listen to it for over 400 years before you respond? The answer is, I believe, that it took that long for His people to finally admit they were slaves.

Things had actually gone quite well for the Israelites when they first came to Egypt. One of their own, their brother Joseph, was in charge. The land was in the beginning, a place in which they could prosper and flourish, and so they did. Then eventually there arose a Pharaoh who *"knew not Joseph";* a Pharaoh who did not understand the relationship of God's people to the world's system of commerce symbolized by Egypt. The moral values of God and His covenant people had become unfamiliar to the leadership of the world's system. They did not share their values, or for that matter even care what they were. They simply did not understand the history of the system that had brought prosperity to them and saved their nation from famine in the beginning. They had prospered through the labor of the people of God.

The people of God had hoped it would get better. Perhaps new leadership would improve their lot. Perhaps if they produced more the world system would recognize their efforts and reward them with favor. They hoped from generation to generation until finally hope was displaced with despair. They came to grips with the reality that it was not going to get any better. They had to deal with the unequivocal truth that they were in bondage. Then and only then did they cry out to their God. This time when they quit looking to the very system that had entrapped them for deliverance, and they called on the Name of the Lord— then He heard from heaven and He began to intervene.

My prayer is that you have come to this same revelation. God is calling His people to separate themselves from the world and its systems. Not commerce all together. We're called as the people of God to *"do business until He returns"* (Luke 19:13), but we're called to do it His way. If you've come to the same realization that the children of Israel did in Egypt thousands of years ago, and decided that you're in financial bondage I say, good for you! The first step in deliverance is the acknowledgment of bondage. Have the courage to break ties with Egypt and step into the wilderness. Renounce credit. Refuse to live on it any longer. I know the wilderness may look formidable, but just follow the *"cloud by day and the pillar of fire by night"*. Let the Lord lead you on this journey to financial freedom and deliverance. *"Destiny is no matter of chance. It is a matter of choice: It is not a thing to be waited for, it is a thing to be achieved"* — William Jennings Bryan.

Your destiny in Jesus Christ is freedom. Spiritual, physical, and financial freedom. When we begin to bear the fruits of repentance and turn from the bondage of debt and the pursuit of materialism, God hears our cry and sends us a deliverer. Jesus taught that when He ascended to go to the Father, the Kingdom of God would come among us—to the earth and it would coexist for an undetermined period with the kingdom of the world. After all the prophetic events have been fulfilled, it would overtake the world's kingdom and become fully manifest on the earth. One of these significant prophetic events would be the development of a world system the prophets refer to as *Babylon*. I believe that the components of this *Babylonian* System are in place and I pray that all God's people come out of it so that they do not partake of her plagues (Revelation 18:4) and find deliverance and financial healing in God's Kingdom among us. What we do with money and our relationship to it has eternal significance for us.

Turn from Egypt I pray and pursue God's land of promise where abundance flows—without bondage. Remember the words of Moses to God's people on the banks of the Red Sea.

"...Do not be afraid. Stand still, and see the salvation of the Lord, which He will accomplish for you today. For the Egyptians whom you see today, you shall see again no more forever. The Lord will fight for you, and you shall hold your peace." (Exodus 14:13-14)

Let the Journey begin. Amen!

Epilogue:

Since I began to write this Book last year, many of the financial issues we forecast have come to pass. Americans have finally exhausted their credit limit, and home foreclosures are currently occurring at record levels. The financial institutions that endorsed sloppy loan underwriting requirements "(better known as "sub-prime" mortgages) are having huge liquidity problems as they move to get "nonperforming" assets off of their balance sheets. Citigroup, which is one of the largest financial institutions in the world, has turned to the Sheiks of Dubai for additional capital. They have obliged them with several billion "oil dollars" (they currently take in 300 million of them a day), with which they have bought stock in their bank and become its largest share-holder. This by the way is prophetic. Watch out because Babylon here we come. The rise of a world financial system that is vehemently against Christians (of the spirit of the Anti-Christ) is at hand.

There are other similar stories throughout the financial sector of the American economy. Suffice it to say that their collective impact on the economy of the world is becoming very damaging. We have witnessed a run on investment banker Bearn Stearns that was reminiscent of the 1930's when Banks collapsed right and left. In this case there was one lender who had not been damaged by loose lending practices; namely JP Morgan Chase & Co. They were able to join forces with the Federal Reserve Bank and save some semblance of the original company although the stockholders who watched their stock value go from $100+ to $10 per share might beg to disagree. What happened to Bearn Stearns was a classic case of panic. People became afraid that the institution would not survive therefore they decided to get their money out. The result was a run on the bank that caused its collapse. This whole episode should serve to show how tenuous the current financial climate is. We have built a huge house on shifting sand and it would appear that it is about to come crashing down.

Americans have financed the growth of the world's economy with their voracious appetite to consume, and now the bill has come due. It appears they cannot pay it. Economically the nation has entered into a condition the Bible calls a *"famine"*. Biblically speaking a famine is a natural condition that occurs when there is not enough provision. The Patriarchs of the Old Testament were in the livestock business and livestock eat grass. When there is no rain there is no grass and the source of their provision literally and figuratively dries up. Many of you feel like the source of your provision has dried up due to the adverse economic climate that you currently find yourself in.

In Genesis we've learned that our great benefactor and conduit of all financial provision to His people is Abraham. God basically "calls him out" when He says to him on Haran. "…"*Get out of your country, From your family And from your father's house, To a land that I will show you. I will make you a great nation; I will bless you And make your name great; And you shall be a blessing—*" (Genesis 12:1-2, NKJV). Abraham is obedient to the word of God (a characteristic for which he would become well-known), and he heads off to Canaan to a country which he has never seen. When he gets there God says, "This is it." He looks around, thanks God by building an altar to Him and giving Him an offering. Then immediately he has to move on to Egypt because the land is in a drought so bad that there is not enough grass to feed his sheep.

Wait a minute! If I had traveled all that way, left a perfectly good home and a successful business back home, and gone totally on faith to a place I'd never heard of before that was supposed to be my inheritance, only to find it in famine…I would have a hard time being thankful; but not Abraham, because he knew the nature of

God. He understood that God would never "bless him" with something that was going to be a liability. His inheritance might be in a season of drought right now but there were better times ahead. Everything that God gives us has unspeakable potential. We have to develop it with our faith and our diligence. Abraham went on down to Egypt and probably picked up some sheep cheap because of the other herdsmen who had to travel further south who could not see the potential in a famine, and their pessimism made them willing sellers.

Adversity creates opportunity. God's people need to look around at the wreckage of the US economy, and find the hidden opportunities that are going to be there. Only the faith filled mind will be able to see them. The fear filled mind will only see smoldering wreckage. To those who have not followed the patterns of the world by being sensitive to debt, these opportunities will be of the "once in a lifetime" category. You will be able to buy the assets of those who have become drunk on the wine of easy credit for a song. Abraham knew the famine would not last forever. He bought livestock while they were cheap. We should learn from his example.

To those of us who are locked into the wreck because we didn't have time to escape debt, the Bible also has *Good News*. First and foremost is the fact that God is quick to mend the lives of people who genuinely repent and turn from the error of their ways. All we have to do is ask God to help us and He will. It's that simple. The grace of God is not just about forgiveness…it's about supernatural power from beyond us, of the non-physical realm He refers to as the "Kingdom of God". Its purpose is to help us in a time of need, regardless of what that need is (Hebrews 4:16). We just need His guidance to get us into the place of our Promised Land inheritance, and His grace to help us survive the journey. He and He alone will guide us through the pitfalls of the financial wilderness we currently find ourselves in.

Secondly, we can learn from Abraham's son Isaac in Genesis Chapter 26, who by now had become the heir to the covenant. He was full grown and his father had been *"gathered to his fathers"*; an Old Testament euphemism for death. Isaac was on his own and was making decisions based on what he had learned from his father, just like the rest of us. Another famine has hit, and Isaac finds himself right in the middle of it. He does what his father did. He starts gathering up the livestock to head south to Egypt and lay low till conditions improve. But the Lord *"appears to him"* and tells him to remain in the place of his inheritance and He would bless him. He reminds him of the covenant He has made with his father and that by being the heir he is covered under the same agreement. And that the terms of the covenant are that God would bless him and He would bless his children and that through Him all the peoples of the earth would be blessed.

It seems that God is trying to tell us that in the early days of Abraham's sojourning, the covenant was not fully in place. Therefore for a season Abraham had to go move out of the place of his inheritance to escape adverse natural circumstances. But for his son Isaac, the situation was entirely different. Oh...the adversity of Isaac's drought was just as severe as the adversity of Abraham's, but the difference was that in Isaac the covenant had now become fully established. Now it was the covenant and not the circumstance that would dictate Isaac's blessing. Unlike his father, he was to refuse to allow famine to move him but was to place his faith in the agreement God had made with his father that was now passed on to him.

If you're in adversity financially right now and you've vowed to come out of debt, place your confidence in the covenant. God is a covenant maker and a covenant keeper. Don't be moved by your circumstance, but hold on to the Word of God and His promises. He will be your sustainer. Isaac sowed in famine by the Word of God, and the results were miraculous. *"Then Isaac sowed in that land, and reaped in the same year a hundredfold; and the Lord blessed him. The man began to prosper, and continued prospering until he became very prosperous; for he had possessions of flocks and possessions of herds and a great number of servants. So the Philistines envied him. Now the Philistines had stopped up all the wells which his father's servants had dug in the days of Abraham his father, and they had filled them with earth."* (Genesis 26:12-15, NKJV).

God is calling His people to remain steadfast and sow in famine right where they are. He will bless them so radically that the world will become envious. Come out of the pattern of the world and listen for God's guidance. A season of harvest is at hand if we will only be obedient and believe.

Envy will lead to further separation:

Another Spiritual truth that will become more and more pronounced as Christ's appearing comes closer and closer is the Principle of Sanctification. Jesus said, "*"Do not think that I came to bring peace on earth. I did not come to bring peace but a sword. For I have come to 'set a man against his father, a daughter against her mother, and a daughter-in-law against her mother-in-law'; and 'a man's enemies will be those of his own household.'"* (Matthew 10:34-36, NKJV). He does not mean that He came to divide families. What He meant was He came to facilitate the separation of two competing Kingdoms. The Kingdom of God and what the Bible broadly refers to as the *"world"*. If a father is a non-believer and his son becomes redeemed by faith in Christ, they will likely become more distant as the pressures of a failing and futile world increase. To be sanctified merely means to be "set-apart" or brought into a condition of Holiness. I believe that in the coming days and months, God's economic system is going to be increasingly separate from that of the world's.

The "end-times" transference of wealth that is indicated in Proverbs 13:22 *"A good man leaves an inheritance to his children's children, But the wealth of the sinner is stored up for the righteous."*, is about to occur. Even in *"perilous times "*, God's people are going to prosper...at least to those who separate themselves from the world and its systems. I believe this prosperity, in what otherwise would have to be called a recession or perhaps even a depression, will lead to wide spread envy and jealousy amongst those who are not saved. True peace on earth can therefore only come when He returns to bring it. The First Advent of Christ is about separation from the world for His followers. The Second Advent is about establishing His Kingdom on earth in a physical form called the Millennial Reign of Christ, where He will return in the flesh and reign on the earth for a thousand years. There will be true peace on earth then and only then.

Until then there will be ever increasing friction between the Trinity Godhead and Satan, the Adversary. This means many

Christian businesses are going to be moved out of one bank and placed in another. God is going to continually shake His people and force them to get into position. This may feel more like judgment than salvation at times. But if we will wait patiently on the Lord and trust in Him, we will eventually see His hand on us and our businesses. As God calls us to *"come out of (Babylon) My people least you commit sin with her and partake of her plagues"* (Revelation 18:4), we need to be ready to break some business relationships and pursue new ones in some cases. Trust God to move us into the position He wants us in to fulfill His promise to us.

As we have said earlier, the wilderness journey can be a little intimidating, but it is designed to demonstrate both God's power and His commitment to us. There is no question that we will make it if we just trust in Him and come apart from the world and its systems. The time to act is now. There is an urgency in God's calling to His people, and Pharaoh will be compelled to release them before the last act is concluded. Again…trust in Him and follow His leading to the place of His provision.

"And Moses said to the people, "Do not be afraid. Stand still, and see the salvation of the Lord, which He will accomplish for you today. For the Egyptians whom you see today, you shall see again no more forever. The Lord will fight for you, and you shall hold your peace."" (Exodus 14:13-14, NKJV)

Appendix:

For Financial forms you can use for budgeting and debt reduction planning, go to:

www.financialexodus.com .ORG

Printed in the United States
121950LV00003B/250-354/P